# R. Gupta's®
## POPULAR MASTER GUIDE

# KVS
## Kendriya Vidyalaya Sangathan

# ENGLISH TEACHER
## Recruitment Exam

by
RPH Editorial Board

**2019**
EDITION

# RAMESH PUBLISHING HOUSE, New Delhi

**Published by**

O.P. Gupta *for* Ramesh Publishing House

**Admin. Office**

12-H, New Daryaganj Road, Opp. Officers' Mess,
New Delhi-110002 ① 23261567, 23275224, 23275124

E-mail: info@rameshpublishinghouse.com
Website: www.rameshpublishinghouse.com

**Showroom**

● Balaji Market, Nai Sarak, Delhi-6 ① 23253720, 23282525
● 4457, Nai Sarak, Delhi-6, ① 23918938



**Book Code: R-1145**

**ISBN: 978-81-7812-876-4**

**HSN Code: 49011010**

# Scheme of Written Examination

| Test Duration | 150 Minutes |
| --- | --- |
| Total Questions | 150 Objective type Multiple Choice Questions |
| Total Marks | 150 Marks |

| Section Name | Marks per Question | No. of Questions |
| --- | --- | --- |
| **Part-I :** | | |
| 1. General English | 01 mark | 10 |
| 2. General Hindi | per question | 10 |
| **Part-II :** | | |
| 1. General Knowledge & Current Affairs | | 10 |
| 2. Reasoning Ability | 01 mark | 10 |
| 3. Computer Literacy | per question | 10 |
| 4. Pedagogy | | 20 |
| 5. Subject Concerned (English) | | 80 |

### INTERVIEW: 60 Marks

**Note:** The final merit list will be based on the performance of the candidates in Written Test and Interview. The weightage of Written Test and Interview will be 85:15.

# CONTENTS



❏ ❏ ❏

# KVS—PGT Teacher Recruitment Exam 2017*

## Subject : English

**Directions (Q. Nos. 1 to 8):** *In each of the following sentences, identify the underlined clause.*

1. Farming depends on water, <u>which will be available only during the monsoons</u>.
   A. Principal clause
   B. Adjective/Relative clause
   C. Noun clause
   D. Adverb clause

2. I found at last the book <u>when I had lost all hope</u>.
   A. Principal clause
   B. Adjective/Relative clause
   C. Noun clause
   D. Adverb clause

3. I cannot work <u>unless there is complete calm and quiet</u>.
   A. Principal clause
   B. Adjective/Relative clause
   C. Noun clause
   D. Adverb clause

4. The teacher told the students <u>that their result was quite good</u>.
   A. Principal clause
   B. Adjective/Relative clause
   C. Noun clause
   D. Adverb clause

5. He asked questions <u>for which there were no answers</u>.
   A. Principal clause
   B. Adjective/Relative clause
   C. Noun clause
   D. Adverb clause

6. Ram wears a shawl <u>whereas Sham wears a coat</u>.
   A. Principal clause
   B. Adjective/Relative clause
   C. Noun clause
   D. Adverb clause

7. <u>Whose car has been stolen</u> still remains a mystery.
   A. Principal clause
   B. Adjective/Relative clause
   C. Noun clause
   D. Adverb clause

8. That he may fall ill <u>worries me</u>.
   A. Principal clause
   B. Adjective/Relative clause
   C. Noun clause
   D. Adverb clause

**Directions (Q. Nos. 9 to 16):** *Complete the paragraph given below by filling in the blanks with the help of options that follow:*

From my sixty year _(9)_ to my sixteenth I was at school, _(10)_ taught all sorts _(11)_ things except religion. I may say that I _(12)_ to get from _(13)_ teachers what they could _(14)_ given me. And yet I kept on _(15)_ up things without any effort on _(16)_ part.

9. A. up          B. in
   C. on          D. for

10. A. be          B. being
    C. been        D. am

11. A. on          B. in
    C. of          D. with

12. A. fail        B. failed
    C. fails       D. failing

13. A. a           B. the
    C. any         D. some

14. A. has         B. had
    C. have        D. having

15. A. pick        B. picked
    C. picks       D. picking

16. A. his         B. their
    C. her         D. my

---

**Directions (Q. Nos. 17 to 21):** *Read the passage given below and answer the questions that follow with the help of given options:*

The body should function rightly, perfectly. It is an art, it is not austerity, you are not to fight with it, you are simply to understand it. And the body is so wise, and wiser than your mind, remember, because the body has existed longer than the mind. The mind is a very new arrival, just a child.

The body is very ancient, because you moved once as a rock; the body was there, the mind was fast asleep. Then you became a tree; the body was there, with all its greenery and flowers. The mind was fast asleep still, not so asleep as in the rock but still asleep. You became an animal, a tiger, the body was so alive with energy, but the mind was not functioning. You became a bird, you became a man. The body has been functioning for millions of years.

The body has accumulated much wisdom, the body is wise. So, if you eat too much, the body says, 'Stop!' The mind is not so wise. The mind says, 'The taste is beautiful—a little more'. And if you listen to the mind, then the mind becomes destructive to the body, this way or that. If you listen to the mind, first it will say, 'Go on eating', because mind is foolish, a child. He does not know what he is saying. He is a new arrival; he has no learning in him.

He is not wise, he is yet a fool. Listen to the body. When the body says, 'Hungry,' eat. When the body says, 'Stop,' stop.

17. Study the following statements:
    1. Man created trees to satisfy his needs.
    2. Plant life evolved into animal life.
    A. (1) is true and (2) is false
    B. Both (1) and (2) are true
    C. (2) is true and (1) is false
    D. Both (1) and (2) are false

18. How does the author establish body's superiority over mind?
    A. Body can be seen while the mind can't be
    B. Mind depends on the body for everything it wants
    C. Body came into existence earlier than mind
    D. All human activities are controlled by the mind

19. Which word among the following means the same as 'accumulated'?
    A. assembled          B. saved
    C. collected          D. decided

20. Choose the correct sequence in which the evolution of life has taken place.
    A. Man → Plants → Animals → Mind
    B. Plants → Animals → Man → Mind
    C. Animals → Man → Plants → Mind
    D. Mind → Man → Plants → Animals

21. Which of the following statements is not true?
    A. Mind also underwent an evolution when body did
    B. Mind of a tiger is non-functional
    C. When we get obese our mind is responsible for it
    D. Mind guides us in all of our activities

**Directions (Q. Nos. 22 to 56):** *Answer the questions/ complete the statements given below with the help of options that follow:*

22. Conflict between desire for vengeance and voice of conscience leads to the downfall of the tragic protagonist in Shakespeare's ...... .
    A. *Othello*
    B. *Hamlet*
    C. *Antony and Cleopatra*
    D. *Macbeth*

23. In 'The Tempest', Prospero frees Ariel from the witch Sycorax but has enslaved:
    A. Trinculo          B. Stephano
    C. Caliban          D. Boatswain

24. Wordsworth comes out of a mood of despondency in his poem 'Resolution and Independence' by interacting with a:
    A. little cottage girl
    B. boatman
    C. leech gatherer
    D. girl called Lucy

25. One aspect of Romantic Poetry is its interest in medieval romance and ballad which find their best proponent in:
    A. William Blake      B. Thomas Moore
    C. Byron          D. Sir Walter Scott

26. Shakespeare addresses the themes of ........... in his sonnets.

A. peace, time, beauty and wealth
B. harmony, wealth, love and conflict
C. love, beauty, time and loyalty
D. honesty, wealth, time and beauty

27. "Kill Claudio"
Who made this demand and in which play of Shakespeare?
A. Jessica in the Merchant of Venice
B. Ophelia in Hamlet
C. Beatrice in Much Ado About Nothing
D. Olivia in Twelfth Night

28. Byron's greatness as a poet lies in his satires. Which of the following poems of Byron is not a satire?
A. Beppo
B. The Vision of Judgement
C. Childe Harold's Pilgrimage
D. Don Juan

29. Tennyson's poem .............. is not merely a pastoral elegy but also a deeply philosophical reflection on religion, science and immortality.
A. In Memorium        B. Locksley Hall
C. The Princess        D. Maud

30. Where was Hamlet studying when he was summoned to Denmark on the death of his father?
A. Germany        B. France
C. England        D. Athens

31. In 'Frost at Midnight' Coleridge promises his infant son that he would learn about God:
A. by visiting holy places
B. through interaction with nature
C. through teachings at school
D. through Sunday visits to church

32. 'She dwells with Beauty-Beauty that must die'. In which ode of Keats does this line occur?
A. Grecian Urn        B. Psyche
C. Nightingale        D. Melancholy

33. In Julius Caesar, after Brutus' presumed dealth, his wife, Portia .................. .
A. goes into hiding   B. remarries
C. goes into exile    D. commits suicide

34. Apart from Mark Antony, and Octavius Caesar who was the third member of the triumvirate which ruled Roman Empire in the play Antony and Cleopatra?

A. Pompey        B. Lepidus
C. Agrippa        D. Enobarbus

35. Some critics call him ineffectual, yet along with Blake, ................. is the nearest example of poet as a prophet. In life he suffered more than Blake.
A. Sir Walter Scott   B. John Keats
C. P.B. Shelley        D. Coleridge

36. In 'As You Like It' who said to whom the following?
"All the world is a stage".
A. Jacques to Duke Senior
B. Touchstone to Celia
C. Adam to Duke Fredrick
D. Rosalind to Orlando

37. By which Spanish novelist was the famous character, Sancho Panza created?
A. Galdos        B. Rosa Montero
C. Cervantes     D. Javier Marias

38. That poetry should portray 'the naked and native dignity of man' was pronounced by:
A. Wordsworth    B. M. Arnold
C. Coleridge     D. Shelley

39. An often used phrase, 'tilting at windmills' was inspired by:
A. Moll Flanders  B. Tom Jones
C. Kim            D. Don Quixote

40. What is common between "The White Devil" and "The Duchess of Malfi"?
A. Both plays are based on Holinshed
B. Both are written by Beaumont and Fletcher
C. Both have been characterised as dark comedies
D. Both show life as pitiless, cruel and corrupt

41. Match the following books written by Graham Greene with their setting.

| Book | Setting |
|---|---|
| (a) Journey without maps | (i) Mexico |
| (b) The Lawless Roads | (ii) Sierra Leone |
| (c) The Heart of the Matter | (iii) Indochina |
| (d) The Quiet American | (iv) Liberia |

|     | (a)    | (b)    | (c)    | (d)    |
|-----|--------|--------|--------|--------|
| A.  | (ii)   | (iii)  | (i)    | (iv)   |
| B.  | (i)    | (ii)   | (iii)  | (iv)   |
| C.  | (iii)  | (ii)   | (iv)   | (i)    |
| D.  | (iv)   | (i)    | (ii)   | (iii)  |

**42.** Which of these works of Wole Soyinka, a Nigerian writer is a novel?
A. Ake : The Years of Childhood
B. The Man Died : Prison Notes
C. The Interpreters
D. The Open Sore of a Continent

**43.** Which of the following books written by Nadine Gordimer is not a novel?
A. The House Gun    B. July's People
C. Burger's Daughter D. The Lying Days

**44.** Which novel written by Faulkner is about World War I and its aftermath?
A. The Sound and Fury
B. Soldier's Pay
C. Sanctuary
D. Sartoris

**45.** In Arthur Miller's 'Death of a Salesman', the unsuccessful salesman, Willy Loman on return from a failed business trip shows his unhappiness even with his family because:
A. his wife suggests that he should talk to his boss for a transfer
B. his younger son, Happy is not doing well academically
C. his eldest son, Biff has no career prospects
D. his neighbour Charley always finds faults with him

**46.** Which is the last novel in Chinua Achebe's 'The African Trilogy'?
A. A Man of the People
B. The Trouble with Nigeria
C. Arrow of God
D. Hopes and Impediments

**47.** Which African writer wrote the following in their work. 'Leaving School II'?
'Truth isn't always beauty, but the hunger for it is'.
A. Wole Soyinka      B. Nuruddin Farah
C. Nadine Gordimer   D. Buchi Emecheta

**48.** Walt Whitman's 'Song of Myself' was first included in:
A. Drum Taps         B. Leaves of Grass
C. Poems by Walt Whitman
D. November Boughs

**49.** Who said the following in one of his works? 'When we are not sure, we are alive'.
A. Thomas Hardy      B. Byron
C. Graham Greene     D. T.S. Eliot

**50.** Which novel written by Chetan Bhagat deals with a love triangle, corruption and is a journey of self-discovery?
A. Five Point Someone
B. Revolution 2020
C. Half Girlfriend
D. One Indian Girl

**51.** 'Interpreter of Maladies' deals with the difficulties of communication. This book of nine short stories was written by:
A. Jhumpa Lahiri     B. Kiran Desai
C. Arvind Adiga      D. Chetan Bhagat

**52.** Of Indian writers writing in English who wrote the poem, 'On The Death of A Poem' which uses a court metaphor?
A. Gieve Patel       B. Shiv K. Kumar
C. A.K. Mehrotra     D. A.K. Ramanujan

**53.** Which poem written by K.N. Daruwala opens with the line given below?
'Corn is great, on the cob or otherwise'.
A. Bars              B. Before the Word
C. At War            D. Migrations

**54.** 'Talkative Man', 'Under the Benyan Tree', 'A Horse and Two Goats' are all written by:
A. R.K. Narayan      B. Amitav Ghosh
C. Raja Rao          D. Amish Tripathi

**55.** Mulk Raj Anand's novel which deals with the rise of communism is:
A. The Big Heart
B. Across the Black Waters
C. The Sword and the Sickle
D. Untouchable

**56.** Of the following Indian writers writing in English who does not belong to Indian diaspora?
A. Kiran Desai       B. Salman Rushdi
C. V.S. Naipaul      D. Kiran Nagarkar

**Directions (Q. Nos. 57 to 62):** *Read the passage given below and answer the questions/complete the statements that follow with the help of given options.*
Fortunately we do not have to rely on such peekaboo evidence to know more of chimpanzee nature. They have been studied intensively in captivity, in a great variety of ways, because their close relationship to ourselves makes them so exceptionally important; the only drawback is that captive apes are, after all, not leading natural lives. They are, as everybody has noted, highly emotional and sensitive animals, and one needs very little experience of chimpanzees to realize the force of

their interest in, and reliance on, other chimpanzees or such near-chimps as human beings. It is hard to convey the meaning of this briefly. You might almost say that chimpanzees are like us, but more so, in the degree to which their behaviour relates to that of others. Dominance is present, with the larger male tending to dominate a female. This is not invariable, however, and a female can use the advantages of her sex temporarily to dominate a usually dominant male. Furthermore, dominance is less obvious than in the monkeys: one gets the impression that the more forceful and positive individuals are not simply the most blatantly aggressive, and that the interplay of personalities has a complexity that suggests the human. A chimpanzee group, in other words, has, like other primate groups, a definite arrangement of its individuals which rules activity, but which depends on other considerations besides brutishness. It is unsafe to humanize such traits, but they give the appearance of amiability, general vigour, self-confidence and so on. Special friendships and enmities are plain. I might say that Professor Robert M. Yerkes, the great authority on chimps, never hesitated to emphasize the humanness of chimpanzee personality and responsiveness.

**57.** Why do we need to study them?
  A. Man is closely related to them
  B. They may add to our knowledge of the animal world
  C. They are fun to watch
  D. We can find out how man evolved from the apes

**58.** Study the following statements:
  1. Chimpanzees take interest in human beings.
  2. Their social life is so much like that of human beings.
  A. (1) is true and (2) is false
  B. Both (1) and (2) are true
  C. (2) is true and (1) is false
  D. Both (1) and (2) are false

**59.** Which one of the following words means the same as 'intensively'?
  A. hopefully    B. strongly
  C. largely    D. deeply

**60.** Why is it incorrect to study them in captivity?
  A. They don't behave in the natural way in the cage

  B. Here they don't get food in the natural way
  C. They don't like to be stared at
  D. They are likely to get emotional

**61.** What is common between chimpanzees and humans?
  A. Both want to enjoy freedom
  B. Males try to dominate the females
  C. Both like the privacy of captivity
  D. The strong ones are very aggressive

**62.** How have the researchers studied the nature of chimpanzees?
  A. They have given them a casual look
  B. They have observed their behaviour in the labs
  C. They have studied them in the zoos
  D. They have studied them deeply in the cages

**Directions (Q. Nos. 63 to 70):** *Complete the sentences given below with the help of options that follow each of them.*

**63.** I hope you ............ all this by tomorrow.
  A. do not forget    B. would not forget
  C. had not forgotten  D. have not forgotten

**64.** You would be ill if you ............ so much.
  A. will have eaten    B. have had eaten
  C. would have eaten  D. ate

**65.** I scolded my son ............ he is sulking.
  A. so it is why    B. and that's how
  C. so that is why    D. but it is when

**66.** If you were a fish, the cat ............ caught you.
  A. would have    B. will have
  C. would have had  D. have had

**67.** If you ......... with him he will give you a pen.
  A. would go    B. will have gone
  C. will go    D. go

**68.** By next June, he ............ his next novel.
  A. have had written
  B. will have written
  C. should have been writing
  D. had written

**69.** How many times have I ............ ?
  A. told you not to do that
  B. told you to have done that
  C. to tell you not do that
  D. tell you I will not do that

**70.** Can you tell me ............ ?
  A. how are you so sad
  B. why you are so sad

C. why are you so sad

D. why will you be so sad

**Directions (Q. Nos. 71 to 76):** *Read the passage given below and answer the question/complete the statements that follow with the help of given options.*

The bombing of Hiroshima and Nagasaki provides our only direct experience of the consequences of nuclear explosions on cities. Those events have taught us a great deal about the potential physical and biological impact of a nuclear war. But it must be remembered that the cities of Hiroshima and Nagasaki experienced only a single explosion each of a weapon much smaller in yield than many of those stockpiled in world nuclear arsenals today. The bomb dropped on Hiroshima released energy equalling 20 kilo-tons of chemicals explosive.

It must be remembered that the environmental impact of the Hiroshima and Nagasaki bombs was geographically limited, and survivors were almost immediately able to obtain medical and other assistance from outside. Thus, the impact of those bombs, though devastating for the people directly affected, was much more limited than might be expected in a full-scale war.

The deployment of increasing numbers of powerful weapons since Hiroshima and Nagasaki prompts the question: "What will happen if many modern nuclear weapons are exploded ?" It is obvious that the consequences will be far more severe than in 1945. The most important fact is that the consequences can be of a kind that were not even contemplated until recently, *i.e.*, the possibility that smoke from massive nuclear-ignited urban fires can cause a worldwide disruption in the planet's weather and climate.

**71.** What lesson have we learnt from the bombings of Hiroshima and Nagasaki?

A. We saw what happens when a nuclear explosion takes place

B. We saw the effect of nuclear explosion on life and property

C. It was not a theoretical phenomenon, but bombs were actually dropped

D. We learnt how to prepare in the event of a nuclear war

**72.** Study the following statements:

1. The bomb dropped on Hiroshima had twenty kilotons of chemical energy.

2. Both the bombs were biological weapons.

A. (1) is true and (2) is false

B. Both (1) and (2) are true

C. (2) is true and (1) is false

D. Both (1) and (2) are false

**73.** Study the following statements:

1. A full scale nuclear war will affect global climate.

2. In Hiroshima and Nagasaki the impact on the people was limited.

3. We have now realised how destructive a nuclear war in future will be.

A. (1) is true and (2) is false

B. (3) is true and (1) is false

C. (2) is true and (3) is false

D. All (1), (2) and (3) are true

**74.** Why would a nuclear war in future be much more devastating?

A. More countries have nuclear stockpiles today

B. Day by day the number of conflicts in the world is increasing

C. Nuclear explosions over Hiroshima and Nagasaki were small ones

D. Today we have bigger bombs which can cause far more damage

**75.** Which of the following statements is not true?

A. Area affected by Hiroshima and Nagasaki bombings was limited

B. Help could be provided to the survivors

C. It did not have a vast impact on environment

D. Nuclear proliferation has stopped

**76.** What does the word 'prompts' mean here? (Para 3)

A. raises          B. replies

C. affects          D. influences

**Directions (Q. Nos. 77 to 84):** *In each of the following sentences there is an error. Identify the part containing the error.*

**77.** (A) During the winter months / (B) food and firewood / (C) were scarcely / (D) available.

**78.** (A) I have lost / (B) count how many times / (C) I have / (D) broken my glasses.

**79.** (A) The report that covers / (B) many areas have / (C) established / (D) that situation is comic.

**80.** (A) I do not want to be rude, / (B) it is simple / (C) that we have to be careful / (D) who we give this information to.

**81.** (A) The roadside vendors / (B) do not know / (C) how much longer / (D) would they be able to stay.

**82.** (A) Last but not / (B) the least / (C) Ram is our / (D) most promising player.

**83.** (A) Due to / (B) heavy rains on the area / (C) the match had to be / (D) cancelled.

**84.** (A) It is earth's / (B) magnetic field / (C) that made / (D) a compass work.

**Directions (Q. Nos. 85 to 92):** *Read the passage given below and answer the question/complete the statements that follow with the help of given options.*
It was once believed that being overweight was healthy, but now-a-days few people subscribe to this viewpoint. While many people are fighting the battle to reduce weight, studies are being conducted concerning the appetite and how it is controlled by both emotional and biochemical factors. Some of the conclusions of these studies may give insights into how to deal with weight problems. For example, when several hundred people were asked about their eating habits in times of stress, 44 per cent said they reacted to stressful situations by eating. Further investigations with both humans and animals indicated that it is not food which relieves tension but rather the act of chewing.

A test in which subjects were blindfolded showed that obese people have a keener sense of taste and crave more flavourful food than non-obese people. When deprived of the variety and itnensity of tastes, obese people are not satisfied and consequently eat more to fulfill this need. Blood samples taken from people after they were shown a picture of food revealed that overweight people reacted with an increase in blood insulin, a chemical associated with appetite. This did not happen with average-weight people.

In another experiment, results showed that certain people have a specific, biologically induced hunger for carbohydrates. Eating carbohydrates raises the level of serotonin, a neurotransmitter in the brain. Enough serotonin produces a sense of satiation, and hunger for carbohydrates subsides.

Exercise has been recommended as an important part of a weight-loss program. However, it has been found that mild exercise, such as using stairs instead of the elevator, is beetter in the long run than taking on a strenuous programme, such as jogging, which many people find difficult to continue over periods of time and which also increases appetite.

**85.** Study the following statements:
1. We want to eat more when we are emotionally stressed.
2. Our need for food is controlled by metabolic functions.
   A. (1) is true and (2) is false
   B. Both (1) and (2) are true
   C. (2) is true and (1) is false
   D. Both (1) and (2) are false

**86.** Which of the following statements is true?
   A. Thin people fall ill more often
   B. Food relieves stress in both humans and animals
   C. Fat people can judge taste and flavour better
   D. Insulin has no effect on people of average weight

**87.** Insulin in the blood increases:
   A. the desire for food
   B. to neutralise the fattening effect of food
   C. when overweight people look at food
   D. when the blood sugar levels are low

**88.** When under stress:
   A. fat people suffer more
   B. a good number of people want to eat
   C. thin people don't rush to eat
   D. 56 per cent of the people keep their cool

**89.** Which word means the same as 'subscribe'?
   A. support      B. gain
   C. contribute      D. persuade

**90.** How are people trying to reduce weight?
   A. through exercise
   B. by controlling their hunger
   C. through diet control
   D. by using weight loss gadgets

**91.** Which of the following statements is true?
   A. Our intake of food relieves us of our stress
   B. It is spicy food that makes people fat
   C. Fat people like to eat more
   D. Slim people crave for spicy food

**92.** Which of the following statements is not true?
   A. If food is tasty even fat people eat less
   B. Fat people enjoy food more than slim people
   C. Light exercise is beeter than strenuous one
   D. Fat people remain fat even if they don't eat

**Directions (Q. Nos. 93 to 100):** *Voice in each of the following sentences has been changed. Choose the option in which it has been changed correctly.*

93. Who took it?
    A. Who was it taken by
    B. By whom was it taken?
    C. It was taken by whom?
    D. It was taken by who?

94. This letter was not written by Jane.
    A. Jane did not write this letter.
    B. Who wrote this letter to Jane?
    C. Jane had not written this letter.
    D. Jane wrote this letter.

95. Someone may steal the cycle.
    A. The cycle will be stolen.
    B. The cycle may be stolen.
    C. A thief may be stealing the cycle.
    D. The cycle will be stolen by a thief.

96. This house will be built.
    A. We will be built this house.
    B. We will get this house built.
    C. We shall build this house.
    D. We need to build this house.

97. We have been shown several books.
    A. The librarian has shown as several books.
    B. We have seen several books.
    C. The librarian has been shown several books.
    D. We have shown several books.

98. How will you watch him?
    A. How will he be watched by you?
    B. Who will be watched by him?
    C. By whom will he be watched?
    D. You will be watched by whom?

99. Sita married Ram.
    A. Ram was married by Sita.
    B. Sita was married to Ram.
    C. Sita was married by Ram.
    D. Ram was married to Sita.

100. I am playing tennis.
    A. Tennis is played by me.
    B. Tennis is playing by me.
    C. Tennis is being played by me.
    D. I am being played.

## ANSWERS

| 1 | 2 | 3 | 4 | 5 | 6 | 7 | 8 | 9 | 10 |
|---|---|---|---|---|---|---|---|---|----|
| B | D | D | C | B | D | C | A | A | B |

| 11 | 12 | 13 | 14 | 15 | 16 | 17 | 18 | 19 | 20 |
|----|----|----|----|----|----|----|----|----|----|
| C | B | B | C | D | B | C | B | C | B |

| 21 | 22 | 23 | 24 | 25 | 26 | 27 | 28 | 29 | 30 |
|----|----|----|----|----|----|----|----|----|----|
| D | B | C | C | D | C | C | C | A | A |

| 31 | 32 | 33 | 34 | 35 | 36 | 37 | 38 | 39 | 40 |
|----|----|----|----|----|----|----|----|----|----|
| B | D | D | B | C | A | C | A | D | D |

| 41 | 42 | 43 | 44 | 45 | 46 | 47 | 48 | 49 | 50 |
|----|----|----|----|----|----|----|----|----|----|
| D | C | B | B | C | C | C | B | C | B |

| 51 | 52 | 53 | 54 | 55 | 56 | 57 | 58 | 59 | 60 |
|----|----|----|----|----|----|----|----|----|----|
| A | D | B | B | C | D | A | B | D | A |

| 61 | 62 | 63 | 64 | 65 | 66 | 67 | 68 | 69 | 70 |
|----|----|----|----|----|----|----|----|----|----|
| B | D | A | D | C | A | D | B | A | B |

| 71 | 72 | 73 | 74 | 75 | 76 | 77 | 78 | 79 | 80 |
|----|----|----|----|----|----|----|----|----|----|
| B | D | A | D | D | A | C | B | B | B |

| 81 | 82 | 83 | 84 | 85 | 86 | 87 | 88 | 89 | 90 |
|----|----|----|----|----|----|----|----|----|----|
| D | B | B | C | B | C | C | B | A | C |

| 91 | 92 | 93 | 94 | 95 | 96 | 97 | 98 | 99 | 100 |
|----|----|----|----|----|----|----|----|----|----|
| C | D | B | A | B | C | A | A | D | C |

# ENGLISH LITERATURE

# SHAKESPEARE'S WORKS

### WILLIAM SHAKESPEARE (16116)

**Life**

1.    He was born on or about 23 April, 1564 at Stratford-on-Avon, Warwickshire.

2.    His father was a prospersons tradesman.

3.    He was sent to a Grammar school where he learnt "small Latin and less Greek."

4.    Later misfortunes overtook the family.

5.    In his 19th year, he married Anne Hathaway, who was eight years his seniors.

6.    His marriage seems to have been an unhappy one.

7. *(i)* There are several anecdotes why he left for London, but we need not study them here.

*(ii)* It is almost certain that he went to London in or about 1587 to seek fortunes there.

8.    It was the time when drama was being popularized by the University Wits.

9. *(i)* There are again several stories how he came on the stage, but what we are concerned here is that soon he gained popularity and appeared on the stage as an actor.
For example, he acted in Ben Jonson's "Everyman in His Humour."

*(ii)* Soon alongwith being an actor, he became a playwright also.

10. It is certain from the deathbed words of Greene who called him an "upstart" that by 1592, Shakespeare had quite established himself as a playwright.

11. Soon he became a shareholder in prestigious theatres such as the Globe and the Blackfriars.

12. *(i)* He also purchased property in London and Stratford.

*(ii)* It is clear that he had become sufficiently prosperous.

13. However, misfortunes were not late in visiting him :

*(i)*  His only son died in 1596.

*(ii)*  His father died in 1601.

*(iii)*  His mother died in 1608.

14. Still, financially he was sound.

15. Between 1610 and 1612 he retired to his hometown, Stratford, where he bought the largest house in the town named the New Place.

16. As his health broke down, he died on 23rd April, 1616.

**Works**

In all, he wrote :

*(i)*  37 plays

*(ii)*  Two narrative poems:

    *(a)*  Venus and Adonis

    *(b)*  Lucrece

*(iii)*  154 sonnets:

    *(a)*  126 addressed to a man—a patron or friend.

    *(b)*  the rest 28 addressed to a dark lady.

His dramatic work is generally divided in four periods:

**1. The First Period (1588-93) :** It was the period of apprenticeship and experiment. It included:

*(i)*  Revision of old plays such as:

    *(a)*  Henry VI

    *(b)*  Titus Andronicus,

*(ii)*  the first comedies such as :

    *(a)*  Love's Labour's Lost

    *(b)*  Two Gentlemen of Verona

    *(c)*  The Comedy of Errors, and

    *(d)*  A Midsummer Night's Dream, and

*(iii)*  the first attempt at writing a tragedy—Romeo and Juliet.

**2. The Second Period (1594-1600) :** It was the period of the great Comedies and Chronicle Plays, such as

- (a) Richard II
- (b) King John
- (c) The Merchant of Venice
- (d) Henry IV Part I
- (e) Henry IV Part II
- (f) Henry V
- (g) The Taming of the Shrew
- (h) The Merry Wives of Windsor
- (i) Much Ado About Nothing
- (j) As You Like It, and
- (k) Twelfth Night

**3. The Third Period (1601-08):** This was the period of his great tragedies and sombre comedies, such as

- (i) Julius Caesar
- (ii) Hamlet
- (iii) All's Well That Ends Well
- (iv) Measure for Measure
- (v) Troilus and Cressida
- (vi) Othello
- (vii) King Lear
- (viii) Macbeth
- (ix) Antony and Cleopatra
- (x) Coriolanus
- (xi) Timon of Athens

**4. The Fourth Period (1608-12):** This was the period of later comedies or what are known as "Dramatic Romances"—

- (a) (i) Cymbeline
  - (ii) The Tempest
  - (iii) Winter's Tale
- (b) There are two other plays of this period which are only partly written by Shakespeare
  - (i) Pericles
  - (ii) Henry VIII

(**Note :** Henry VIII was completed by his friend, Fletcher (1579-1625) after his death.)

**Characteristics :** Characteristics of Shakespeare's works can be studied from two angles:

- (i) According the periods of their production.
- (ii) As general characteristics of his overall work.

**According to the Periods**

**1. The First Period (1588-93) :** According to Hudson, "The work of this period as a whole is extremely slight in texture; the treatment of life in it is superficial; there is little depth of thought or characterisation; and the art is marked immature."

**Hudson goes on :** "The prominence of rime in the dialogue, the stiffness of the blank verse, and the constant use of puns, conceits and other affectations, are among its outstanding technical features."

**2. The Second Period (1594-1600):** Hudson observes: In this period, "The characterisation and humour have become deep and penetrative, and there is a great growth in the weight of thought. Shakespeare has also outgrown, or is fast outgrowing, the immaturities of his former style. The youthful crudeness, extravagance, and strain are disappearing, rime is largely abandoned for prose and black verse, and the black verse itself has lost it stiffness, and is free and flexible."

**3. The Third Period (1601-08):** As per Hudson, "In this period all Shakespeare's powers—his dramatic power, his intellectual power and his power of expression—are at their highest."

**4. The Fourth Period (1608-12):** To quote Hudson again, "They show very fully the decline of Shakespeare's dramatic powers. They are often careless in construction and unsatisfactory in characterisation, while in style and versification they will not bear comparison with the work of preceding ten years."

**Shakespeare's Characteristics in General**

1. No single writer has contributed to literature as much literary work as Shakespeare has done.

2. There is "infinite variety" in his work.

3. He was indisputably a versatile genius—a deft master both at prose and verse of all kinds:

- (i) blank verse
- (ii) rhyme
- (iii) dramatic verse
- (iv) narrative verse, etc.

4. He is the most often quoted among all the English writers.

5. He is one of the greatest poets and dramatists of the world, probably the greatest.

6. It is said that he is the only man in the history of mankind who has said all that is worth-saying.

7.   He himself might not be a great thinker, but he could reproduce the borrowed matter in an original form such as none else perhaps could do.

8.   No other writer, not even Dickens, has been able to produce so many living and throbbing characters as he has done.

9.   It is estimated that he coined more than 15000 (some say, about 18000) words which he contributed to the English language.

10. He is the single writer who has given such a solid footing to the English language that its undying endurance over the centuries can hardly ever be doubted.

11. Needless to say his command over the language he uses is unrivalled.

12. Though a romantic writer, he is all the same the master of realism.

13. He steered the drama clear of stiff classical rules based on ancient masters, and made it a national movement.

14. With all the brutalities as shown by him like other dramatists, unlike them, he upheld the moral law such that truth triumphs in the long run, though poetic justice is not essentially done.

15. Thus his dramas are true to life and human nature.

16. There is a mixture of tragedy and comedy in his dramas as in life.

17. He is the master of true humour and has genuine sympathy with mankind.

**Shakespeare's Faults :** He is not without faults:

1.   The feeling of hastiness is evident at places in his works.

2.   At places, he uses claptrap methods and means to cater to the 'groundlings', thus sacrificing some of the essential elements of genuine drama, consistency of character and propriety.

3.   As Hudson points out, "At places his psychology is hopelessly crude and unconvincing; his style vicious; his wit forced and poor; his tragic language bombastic."

4.   At some places there are factual errors in his dramas such that the story, plot, scenes and characters start seeing unreal, *e.g.*

*(i)*   The modern Switzerland in 'Winter's Tale' is shown as having a sea-coast.

*(ii)*   There are trees of coconut and palm-dates side by side in 'As You Like It'.

*(iii)*   Sometimes, the "mistaken identity" scenes as in 'The Merchant of Venice' and 'Twelfth Night' seem unreal.

(**Note:** Here are some extracts from some of his works for study :

### Hamlet

(From Act I)

*King:* ....think of us
As of a father, for let the world take note
You are the most immediate to our throne,
And with no less nobility of love
Than that which dearest father bears his son
Do I impart toward you. For your intent
In going back to school in Wittenberg,
It is most retrograde to our desire,
And we beseech you, bend you to remain
Here in the cheer and comfort of our eye,
Our chiefest courtier, cousin, and our son.
*Queen:* Let not thy mother lose her prayers,
Hamlet.
I pray thee stay with us, go not to Wittenberg.
*Hamlet.* I shall in all my best obey you, madam.
*King:* why, 'tis a loving and a fair replay.
Be as ourself in Denmark. Madam, come.
This gentle and unforced accord of Hamlet
Sits smiling to my heart, in grace whereof
No jocund health that Denmark drink today,
But the great cannon to the clouds shall tell,
And the King's rouse the heaven shall bruit again,
Respeaking earthly thunder. Come away.

*Flourish. Exeunt all but Hamlet*

*Hamlet:* O that this too sullied flesh would melt
Thaw, and resolve itself into a dew,
Or that the Everlasting had not fixed,
His cannon 'gainst self-slaughter. O God, God,
How weary, stale, flat, and unprofitable
Seem to me all the uses of this world!
Fie on't, ah, fie, 'tis an unweeded garden
That grows to seed. Things rank and gross in nature
Possess it merely. That it should come to this:
But two months dead, nay, not so much, not two,
So excellent a king, that was to this
Hyperion to a satyr, so loving to my mother

That he might not beteem the winds of heaven
Visit her face too roughly. Heaven and earth,
Must I remember? Why, she would hang on him
As if increase of appetite had grown
By what if fed on; and yet within a month—
Let me not think on't: frailty, thy name is
  woman—
A little month, or ere those shoes were old
With which she followed my poor father's body
Like Niobe. all tears, why she, even she—
O God, a beast that wants discourse of reason
Would have mourned longer—married with my
  uncle,
My father's brother, but no more like my father
Than I to Hercules. Within a month,
Ere yet the salt of most unrighteous tears
Had left the flushing in her gallèd eyes,
She married O, most wicked speed, to post
With such dexterity to incestuous sheets!
It is not, nor it cannot come to good.
But break my heart, for I must hold my tongue.
*Enter Horatio, Marcellus, and Barnardo.*
*Horatio:* Hail to your lordship!
*Hamlet:* I am glad to see you well.
Horatio—or I do forget myself.
*Horatio:* The same, my lord, and your poor
  servant ever.
*Hamlet:* Sir, my good friend, I'll change that name
  with you.
And what make you from Wittenberg, Horatio?

### Hamlet
(Act III)

*Polonius:* Ophelia, walk you here.—Gracious, so
  please you.
We will bestow ourselves. [*To Ophelia*] Read on
  this book,
That show of such an exercise may colour
Your loneliness. We are oft to blame in this,
'Tis too much proved, that with devotion's visage
And pious action we do sugar o'er
The devil himself
*King:* [*Aside*] O, 'tis too true.
How smart a lash that speech doth give my
  conscience!
The harlot's cheek, beautied with plast'ring art,
Is not more ugly to the thing that helps it

Than is my deed to my most painted word.
O heavy burden!
*Polonius:* I hear him coming. Let's withdraw, my
  lord.

  [*Exeunt King and Polonius.*]
  *Enter Hamlet.*
*Hamlet:* To be, or not to be: that is the question:
Whether 'tis nobler in the mind to suffer
The slings and arrows of outrageous fortune,
Or to take arms against a sea of troubles,
And by opposing end them. To die, to sleep—
No more—and by a sleep to say we end
The heartache, and the thousand natural shocks
That flesh is heir to! 'Tis a consummation
Devoutly to be wished. To die, to sleep—
To sleep—perchance to dream: ay, there's the rub,
For in that sleep of death what dreams may come
When we have shuffled off this mortal coil,
Must give us pause. There's the respect
That makes calamity of so long life:
For who would bear the whips and scorns of time,
Th' oppressor's wrong, the proud man's
  contumely,
The pangs of despised love, the law's delay,
The insolence of office, and the spurns
That patient merit of th' unworthy takes,
When he himself might his quietus make
With a bare bodkin? Who would fardels bear,
To grunt and sweat under a weary life,
But that the dread of something after death,
The undiscovered country, from whose bourn
No traveler returns, puzzles the will,
And makes us rather bear those ills we have,
Than fly to others that we know not of?
Thus conscience does make cowards of us all,
And thus the native hue of resolution
Is sickled o'er with the pale cast of thought,
And enterprises of great pitch and moment,
With this regard their currents turn awry,
And lose the name of action.—Soft you now,
The fair Ophelia!—Nymph, in thy orisons
Be all my sins remembered.
*Ophelila:* Good my lord,
How does your honor for this many a day?
*Hamlet:* I humbly thank you; well, well, well.
*Ophelia:* My lord, I have remembrances of yours
That I have longèd long to redeliver.

I pray you now, receive them.

*Hamlet:* No, not I,
I never gave you aught.

*Ophelia:* My honored lord, you know right well
you did,
And with them words of so sweet breath
composed
As made these things more rich. Their perfume
lost,
Take these again, for to the noble mind

### Hamlet
#### (Act IV)

[Scene IV. *A plain in Denmark.*]

*Enter Fortinbras with his Army over the stage.*

*Fortinbras:* Go, Captain, from me great the Danish
king.
Tell him that by his license Fortinbras
Craves the conveyance of a promised march
Over his kingdom. You know the rendezvous.
If that his Majesty would aught with us,
We shall express our duty in his eye;
And let him know so.

*Captain:* I will don't, my lord.

*Fortinbras:* Go softly on.

[*Exeunt all but the Captain.*]

*Enter Hamlet, Rosencrantz, & c.*

*Hamlet:* Good sir, whose powers are these?

*Captain:* They are of Norway, sir.

*Hamlet:* How purposed, sir, I pray you?

*Captain:* Against some part of Poland.

*Hamlet:* Who commands them, sir?

*Captain:* The nephew to old Norway, Fortinbras.

*Hamlet:* Goes it against the main of Poland, sir,
Or for some frontier?

*Captain:* Truly to speak, and with no addition,
We go to gain a little patch of ground
That hath in it no profit but the name.
To pay five ducats, five, I would not farm it,
Nor will it yield to Norway or the Pole
A ranker rate, should it be sold in fee.

*Hamlet:* Why, then the Polack never will defend
it.

*Captain:* Yes, it is already garrisoned.

*Hamlet:* Two thousand souls and twenty thousand ducats.
Will not debate the question of this straw.

This is th' imposthume much wealth and peace,
That inward breaks, and shows no cause without
Why the man dies. I humbly thank you, sir.

*Captain:* God by you, sir.        [*Exit.*]

*Rosencrantz:* Will't please you go, my lord?

*Hamlet:* I'll be with you straight. Go a little before.

[*Exeunt all but Hamlet.*]

How all occasions do inform against me
And spur my dull revenge! What is a man,
If his chief good and market of his time
Be but to sleep and feed? A beast, no more.
Sure he that made us with such large discourse,
Looking before and after, gave us not
That capability and godlike reason
To fust in us unused. Now, whether it be
Bestial oblivion,° or some craven scruple
Of thinking too precisely on th' event—
A thought which, quartered, hath but on part
wisdom
And ever three parts coward—I do not know
Why yet I live to say, "This thing's to do,"
Sith I have cause, and will, and strength, and
means
To do't. Examples gross as earth exhort me.
Witness this army of such mass and charge,
Let by a delicate and tender prince,
Whose spirit, with divine ambition puffed,
Makes mouths at the invisible event,
Exposing what is mortal and unsure
To all that fortune, death, and danger dare....

Shakespeare writes highly quotable lines which
are pithy and epigrammatic and full of wisdom. Here
are examples from some of his plays:

*From All's Well That Ends Well*

1.  A young man married is a man that's marred.

    II, iii, 315

2.  The web of one life is of a mingled yarn, good
    and ill together.

    IV, iii, 83

3.  There's place and means for every man alive.

    iii, 379

*From 'Antony and Cleopatra'*

1.  There's beggary in the love that can be reckoned.
    —I, i, 5

2.  In Nature's in finite book of secrecy A little I can
    read.        —I, ii, 11

3. Eternity was in our lips and eyes, Bliss in our brows. —I, iii, 135

4. Age cannot wither her, nor custom stale Her infinite variety. —II, ii, 243

5. Music, moody food of us that trade in love. —II, v, 1

6. Though it be honest, it is never good To bring bad news. —II, v, 85

7. We have kissed away kingdom and provinces. —III, viii, 17

**As You Like It**

1. Let us sit and mock the good housewife fortune from her wheel, that her gifts may henceforth be bestowed equally. —I, ii, 35

2. O, how full of briers is this working-day world! —I, iii, 12

3. Beauty provoketh fools sooner than gold. —I, iii, 113

4. Sweet are the uses of adversity,
Which like the toad, ugly and venomous,
Wears yet a precious jewel in his head;
And this our life, exempt from public haunt,
Finds tongues in trees, books in the running brooks,
Sermons in stones and good in everything. —II, i, 12

5. I can such melancholy out a song, as a weasel sucks eggs. —II, v, 12

6. Who doth ambition shun,
And loves to live i' the sun,
Seeking the food he eats,
And pleased with what he gets. —II, v, 38

7. Blow, blow, thou winter wind,
Thou art not so unkind
As man's ingratitude —II, vii, 74

8. Most friendship is feigning, most loving mere folly. —II, vii, 181

**Cymbeline**

1. "Fear no more the heat O' the sun,
Nor the furious winter's rages;
Thou thy wordly task hast done,
Home are gone and ta'en thy wages:

**Hamlet**

1. This sweaty haste
Doth make the night joint-labourer with the day. —I, i, 77

2. But, look, the morn in russet mantle clad,
Walks o'er the dew of you high eastern hill. —I, i, 166

3. With one auspicious and one dropping eye,
With mirth in funeral and with dirge in marriage,
In equal scale weighing delight and dole —I, ii, 11

4. The head is not more native to be heart —I, ii, 47

5. All that live must die,
Passing through nature to eternity. —I, ii, 72

6. Frailty, thy name is woman —I, ii, 146

7. Give it an understanding but no tongue. —I, ii, 249

8. Neither a borrower nor a lender be. —I, iii, 75

9. That one may smile, and smile, and be a villain. —I, v, 108

10. There are more things in heaven a earth, Horatio,
Than are dreamt of in your philosophy. —I, v, 166

11. The time is out of joint. —I, v, 188

12. Brevity is the soul of wit. —II, ii, 90

13. To be honest, as this world goes,
Is to be one man picked out of ten thousand. —II, ii, 179

14. Though this be madness, Yet there is method in't. —II, ii, 211

15. On Fortune's cap we are not the very button. —II, ii, 237

16. There is nothing either good or bad, but thinking makes it so. —II, ii, 259

17. To be or not to be: that is the question. —III, i, 56

18. For to the noble mind
Rich gifts wax poor when givers prove unkind. —III, i, 100

19. O! that this two solid flesh would melt,
Thaw, and resolve itself into a dew..... —I, ii, 129

**King Lear**

1. Nothing will come of nothing. —I, i, 92

2. How sharper them a serpent's tooth it is
To have a thankless child! —I, iv, 312

3. Striving to better, of we mar what's well. —I, iv, 370

4. I am a man
   More sinned against than sinning.
   —III, ii, 59
5. As flies to wanton boys, are we to the gods;
   They kill us for their sport.        —IV, i, 36
6. Wisdom and goodness to the vile seem vile.
   —IV, ii, 38
7. It is the stars,
   The stars alone us, govern our conditions
   —IV, iii, 34
8. How tearful
   And dizzy 'tis to cast one's eyes so low!
   —IV, vi, 12
9. Though tattered clothes small vices do appear;
   Robes and furred gowns hide all.  —IV, vi, 169
10. When we are born, we cry that we are come
    To this great stage of fools.      —IV, vi, 187
11. Men must endure
    There going hence, evening as their coming
    hither:
    Ripeness is all.                     —V, ii, 9
12. The gods are just, and of our pleasant vices
    Make instruments that plague us.  —V, iii, 172
13. The wheel is come full circle.      —V, iii, 176
14. Her voice was ever soft,
    Gentle and low, an excellent thing in woman.
    —V, iii, 274

It is important to elaborate further on Shakespeare. Let us take typically his play "Antony and Cleopatra". Here is a part of Scene *(i)* from Act I :

### Antony and Cleopatra
#### Act I
Scene I. Alexandria. A room in Cleopatra's palace.
*Enter* Demetrius and Philo.
*Phi:* Nay, but this dotage of our general's
O'erflows the measure: those his goodly eyes.
That o'er the files and musters of the war
Have glow'd like plated Mars, now bend, now
      turn,
The office and devotion of their view
Upon a tawny front: his captain's heart,
Which in the scuffles of great fights hath burst
The buckles on his breast, reneges all temper,
And is become the bellows and the fan
To cool a gipsy's lust.

*Flourish. Enter* Antony, Cleopatra, *her Ladies,* the Train with Eunuchs fanning her.
   Look, where they come :
   Take but good note, and you shall see in him
   The tripple pillar of the world transform'd
   Into a strumpet's fool: behold and see.
*Cleo:* If it be love indeed, tell me how much.
*Ant:* There's beggary in the love that can be
      reckon'd.
*Cleo:* I'll set a bourn how far to be beloved.
*Ant:* Then must thou needs find out new heaven,
      new earth.
            *Enter* an Attendant.
*Att:* News, my good lord, from Rome.
*Ant:* Grates me: the sum.
*Cleo:* Nay, hear them, Antony:
Fulvia perchance is angry; or, who knows
If the scarce-bearded Caesar have not sent
His powerful mandate to you, 'Do this, or this;
Take in that kingdom, and enfranchise that;
Perform't or else we damn thee.'
*Ant:* How, my love!
*Cleo:* Perchance! nay, and most like:
You must not stay here longer, your dismission
Is come from Caesar; therefore hear it, Antony.
Where's Fulvia's process? Caesar's
I would say? both?
Call in the messengers. As I am Egypt's queen,
Thou blushest, Antony; and that blood of thine
Is Caesar's homager; else so thy cheek pays shame
When shrill-tongued Fulvia scolds. The
      messengers!
*Ant:* Let Rome in Tiber melt, and the wide arch
Of the ranged empire fall! Here is my space.
Kingdoms are clay: our dungy earth alike
Feeds beast as man: the nobleness of life
Is to do thus: when such a mutual pair
[*Embracing.*
And such a twain can do't, in which I bind,
On pain of punishment, the world to weed
We stand up peerless.
*Cleo:* Excellant falsehood!
Why did he marry Fulvia, and not love her?
I'll seem the fool I am not: Antony
Will be himself.
*Ant:* But stirr'd by Cleopatra.

Now, for the love of Love and her soft hours,
Let's not confound the time with conference
    harsh!
There's not a minute of our lives should stretch
Without some pleasure now. What sport tonight?

Act IV

In Act IV we learn how Antony feels on being "betrayed" by Cleopatra. Here are scene (xii) and part of scene (xiii) (Act IV):

Scene (XII). Another part of the same.
    *Enter* Antony and Scarus.
*Ant:* Yet they are not join'd: where yond pine does stand, I shall discover all: I'll bring thee word
    Straight, how 'tis like to go.          [*Exit.*
*Scar:* Swallows have built
In Cleopatra's sails their nests; the augurers
Say they know not, they cannot tell; look grimly,
And dare not speak their knowledge. Antony
Is valiant, and dejected; and by starts,
His fretted fortunes give him hope, and fear,
Of what he has, and has not,
              [*Alarum afar off, as at a sea fight.*
          *Re-enter* Antony.
*Ant:* All is lost
This foul Egyptian hath betrayed me:
My fleet hath yielded to the foe; and yonder
They cast their caps up and carouse together
Like friends long lost. Triple-turn'd whore! 'tis
    thou
Hast sold me to this novice; and my heart
Makes only wars on thee. Bid them all fly;
For when I am revenged upon my charm,
I have done all. Bid them all fly; begone.
                  [*Exit Scarus.*
O sun, thy uprise shall I see no more:
Fortune and Antony part here; even here
Do we shake hands. All come to this?
The hearts                                          20
That spaniel'd me at heels, to whom I gave
Their wishes, do discandy, melt their sweets
On blossoming Caesar; and this pine is bark'd,
that overtopp'd them all. Betray'd I am:
O this false soul of Egypt! this gave charm,—
Whose eye beck'd forth my wars, and call'd them
    home;
Whose bosom was my crownet, my chief end,—

Like a right gipsy, hath, at fast and loose,
Beguiled me to the very heart of loss.
What, Eros, Eros!
              *Enter* Cleopatra.
                  Ah, thou spell! Avaunt!
*Cleo:* Why is my lor enraged against his love?
*Ant:* Vanish, or I shall give thee thy deserving,
And blemish Caesar's triumph. Let him take thee,
And hoist thee up to the shouting plebeians:
Follow his chariot, like the greatest spot
Of all thy sex; most monster-like, be shown
For poor'st diminutives, for doits: and let
Patient Octavia plough thy visage up
With her prepared nails.          [*Exit Cleopatra.*
                  'Tis well thou'rt gone,
If it be well to live; but better 'twere
Thou fell'st into my fury, for one death
Might have prevented many. Eros, ho!
The shirt of Nessus is upon me: teach me,
Alcides, thou mine ancestor, thy rage:
Let me lodge Lichas on the horns o' the moon;
And with those hands, that grasp'd the heaviest
    club,
Subdue my worthiest self. The witch shall die:
To thy young Roman boy she hath sold me, and
    I fall
Under this plot; she dies for't Eros, ho!     [*Exit.*

Scene XIII. *Alexandria. Cleopatra's place.*

    *Enter* Cleopatra, Charmian, Iras and Mardian.
*Cleo:* Help me, my woman! O, he is more made
Than Telamon for his shield; the boar of Thessaly
Was never so emboss'd.
*Char:* To the monument!
There lock yourself, and send him word you are
    dead.
The soul and body rise not more in parting
That greatness going off.
**Note:** One may find fault with the beloved when he/she is alive.

But on his/her death, one feels the pangs of remorse and the separation. This is how Antony feels on Cleopatra's death.

The extract is from Scene (XIV)
Act IV
*Enter* Mardian.

O, thy vile lady!

She has robb'd me of my sword.

*Mar:* No, Antony;
My mistress loved thee, and her fortunes mingled
With thine entirely.

*Ant:* Hence, saucy eunuch; peace!
She hath betray'd me and shall die the death.

*Mar:* Death of one person can be paid but once,
And that she has discharged: what thou wouldst
　　do
Is done unto thy hand: the last she spake
Was 'Antony! most noble Antony!'
Then in the midst a tearing groan did break
The name of Antony; it is divided
Between her heart and lips: she render'd life,
Thy name so buried in her.

*Ant:* Dead, then?

*Mar:* Dead.

*Ant:* Unarm, Eros; the long day's task is done,
And we must sleep. [*To Mar.*] That thou depart'st
　　hence safe,
Does pay thy labour richly; go 　[*Exit Mardian.*
Off. pluck off:
The seven-fold shield of Ajax cannot keep
The battery from my heart. O, cleave, my sides!
Heart, once be stronger than thy continent,
Crack thy frail case! Apace, Eros, apace.
No more a soldier: bruised pieces, go;
You have been nobly brone. From me awhile.
　　　　　　　　　　　　　　　[*Exit Eros.*
I will o'ertake thee, Cleopatra, and
Weep for my pardon. So it must be, for now
All length is torture: since the torch is out,
Lie down, and stray no farther: now all labour
Mars what it does; yea, very force entangles
Itself with strength: seal them, and all is done
Eros! I come, my queen:—Eros!—Stay for me:
Where souls do couch on flowers, we'll hand in
　　hand,
And with our sprightly port make the ghosts
　　gaze:
Dido and her Aeneas shall want troops,
And all the haunt be ours. Come, Eros, Eros!
　　　　　　　*Re-enter* Eros.

*Eros:* What would my lord?

*Ant:* Since Cleopatra died,
I have lived in such dishonour, that the gods

Detest my baseness. I, that with my sword
Quarter'd the world, and o'er green Neptune's
　　back
With ships made cities, condemn myself to lack
The courage of women; less noble mind
Than she which by her death our Caesar tells
'I am conqueror of myself.' Thou art sworn, Eros,
That when the exigent should come, which now
Is come indeeed, when I should see behind me
The inevitable prosecution of
Disgrace and horror, that, on my command,
Thou then wouldst kill me: do 't; the time is
　　come:
Thou strikest not me, 'tis Caesar thou defeat'st.
Put colour in thy cheek.

*Eros:* The gods withhold me!
Shall I do that which all the Parthian darts,
Though enemy, lost aim, and could not?

*Ant:* Eros,
Wouldst thou be window'd in great Rome and
　　see
Thy master thus with pleach'd arms, bending
　　down
His corrigible neck, his face subdued
To penetrative shame, whilst the wheel'd seat
Of fortunate Caesar, drawn before him, branded
His baseness that ensued?

*Eros:* I would not see 't.

### "Criticism on Antony and Cleopatra"

We have elaborate criticism on Antony and Cleopatra", some of which is given below :

(1)

**F.S. Boas**

"Certainly in consummate delineation of character, and in the superb rhythmical swell of many passages, the work is unsurpassed. But it has a grave share of the defects to which Romantic Drama had been liable from the first, especially when it was drawing upon historical material ....Shakespeare seems to have felt a conscientious obligation to introduce every incident, political, private, mentioned by Plutarch, and the result is a loss of dramatic unity and perspective. The multiplicity of details is bewildering, and no single event stands out boldly as the pivot on which the catastrophe turns.

But this artistic defect is here in part the outcome of a significant peculiarity in Shakespeare's treatment of love as a dramatic theme. Sexual passion is the immediate obect of only three plays, *Romeo and Juliet, Troilus and Cressida and Antony and Cleopatra*. In each case of emotional interest is interwoven with elements of a political nature—the civil strife of Montagues and Capulets, the war between the Greeks and the Trojans, the struggle for the lordship of the Roman world. Thus, Shakespeare even when making an elaborate study of amorous passion, does not isolate it from the wider, more material, issues of surrounding civic or national life. He thus avoids the disastrous pitfall of treating love as the exclusive factor in existence—a method which, according to the nature of the love chosen for analysis, tends to produce an unwholesome sentimentality or a still more unwholesome experience. Shakespeare opens to our view hearts aflame with chaste affection or with sensous desire, but he never cheats himself or others into the belief that sexual relationship is the solitary, imperious concern of all mankind. From the Kaleidoscopic changes of Cleopatra's moods, he turns our gaze to the legions tramping in solid array through the uttermost parts of the earth, or to the council-chambers where the destinies of kingdoms are being decided by the stroke of a pen. We are shown in turn of the most materialistic age in the world's history, the age when Roman civic virtue was, in its death-throes, suffocated by the plethora of its golden spoils from the South and the East.

(2)

**Hazlitt**

Hazlitt's views are very pertinent in regard to Antony and Cleopatra :

"This is a very noble play. Though not in the first class of Shakespeare's productions, it stands next to them, and is, we think, the finest of his Historical plays, that is, of those in which he made poetry the organ of history, and assumed a certain tone of character and sentiment, in conformity to known facts, instead of trusting to his observations of general nature or to the unlimited indulgence of his own fancy. What he has added to the history, is upon a par with it. His genius was, as it were, a match for history as well as nature, and could grapple at will with either. This play is full of that pervading comprehensive power by which the poet could always make himself master of time and circumstances. It presents a fine picture of Roman pride and esteem magnificence: and in the struggle between the two, the empire of the world seems suspended, 'like the swan's down feather', 'That stands upon the swell at full of tide, And neither way inclines.' The characters breath, move and live. Shakespeare does not stand reasoning on what his characters would do or say, but at once *becomes* them, and speaks and acts for them. He does not present us with groups of stage-puppets on poetical machines making set speeches on human life, and acting from a calculation of ostensible motives, but he brings living men and women on the scene, who speak and act from real feelings, according to the ebbs and flows of passion, without the least tincture of the pedantary of logic or rhetoric. Nothing is made out of inference or analogy, by climax and antithesis, but everything takes place just as it would have done in reality, according to the occasion."

(3)

**Paul Stepfer**

Reflecting on the subject of Antony and Cleopatra, Stepfer says,

"The subject of Shakespeare's tragedy is the guilty love of Antony and Cleopatra, a subject that would have presented an almost insuperable difficulty to a poor little poet of a narrow and mediocre type; quite at a loss, and biting his pen the while, he would have said to himself, 'What is to be done? Cleopatra is a very wicked woman, *a monster*, as. Horace calls her,—a mixture of all we must hate and despise, she is a coquette, timid, cowardly, cringing perfidious, tyrannical, cruel and wanton. To interest decent people in such a creature is clearly impossible, except by making a selection from among the contradictory features of her character, and since Plutarch speaks of her as being occasionally geneous, tender and devoted, heroic and sublime, I must convert the conception into the rule, and put an expurgated Cleopatra on the stage.' But Shakespeare reasoned in a very different manner. He started with the notion of Cleopatra as an enhantress, and he trusted with quiet confidence to the power of his poetry, and to his sure knowledge of the human heart, to make the same fascination that she exercised over her lovers be felt by us : her faults, her vices, her crimes—what do they matter? Besides which, it betrays a good deal of simplicity to suppose that certain sins which are repulsive in a man are equally odious when met with in a woman. A man is ugly, and has hard work to atone for his natural ugliness, but, as a poet has said,—and it is no empty compliment, but an astute psychological truth,—women, do what they will, are always charming.

Shakespeare has not deemed it necessary to leave out any of the stains, big or little, in Cleopatra's character, as he was obliged to do in Antony's; and this, instead of depriving the lovely little monster of a single charm, only makes her the more irresistible."

(4)

**A.C. Bradley**

Bradley, who is an acknowledged authority on "Shakespearean Tragedy", says about Antony and Cleopatra,

"A comparison of Shakespearean tragedies seems to prove that the tragic emotions are stirred in the fullest possible measure only when such beauty or nobility of character is displayed or commands unreserved admiration or love; or when, in default of this, the forces which move the agents, and the conflict which results from these forces attain a terrifying and overwhelming power. The four most famous tragedies satisfy one or both these conditons; 'Antony and Cleopatra', though a great tragedy, satisfies neither of them completely. But to say this is not to criticize it. It does not attempt to satisfy these conditions, and then fail in the attempt. It attempts something different, and succeeds as triumphantly as 'Othello' itself. In doing so it gives us what no other tragedy can give and it leaves us, no less than any other, lot in astonishment at the powers which created it."

(5)

**W.J. Courthope**

Courthope has the following opinion on Antony and Cleopatra :

"Antony's character in its extraordinary versatility—orator, soldier and debauchee; a Henry V without his power of self-control—furnished one of those contradictory problems of human nature

which Shakespeare was accustomed to study with the most sympathetic insight; and the meretricious fascination of Cleopatra, as recorded by Plutarch, joined (for she is no Cressida) to a certain greatness of soul and fidelity of passion, must have struck the poet's imagination by its likeness, as well as its contrast, to some woman whose character he painted in the *Sonnets*. The use of the word 'will' in this remarkable play is noticeable. When Antony has left the battle of Actium, to his own dishonour, in pursuit of the flying Cleopatra the queen asks the shrewd, worldly, and calculating Enobarbus, who is introduced into the play as a kind of chorus to comment on Antony and his fortunes: 'Is Antony or we in fault for this?' Enobarbus replies: Antony only, that would make his will Lord of his reason.' (III, XIII) Yet Antony throughout the play recognises that he is acting against his deliberate resolution, under the irresistible influence of passion: 'I followed that I blush to look upon: My very hairs do mutiny; for the white Reprove the brown for rashness, and they them for fear and doting,' (III, XI). So that his conduct is what Iago calls 'merely a lust of the blood and *permission* of the will' (1. III). This is the very helplessness spoken of in *Sonnet* CL: 'O from what power hast thou this powerful might with insufficiency my heart to sway? To make me give the lie to my true sight and swear that brightness doth not grace the day? Whence hast thou this becoming of things ill, that in the very refuse of thy deeds. There is such strength and warrantise of skill. That, in my mind, thy worst all best exceeds?

(6)

**H.A. Taine**

Taine's views on the play are expressed in an impassioned language :

"How much more visible is this impassioned and unfettered genius of Shakespeare in the great characters which sustain the whole weight of the drama! The startling imagination, the furious velocity of the manifold and exuberant ideas, the unruly passion, rushing upon death and crime, hallucinations, madness, all the ravages of delirium bursting through will and reason: such are the forces and ravings which engender them. Shall I speak of dazzling Cleopatra, who holds Antony in the whirlwind of her devices and caprices, who fascinates and kills, who scatters to the winds the lives of men as a handful of desertdust, the fatal Eastern sorceress who sports with life of death, headstrong, irresistible, child of air and fire, whose life is but a tempest, whose thought, ever re-pointed and broken, is like the crackling of lighting."

(7)

**Dowden**

Dowden, the great critic, who is known for the proverbial division of Shakespeare's artistic periods, has the following words to say on Antony and Cleopatra :

"The spirit of the play, though superficially it appears voluptuous, is essentially severe. There is to say, Shakespeare is faithful to the fact. The fascination exercised by Cleopatra, is not so much that of the senses as of the sensuous imagination. A third of the world is theirs. They have left youth behind with is slight, melodious raptures and despairs. Their is the deeper intoxication of middle age, when death has become a reality, when the world is limited and positive when life is urged to yield up quickly its utmost treasures of delight. What may they not achieve of joy who have power and beauty, and pomp, and pleasure all their own? How shall they fill every minute of their time with the quintessence of enjoyment and of glory? 'Let Rome in Tiber melt! and the wide arch of the ran'd empire fall! here is my 'space'.' Only *one* thing they had not allowed for,— that over and above power, and beauty pleasure, and pomp, there is a certain inevitable fact, a law which cannot be evaded. Pleasure sits enthroned as queen; there is a revel, and the lords of the earth, crowned with roses, dance before her to the sound of lascivious flutes. But presently, the scene changes; the hall of revel is transformed to an arena; the dancers are armed gladiators; and as they advance to combat they pay the last homage to their Queen with the words *Morituri te salutant*."

(8)

**Objections by Gervinus**

Gervinus has raised some important objections against the play :

"There arises, moreover, an ethical objection (to this play) which will prejudice the majority of readers against it, and against Coleridge's opinion of it.

Among the *Dramatis Personae* there is no great and noble character, and in the actions of the drama no really elevating feature, either in its politics or in its love-affairs. This play seems to make us intuitively aware how much we should lose in Shakespeare, if, with his confessedly great knowledge of men and nature there did not go, hand in hand, aesthetic excellence (the ideal concentration of actors and actions), and ethical excellence (the ideal height of what is represented as human nature). The poet had to set forth a debased period in his *Antony and Cleopatra*; for the truth of history, he did adequately; but this did not exclude him from giving a glance at a better state of human nature, which, amid so much degradation, might comfort and elevate us. If we recall the *Historical Plays*, where Shakespeare had to depict generations, for the most part degenerate and ruined, we shall find that in Richard II there was, as a compensation, a Gaunt and a Carlisle; and even in Richard III, the few strokes that depicted the sons of Edward, are beneficent counterpoise to the widespread wickedness. Here, however, there is nothing of the kind, and we may even affirm that the opportunity for such a counterbalance has been conspicuously evaded : it would surely have been easy, in the characters of Octavia at least, to keep before us some views of what is more noble in human nature: even if it were only a few traits, which would have exhibited her to us in action, where now she is merely described to us in words."

**Shakespearean Criticism (General)**

There has been a lot of Shakespearean criticism over the centuries. It will be enough to give only a few examples :

(1)

**T.S. Baynes**

According to T.S. Baynes:

"Shakespeare's work alone can be said to possess the organic strength and infinite variety, the troubling fulness, vital complexity, and breathing truth of Nature herself. In points of artistic resource and technical ability—such as copious and expressive diction, freshness and pregnancy of verbal combination, richly modulated verse, and structural skill in the handling of incident and action— Shakespeare's supremacy is indeed sufficiently assured. But, after all, it is of course, in the spirit and substance of his work, his power of piercing to the hidden centres of character, of touching the deepest springs of impulse and passion, out of which emerge the issues of life, and of evolving those issues dramatically with a flawless strength, subtlety, and truth, which raises him so immensely above and beyond not only the best of the play, Wrights who went before him, but the whole line of illustrious dramatists that came after him. It is Shakespeare's unique distinction that he has an absolute command over all the complexities of thought and feeling that prompt action and bring out the dividing lines of character. He sweeps with the hand of a master the whole gamut of human experience from the lowest note to the very top of its compass, from the sportive childish treble of Mamilius, and the pleading boyish tone of Prince Arthur, up to the spectre-haunted terrors of Macbeth, the tropical passion of Othello, the agonised sense and torture spirit of Hamlet, the sustained elemental grandeur, the Titanic force, the utterly tragical pathos of King Lear."

(2)

**George Lord Littleton**

"No other author has ever so copious, so bold, so *creative* an imagination, with so perfect a knowledge of the passions, humours, and sentiments of mankind. He painted all characters. From kings down to peasants, with equal truth and equal force. If human nature were destroyed and no monument were left of it expect his works, other beings might know *what man was* from those writings."

(3)

**Dr. Johnson**

*(i)* Johnson says of Shakespeare, "In tragedy he often writes, with great appearance of toil and study, what is written at last with little felicity, but in his comic scenes, he seems to produce, without labour, what no labour can improve."

*(ii)* Shakespeare's "scenes are occupied only by men, who act and think."

(4)

**T.S. Eliot**

T.S. Eliot defends Johnson's views on Shakespeare. He says,

"This is an opinion which we cannot lightly dismiss. Johnson is quite aware that the alternation of 'tragic' and 'comic' is something more than an alternation; he perceives that something different and new is produced. The interchanges of mingled scenes seldom fail to produce the intended vicissitudes of passion."

(5)

**Hazlitt**

According to Hazlitt,

"His plays alone are properly expressions of the passions, not descriptions of them. His characters are real beings of flesh and blood; they speak like man, not like author."

(6)

**Pope**

*(i)* Commenting on Shakespeare's originality, Pope says,

"If ever any author deserved the name of an *original* it was Shakespeare. Homer himself drew not his art so immediately from the fountains of Nature; it proceeded through Egyptian strainers and channels, and came to him not without some tincture of the learning or some cast of the models, of those before him. The poetry of Shakespeare was inspiration indeed; he is not so much an imitator as an instrument of Nature : and it is not so just to say that he speaks from her, as that she speaks through him."

*(ii)* Pope expresses his opion about Shakespeare's characters in the following words :

"His *characters* are so much Nature herself, that it is a sort of injury to call them by so distant a name as copies of her. Those of other poets have a constant resemblance, which shows that they received them from one another and were but multipliers of the same image : each picture, like a mock rainbow, is but the reflection of a reflection. But every single character in Shakespeare is as much an individual as those in life itself; it is an impossible to find any two alike; as such as from their relation of affinity in any respect appear most to be twins, will upon comparison be found remarkably distinct. To this life and variety of character we must add the wonderful preservation of it, which is such throughout his plays, that, had all the speeches been printed without the very names of the persons, I believe one might have applied them with certainty to every speaker."

(7)

**David Masson**

Commenting on Shakespeare's power of imagination David Masson says,

"Shakespeare is as astonishing for the exuberance of his genius in abstract notions, and for the depth of his analytic and philosophic insight, as for the scope and minuteness of his poetic imagination. It is as if into a mind poetical in *form* there had been poured all the *matter* that existed in the mind of his contemporary Bacon. In Shakespeare's plays, we have thought, history, expedition, philosophy, all within the round of the poet."

(8)

**W. Richardson**

W. Richardson thus comments on Shakespeare's ability to blend the two essential powers of dramatic invention, which mentions in his statement :

"Many dramatic writers of different ages are capable, occasionally, of breaking out, with great fervour of genius, in the natural language of strong emotion. No writer of antiquity is more distinguished for abilities of this kind than Euripides. His whole heart and soul seem torn and agitated by the force of the passion he imitates. He ceases to be Euripides; he is Medis; he is Orestes. Shakespeare, however, is most eminently distinguished, not only by these occasional sallies, but by imitating the passion in all its aspects, by pursuing it through all its windings and labyrinths, by moderating or accelerating its importuosity according to the influence of other principles and of external events, and finally by combining it in a judicious manner with other passions and propensities, or by setting it aptly in opposition. He thus unites the two essential powers of dramatic invention, that of forming characters; and that of imitating in their natural expressions, the passions and affections of which they are composed."

(9)

**Thomas Fuller**

Expressing his views on Shakespeare's in born faculties, Fuller says,

"He was an eminent instance of the truth of that rule, *poeta non fit sed masciture*; one is *not made*, but *born* a poet. Indeed his learning was very little, so that, as Cornish diamonds are not polished by any lapidary, but are pointed and smoothed even as they are taken out of the earth, so nature itself was all the *art* which was used upon him.

Many were the wit-combats betwixt him and Ben Jonson; which two I behold like a Spanish great galleon and an English man of war; Master Jonson (like the former) was built far higher in learning; solid but slow in his performances. Shakespeare, with the English man of war, lesser in bulk, but lighter in sailing, could turn with all tides, tack about, and advantage of all winds, by the quickness of his wit and invention."

(10)

**A.C. Swinburne**

Expressing his views on Shakespeare's tragic art which owed a lot to Marlowe and on his broad and all empracing humanity, Swinburne says,

"Through all the forenoon of our triumphant day till the utter consummation and ultimate ascention of dramatic poetry incarnate and transfigured in the master-singer of the world, the quality of his tragedy was at that of Marlowe's broad, single and intense; large of hand, voluble of tongue, direct of purpose. With the dawn of its latter epoch a new power comes upon it, to find clothing and expression in new forms of speech and after a new style. The language has put off it foreign decoration of lyrics and elegiac ornament; it has found already its infinite gain in the loss of those sweet superfluous graces which encumbered the march and enchained the utterance of its childhood. The figures which it invests are now no more types of a single passion, the incarnations of a single thought. They now demand a scrutiny which tests the power of a mind and tries the value of a judgement; they appeal to something more than the instant apprehension which sufficed to respond to the immediate claim of those that went before them. Romeo and Juliet were simply lovers, and their name brings back to us no further thought than of their love and the lovely sorrow of its end; Antony and Cleopatra shall be before all things lovers, but the thought of their love and its triumphant tragedy shall recall other things beyond number—all the forces and fortunes of mankind, all the chance and all the consequence that waited on their imperial passion, all the infinite variety of qualities and power wrought together and welded into the frame and composition of that love which shook from end to end nations and kingdoms of the earth".

(11)

**F.W. Robertson**

Commenting on Shakespeare's genuine humanity and earthiness, Robertson says,

"What I admire in Shakespeare, however, is that his loves are all human—no earthliness hiding itself from itself in sentimental transcendentalism—no loves of the angels, which are the least angelic things, I believe, that float in the clouds, though they do look down upon mortal feelings with contempt just as the dark volumes of smoke which issue from the long chimney of a manufactory might brood very sublimely over the town which they blacken, and fancy themselves far more ethereal than those vapours which steam up from the earth by day and night. Yet these are pure water and those are destined to condense in black soot. So are the transcendentalisms of affection. Shakespeare is healthy, true to Humanity in this.........You always know that you are on an earth which has to be refined, instead of floating in the empyrean with wings of wax. Therein he is immeasurably greater than Shelley. Shelleyism is very sublime, sublimer a good deal than God, for God's world is all wrong and Shelley is all right—much purer than Christ, for Shelley can criticise Christ's heart and life—nevertheless, Shelleyism is only atmospheric profligacy at coin a Montgomeryism. I believe this to be one of Shakespeare's most wondrous qualities—the humanity of the nature and heart. There is a spirit of sunny endeavours about him, and an aquiescence in things as they are—not incompatible with a cheerful resolve to make them better."

(12)

**Matthew Arnold**

Expressing his views on Shakespeare's power of prosody and expression, Arnold says,

"Let me have the pleasure of quoting a sentence about Shakespeare, which I met my accident not long ago in the *Correspondent*, a French review which not a dozen English people, I suppose, look at. The writer is praising Shakespeare's prose. 'With Shakespare,' he says, 'prose come in whenever the subject, being more familiar is unsuited to the majestic English iambic.' And the goes on : 'Shakespeare is the king of poetic rhythm and style, as well as the king of the realm of thought along with his dazzling prose. Shakespeare has succeeded in giving us the most varied, the most harmonious verse which has ever sounded upon the human ear since the verse of the Greeks. M. Henry Cochin, the writer of this sentence, deserves our gratitude for it; it would not be easy to praise Shakespeare, in a single sentence, more justly."

(13)

**Poetic Effusions**

Some writers have gone wildly ecstatic in expressing themselves poetically on Shakespeare :

*(i)*

**Milton**

"The Sweetest Shakespeare, Fancy's Child!'"

*(ii)*

**W.W. Story**

"And such was Shakespeare, whose strong soul could climb
Steeps of sheer-terrors, sound the ocean grand
Of passions deep, or over Fancy's strand
Trip with his fairies, keeping step and time.
His too the power to laugh out full and clear,
With unembittered joyance, and to move
Along the silent, shadowy paths of love
As tenderly as Dante, whose austere
Stern spirit through the world below, above,
Unsmiling strode, to tell the tidings here."

*(iii)*

**Garrick**

"When Learning's Triumph o'er her barb'rous Foes
First rear'd the stage, immortal Shakespeare rose;
Each change of many-coloured Life he drew,
Exhausted World, and then imagin'd new."

*(iv)*

**M. Arnold**

"Others abide our question :
Thou art free."

# ROMANTIC PERIOD

## PERCY BYSSHE, SHELLEY (1792-1822)

### Life

1. He was born in Sussex in 1792.
2. His parents belonged to the class of nobility.
3. As a child, Shelley was highly fanciful like Blake.

### Education

*(i)* After having got a brutal treatment in his Scotch public school, he joined Eton. But being a highly sensitive boy who held self-respect above anything else, he revolted against the tyrannical system in the new school.

*(ii)* Of course, he was ridiculed and called 'Mad Shelley' by other boys.

*(iii) (a)* While at Oxford, he published his pamphlet "The Necessity of Atheism."

*(b)* In writing this, he was influenced by the philosophy of Hume.

*(c)* He was expelled from the university for this.

### Marriage

1. *(i)* First Shelley married Harriet Westbrook, a mere school girl whose parents never agreed to this marriage.
   *(ii)* Even Shelley's own parents disinherited him for this.
2. *(i)* Later, as Shelley came under the influence of Godwin—an anarchist philosopher—he eloped with his daughter, Mary, who later wrote "Frankenstein's Monster" which is so famous for its title if not much for its contents.
   *(ii)* Sadly, this elopement, however, led to Harriet's well-known suicide.

### Exile

1. Just as Byron had earlier left England in 1816, never to return, Shelley did the same in 1818, though for reasons of health mainly and partly of hostility against his ideology of revolt, anarchism or cynicism (whatever we may call it), etc.
2. His shifting to Italy proved a boon, since—
   *(i)* here he wrote his best poetry
   *(ii)* here he was able to get the friendship of such personalities as: *(a)* Byron *(b)* Leigh Hunt *(c)* Trelawney, etc.

### Death

Shelley met with a tragic death in 1822 while sailing in a boat off the Italian coast.

### Works

1. *Alastor (or the Spirit of Solitude) (1816):*
   *(i)* It expresses Shelley's endless love for wandering in search of a dream girl who is the model of beauty.
   *(ii)* The poem is illusory in nature and lacks reality.
2. *Prometheus Unbound (1818-20):*
   *(i)* In this lyrical drama whilst Prometheus steals fire from heaven for mankind, Shelley, according to Long, "is the prophet of science and evolution."
   *(ii)* Studied in the proper prospective, the work suggests hope and promise for goodness to prevail at last.
   *(iii)* In his poem "The Cloud" Shelley takes recourse to exact geographical phenomenon. Similar is the case in 'Ode to the West Wind'. Because of his correct use of geographical and scientific facts, he is sometimes called "the scientist poet."
3. *Other Revolutionary works:* Besides Promentheus, Shelley's other revolutionary works are:
   *(i)* Queen Mab (1813)
   *(ii)* The Revolt of Islam (1818)
   *(iii)* The Witch of Atlas (1820)
   *(iv)* Hellas (1821)
4. "Epipsychidion" (1821) is Shelley's work of Platonic love.
5. Perhaps Shelley's only work based on reality is his drama "The Cenci". Here below is an extract:

#### Beatrice's Last Words

*Beatrice:* Farewell, my tender brother. Think
Of our sad fate with gentleness, as now:
And let mild, pitying thoughts lighten for thee

Thy sorrow's load. Err not in harsh despair,
But tears and patience. One thing more, my child:
For thine own sake be constant to the love
Thou bearest us; and to the faith that I,
Though wrapped in a strange cloud of crime and
    shame,
Lived ever holy and unstained. And though
Ill tongues shall wound me, and our common
    name
Be as a mark stamped on thine innocent brow
For men to point at as they pass, do thou
Forbear, and never think a thought unkind
Of those, who perhaps love thee in their graves.
So mayest thou die as I do; fear and pain
Being subdued. Farewell! Farewell! Farewell!
*Bernardo:* I cannot say, farewell!
*Camillo:* Oh, Lady Beatrice!
*Beatrice:* Give yourself no unnecessary pain,
My dear Lord Cardinal. Here, Mother, tie
My girdle for me, and bind up this hair
In any simple knot; ay, that does well.
And yours I see is coming down. How often
Have we done this for one another! Now
We shall not do it any more. My Lord,
We are quite ready. Well, 'tis very well.

(End to The Cenci.)

6.   *Adonais:* It is an elegy written on the death of Keats and is one of Shelley's most widely known poems.

### Lyrics

*(i)* That Shelley is probably the greatest lyricist in English needs no emphasis.

*(ii)* Some of his famous lyrics are:

  *(a)*  The Cloud
  *(b)*  To A Skylark
  *(c)*  Ode to the West Wind
  *(d)*  To Night

**Other works**

Some of his other works are :
1.   Hymn to Intellectual Beauty
2.   Sensitive Plant
3.   "Lament" with the first line—"O world, O life, O time"

Shelley and Wordsworth: Comparing Shelley with Wordsworth, Long says, "Wordsworth found and Shelley lost himself in nature."

**Note:** Here are some extracts from his works:

*(i)*  **From Alastor**

    Earth, ocean, air, belovèd brotherhood!
    If our great Mother has imbued my soul
    With aught of natural piety to feel
    Your love, and recompense the boon with mine;
    If dewy morn, and odorous noon, and even,
    With sunset and its gorgeous ministers,
    And solemn midnight's tingling silentness;
    If autumn's hollow sighs in the sere wood,
    And winter robing with pure snow and crowns
    Of starry ice the grey grass and bare boughs;
    If spring's voluptuous pantings when she
    breathes
    Her first sweet kisses, have been dear to me;
    If no bright bird, insect, or gentle beast
    I consciously have injured, but still loved
    And cherished these my kindred; then forgive
    This boast, belovèd brethren, and withdraw
    No portion of your wonted favour now!
    Mother of this unfathomable world!
    Favour my solemn song, for I have loved
    Thee ever, and thee only; I have watched
    Thy shadow, and the darkness of thy steps,

*(ii)*  Passionless?—no, yet free from guilt or pain,
    Which were, for his will made or suffered
    them,
    Nor yet exempt, though ruling them like
    slaves,
    From chance, and death, and mutability,
    The clogs of that which else might oversoar
    The loftiest stars of unascended heaven,
    Pinnacled dim in the intense inane.

(Prometheus, end of Act iii.)

E. Blunden says of Shelley, "Shelley did not take up every subject for verse in the solemn, neutral way which we scholiasts are liable to ascribe to him. Much has been written on his address *To a Skylark*, and much without proper recognition of his actual occasion. Shelley, in that poems, was *talking*, at least at the point of departure. He was capable, there, of joking (for there is a free state of mind, which may not resemble the comic spirit of the *New Yorker,* or perhaps it may—but it is truly random); he did not start as an automatic machine delivering the weight and fortune for skylarks.

Hail to thee, blithe Spirit!

A skylark: but he refuses to believe the natural historians's limited definition. 'Bird thou never wert.' He also rejects the Shakespearean location of Heaven, or else is willing to play upon the neighbourhood ('Hark, hark, the lark at Heaven's gate sings') with his

That *from Heaven, or near it,*
Pourest thy full heart....

The numerous comparisons in the poem, which have been treated like realistic equations, are in fact so much talk, the gestures of a mind in play, the sportive balloon-flying of one who does not really wish to catch his lark.

There are several surviving protests against Shelley. He ought at all costs to have finished *The Boat on the Serchio*, a poem which, so far as it goes, seems to combine all his mystery and concept of our universe, and all his social grace and observation. When he set out on his last voyage, *mutatis mutandis* this is how he went; the biographers need not deplore the want of a log-book or a dictaphone; here is the voice, stir, and fascination of Shelley putting out to sea. Another complaint is that he set sail at such an inauspicious moment. He was, at the time, entering upon a new chapter of intellectual astuteness. In his last long poem, *The Triumph of Life*, though the confusion and agglomeration of his younger manner have not quite disappeared, there is a sinewy manner have not quite disappeared, there is a sinewy and ironic force which makes him jump almost a century. But apart from that, he was beginning, to live, and to cease to be 'at war with life'. Disturbance still embittered him, but exceptionally: a faultless ease was stealing upon his poetry,

The clearest echoes of the hills,
The softest notes of falling rills,
The melodies of birds and bees,
The murmurings of summer seas,
And pattering rain, and breathing dew,
And airs of evening; and it knew
That seldom-heard mysterious sound
Which, driven on its diurnal round,
As it floats through boundless day,
Our world enkindles on its way."

(**Note :** Please see more poems and extracts from Shelley to have a fair appraisal of his poetic art :

### *From* Song to the Men of England

Men of England, wherefore plough
For the lords who lay ye low?
Wherefore weave with toil and care
The rich robes your tyrants wear?

Wherefore feed, and clothe, and save,
From the cradle to the grave,
Those ungrateful drones who would
Drain your sweat—nay, drink your blood?

Wherefore, Bees of England, forge
Many a weapon, chain, and scourge,
That these stingless drones may spoil
The forced produce of your toil?

Have ye leisure, comfort, calm,
Shelter, food, love's gentle balm?
Or what is it ye buy so dear
With your pain and with your fear?

The seed ye sow, another reaps;
The wealth ye find, another keeps;
The robes ye weave, another wears;
The arms ye forge, another bears.

Sow seed,—but let no tyrant reap;
Find wealth,—let no impostor heap;
Weave robes,—let not the idle wear;
Forge arms,—in your defence to bear.

### Ozymandias

I Met a traveller from an antique land
Who said : Two vast and trunkless legs of stone
Stand in the desert.... Near them, on the sand,
Half sunk, shattered visage lies, whose frown,
And wrinkled lip, and sneer of cold command,
Tell that its sculptor well those passions read
Which yet survive, (stamped on these lifeless
      things,)
The hand that mocked them and the heart that
      fed :
And on the pedestal these words appear:
'My name is Ozymandias, king of kings:
Look on my works, ye Mighty, and despair!'
Nothing beside remains. Round the decay
Of that colossal wreck, boundless and bare
The lone and level sands stretch far away.

### Stanzas Written in Dejection, Near Naples

The sun is warm, the sky is clear,

The waves are dancing fast and bright;
Blue isles and snowy mountains wear
    The purple noon's transparent might;
    The breath of the moist earth is light
Around its un-expanded buds;
    Like many a voice of one delight,
    The winds, the birds, the ocean floods,
The City's voice itself is soft Solitude's.
"I see the Deep's untrampled floor
    With green and purple seaweeds strown;
I see the waves upon the shore,
     Like light dissolved in star-showers, thrown:
    I sit upon the sands alone,—
   The lightning of the noontide ocean
    Is flashing round me, and a tone
   Arises from its measured motion,
How sweet! did any heart now share in my
   emotion.

   Alas! I have nor hope nor health,
    Nor peace within nor calm around,
   Nor that content surpassing wealth
    The sage in meditation found,
    And walked with inward glory crowned—
   Nor fame, nor power, nor love, nor leisure.
    Others I see whom these surround—
Smiling they live, and call life pleasure;—
To me that cup has been dealt in another measure.

   Yet now despair itself is mild,
    Even as the winds and waters are;
I could lie down like a tired child,
    And weep away the life of care
    Which I have borne and yet must bear,
Till death like sleep might steal on me,
    And I might feel in the warm air
My cheek grow cold, and hear the sea
Breathe o'er my dying brain its last monotony.

Some might lament that I were cold,
    As I, when this sweet day is gone,
   Which my lost heart, too soon grown old,
    Insults with this untimely moan;
    They might lament—for I am one
Whom men love not, and yet regret
    Unlike this day, which when the sun
Shall on its stainless glory set,

Will linger, though enjoyed like joy in memory
                 yet. "

### The Cloud

I bring fresh showers
    for the thirsting flowers,
From the seas and the streams,
I bear light shade
    for the leaves when laid
In their noonday dreams.

From my wings are shaken the dews that waken
    The sweet buds every one,
When rocked to rest on their mother's breast,
    As she dances about the sun,
I wield the flail of the lashing hail,
    And whiten the green plains under,
And then again I dissolve it in rain,
    And laugh as I pass in thunder.

I sift the snow on the mountains below,
    And their great pines groan aghast;
And all the night 'tis my pillow white,
    While I sleep in the arms of the blast.
Sublime on the towers of my skiey bowers,
    Lightning my pilot sits;
In a cavern under is fettered the thunder,
    It struggles and howls at fits;
Over earth and ocean, with gentle motion,
    This pilot is guiding me,
Lured by the love of the genii that move
    In the depths of the purple sea;
Over the rills, and the crags, and the hills,
    Over the lakes and the plains,
Wherever he dreams, under mountain or stream,
    The Spirit he loves remains;
And I all the while bask in Heaven's blue smile,
    Whilst he is dissolving in rains.

The sanguine Sunrise, with his meteor eyes,
    And his burning plumes outspread,
Leaps on the back of my sailing rack,
    When the morning star shines dead;
As on the jag of a mountain crag,
    Which an earthquake rocks and swings,
An eagle alit one moment may sit
    In the light of its golden wings.
And when Sunset may breathe, from the lit sea
    beneath,

Its ardours of rest and of love,
And the crimson pall of eve may fall
    From the depth of Heaven above,
With wings folded I rest, on mine aery nest,
    As still as brooding dove.

That orbed maiden with white fire laden,
    Whom mortals call the Moon,
Glides glimmering o'er my fleece-like floor,
    By the midnight breezes strewn;
And wherever the beat of her unseen feet,
    Which only the angels hear,
May have broken the woof of my tent's thin roof,
    The stars peep behind her and peer;
And I laugh to see them whirl and flee,
    Like a swarm of golden bees,
When I widen the rent in my wind-built tent,
    Till the calm rivers, lakes, and seas,
Like strips of the sky fallen through me on high,
    Are each paved with the moon and these.

I bind the Sun's throne with a burning zone,
    And the Moon's with a girdle a pearl;
The volcanoes are dim, and the stars reel and
    swim,
    When the whirlwinds my banner unfurl.
From cape to cape, with a bridge-like shape,
    Over a torrent sea,
Sunbeam-proof, I hang like a roof,—
    The mountains its column be.

The triumphal arch through which I march
    With hurricane, fire, and snow,
When the Powers of the air are chained to my
    chair,
    Is the million-coloured bow;
The sphere-fire above its soft colours wove,
    While the moist Earth was laughing below.

I am the daughter of Earth and Water,
    And the nursling of the Sky;
I pass through the pores of the ocean and shores;
    I change, but I cannot die.
For after the rain when with never a stain
    The pavilion of Heaven is bare,
And the winds and sunbeams with their convex
    gleams
    Built up the blue dome of air,

I silently laugh at my own cenotaph,
    And out of the caverns of rain,
Like a child from the womb, like a ghost from the
    tomb,
    I arise and unbuild it again.

### To Night

Swiftly walk o'er the western wave,
Spirit of Night!
Out of the misty eastern cave,
Where, all the long and lone daylight,
Thou wovest dreams of joy and fear,
Which make thee terrible and dear,—
    Swift be thy flight!

Wrap thy form in a mantle gray,
Star-inwrought!
Blind with thine hair the eyes of Day;
Kiss her until she be wearied out,
Then wander o'er city, and sea, and land,
Touching all with thine opiate wand—
    Come, long-sought!

When I arose and saw the dawn,
I sighed for thee;
When light rode high, and the dew was gone,
And noon lay heavy on flower and tree,
And the weary Day turned to his rest,
Lingering like an unloved guest,
    I sighed for thee.

Thy brother Death came, and cried,
    Wouldst thou me?
Thy sweet child Sleep, the filmy-eyed,
Murmured like a noontide bee,
Shall I nestle near thy side?
Wouldst thou me?—And I replied,
    No, not thee!

Death will come when thou are dead,
    Soon, too soon—
Sleep will come when thou art fled;
Of neither would I ask the boon
I ask of thee, beloved Night—
Swift be thine approaching flight,
    Come soon, soon!

### To A Skylark

Hail to thee, blithe Spirit!
    Bird thou never wert—

That from heaven or near it
Pourest thy full heart

In Profuse strains of unpremediated art.

Higher still and higher
From the earth thou springest,
Like a cloud of fire;
The blue deep thou wingest,

And singing still dost soar, and soaring ever singest.

In the golden light'ning
Of the sunken sun,
O'er which clouds are bright'ning,
Thou dost float and run,

Like an unbodied joy whose race is just begun.

The pale purple even
Melts around thy flight;
Like a star of heaven,
In the broad daylight

Thou art unseen, but yet I hear thy shrill delight—

Keen as are the arrows
Of that silver sphere
Whose intense lamp narrows
In the white dawn clear,

Until we hardly see, feel that it is there.

All the earth and air
With thy voice is loud,
As, when night is bare,
From one lonely cloud

The moon rains out her beams, and heaven is overflow'd.

What thou art we know not;
What is most like thee?
From rainbow clouds there flow not
Drops so bright to see,

As from thy presence showers a rain of melody—

Like a poet hidden
In the light of thought,
Singing hymns unbidden,
Till the world is wrought

To sympathy with hopes and fear it heeded not:

Like a high-born maiden

In a palace tower,
Soothing her love-laden
Soul in secret hour

With music sweet as love, which overflows her bower:

Like a glow-worm golden
In a dell of dew,
Scattering unbeholden
Its aerial hue

Among the flowers and grass which screen it from the view:

Like a rose embower'd
In its own green leaves,
By warm winds deflower'd,
Till the scent it gives

Makes faint with too much sweet these heavy wing'd thieves:

Sound of vernal showers
On the twinkling grass,
Rain-awaken'd flowers—
All that ever was

Joyous, and clear and fresh—thy music doth surpass.

Teach us, sprite or bird,
What sweet thoughts are thine:
I have never heard
Praise of love or wine

That panted forth a flood of rapture so divine.

Chorus hymeneal,
Or triumphal chaunt
Match'd with thine would be all
But an empty vaunt—

A thing wherein we feel there is some hidden want.

What objects are the fountains
Of thy happy strain?
What fields, or waves, or mountains?
What shapes of sky or plain?

What love of thine own kind? what ignorance of pain?

With thy clear keen joyance
Languor cannot be:

Shadow of annoyance
    Never came near thee:

Thou lovest, but ne'er knew love's sad satiety.

Waking or asleep,
    Thou of death must deem
Things more true and deep
    Than we mortals dream,

Or how could thy notes flow in such a crystal stream?

We look before and after,
    And pine for what is not:
Our sincerest laughter
    With some pain is fraught;

Our sweetest songs are those that tell of saddest thought.

Yet, if we could scorn
    Hate and pride and fear,
If we were things born
    Not to shed a tear,

I know not how thy joy we ever should come near.

Better than all measures
    Of delightful sound,
Better than all treasures
    That in books are found,

Thy skill to poet were, thou scorner of the ground!

Teach me half the gladness
    That thy brain must know;
Such harmonious madness
    From my lips would flow,

The world should listen then, as I am listening now.

### Ode to the West Wind

#### I

O wild West Wind, thou breath of Autumn's being,
Thou from whose unseen presence the leaves
    dead
Are driven like ghosts from an enchanter fleeing,

Yellow, and black, and pale, and hectic red,
Pestilence-stricken multitudes! O thou
Who chariotest to their dark wintry bed

The winged seeds, where they lie cold and low,

Each like a corpse within its grave, until
Thine azure sister of the Spring shall blow

Her clarion o'er the dreaming earth, and fill
(Driving sweet buds like flocks to feed in air)
With living hues and odours plain and hill;

Wild Spirit, which art moving everywhere;
Destroyer are preserver; hear, O, hear!

#### II

Thou on whose stream, 'mid the steep sky's
    commotion,
Loose clouds like earth's decaying leaves are
    shed,
Shook from the tangled boughs of Heaven and
    Ocean,

Angels of rain and lightning! there are spread
On the blue surface of thine aery surge,
Like the bright hair uplifted from the head

Of some fierce Maenad, even from the dim verge
Of the horizon to the zenith's height,
The locks of the approaching storm. Thou dirge

Of the dying year, to which this closing night
Will be the dome of a vast sepulchre,
Vaulted with all thy congregated might

Of vapours, from whose solid atmosphere
Black rain, and fire, and hail, will burst: O, hear!

#### III

Thou who didst waken from his summer dreams
The blue Mediterranean, where he lay,
Lulled by the coil of his crystalline streams,

Beside a pumice isle in Baiae's bay,
And saw in sleep old palaces and towers
Quivering within the wave's intenser day,

All overgrown with azure moss, and flowers
So sweet, the sense faints picturing them! Thou
For whose path the Atlantic's level powers

Cleave themselve into chasms, while far below
The sea-blooms and the oozy woods which wear
The sapless foliage of the ocean, know

Thy voice, and suddenly grow gray with fear,
And tremble and despoil themselves :O, hear!

**IV**

If I were a dead leaf thou mightest bear;
If I were a swift cloud to fly with thee;
A wave to pant beneath thy power, and share

The impulse of thy strength, only less free
Than thou, O uncontrollable! If even
I were as in my boyhood, and could be

The comrade of thy wanderings over Heaven,
As then, when to outstrip thy skiey speed
Scarce seemed a vision—I would ne'er have
       striven

As thus with thee in prayer in my sore need.
O! lift me as a wave, a leaf, a cloud!
I fall upon the thorns of life! I bleed!

A heavy weight of hours has chained and bowed
One too like thee—tameless, and swift, and
       proud.

**V**

Make me thy lyre, even as the forest is:
What if my leaves are falling like its own?
The tumult of thy mighty harmonies

Will take from both a deep autumnal tone,
Sweet though in sadness. Be thou, spirit fierce,
My spirit! Be thou me, impetuous one!

Drive my dead thoughts over the universe,
Like withered leaves, to quicken a new birth;
And, by the incantation of this verse,

Scatter, as from an unextinguished hearth
Ashes and sparks, my words among mankind!
Be through my lips to unawakened earth

The trumpet of a prophecy! O wind,
If Winter comes, can Spring be far behind?
*Percy Bysshe Shelley*

## WILLIAM WORDSWORTH
## (1770-1850)

**Life**

1.   He was born at Cockermouth, Cumberland.
(A poet/critic has called him "the gander of
Cockermouth").

2.   He got education at Hawkeshead School,
Lancashire, and Cambridge.

3.   He paid two visits to France :
 *(i)*  The first time in 1790
 *(ii)*  The second time in 1791-92.
Long divides his life into four periods :
 *(i)*  *1770-87:* It belongs to his childhood and
       youth-Cumberland.
 *(ii)*  *1787-97:* This period covers :
       *(a)*  his life at Cambridge
       *(b)*  his travels abroad which enabled him
             to be influenced by the revolutionary
             ideas.
(**Note:** We know that his revolutionary
enthusiasm died soon with :
 *(i)*  the excesses of the Revolution including
       what is called "The Reign of Terror,"
 *(ii)*  the rise of tyrannical Napoleon
 *(iii)*  *1797-99:* This period was very significant
       as it enabled him to understand his own
       abilities and take full advantage of them.
 *(iv)*  *1799-1850:* It was practically a period of
       retirement in the lake region of his birth
       and childhood and to remain in direct touch
       with nature.

**Works**

1.   His "Lyrical Ballads"—a book which is
often considered the start of the Revival of
Romanticism in England appeared in 1798.

2.   His Preface to the Lyrical Ballads is
considered important in the history of Criticism of
English literature.

3. *(i)*  He intended to write a single great poem
       under the caption "The Recluse."
 *(ii)*  The poem was intended to give a
       comprehensive treatment of: *(a)* nature, *(b)*
       man and (c) society.
 *(iii)*  His intention was that his "The Prelude"—
       the Growth of a Poet's Mind—should
       introduce the Recluse.
 *(iv)*  *(a)*  The first book of The Recluse "The
             Home at Grasmere" was published
             posthumously in 1888.
       *(b)*  The name of the second book was 'The
             Excursion.'
       *(c)*  The third was never completed by the
             poet.

His most famous poems are :
1. The Prelude
2. Tintern Abbey
3. Ode on Intimations of Immortality.
4. Ode to Duty or Education of Nature
5. The Rainbow
6. The Solitary Reaper
7. Michael
8. To a Skylark
9. Yarrow Revisited
10. Lucy Gray
11. She Dwelt Among the Untrodden Ways
12. Daffodils

He also wrote a large number of sonnets such as :
1.　On Milton
2.　On Westminster Bridge
3.　The World is Too Much With Us, etc.

**Important characteristics of his poetry and philosophy :**

1.　He was a great lover of nature.

2.　He felt the presence of a spirit in nature, that is, the spirit of nature.

3.　He believed in pantheism.

4.　He believed that nature could bestow peace, sympathy, love, joy and other virtues on man.

5.　He did not like to depict nature "red in tooth and claw."

6.　He believed that nature gave purity to man and ennobled his heart.

7.　He was a great lover of the common man and the rustic and rural life.

8.　He loved the child and thought that because of its innocence, purity of thought and nearness to God, childhood was the golden period of human life.

9.　He loved all creation and all kinds of creatures, including the smallest and most insignificant animals and insects.

10. He believed that "nature never did betray the heart that loved her."

11. He himself practised what he preached and spent most of his time in the company of nature.

12. His poetry is full of :
　*(i)* vivid descriptions of scenes of nature.
　*(ii)* simple human affections.
　*(iii)* fervent adulations of childhood and love of animals.
　*(iv)* depictions of country and village life.
　*(v)* sweet and haunting music.
　*(vi)* personal reminiscences and memories
　*(vii)* autobiographical tones
　*(viii)* adulation of simplicity and homeliness.
　*(ix)* tones of true theism and fervent faith in greatness, goodness and benignity of nature.

13. Although much of his later poetry is dull and interesting, yet it contains flashes of imaginative lines and good poetry.

14. Here are some extracts from his poetry.

### Lucy

A slumber did my spirit seal;
I had no human fears:
She seemed a thing that could not feel
The touch of earthly years.
No motion has she now, no force;
She neither hears nor sees;
Rolled round in earth's diurnal course,
With rocks, and stones, and trees.

(**Note:** It is still a matter of conjecture regarding the real child "Lucy" whose death the poet recalls in poem after poem belonging to this class).

### The French Revolution

As it Appeared to Enthusiasts at its Commencement.

Oh! pleasant exercise of hope and joy!
For mighty were the auxiliars which then stood
Upon our side, we who were strong in love!
Bliss was it in that dawn to be alive,
But to be young was very heaven!—Oh! times,
In which the meagre, stale, forbidding ways
Of custom, law, and statute, took at once
The attraction of a country in romance!
When Reason seemed the most to assert her rights,
When most intent on making of herself
A prime Enchantress—to assist the work
Which then was going forward in her name!
Not favoured spots alone, but the whole earth,
The beauty wore of promise, that which sets
(As at some moment might not be unfelt
Among the bowers of paradise itself)
The budding rose above the rose full blown.
What temper at the prospect did not wake

To happiness unthought of? The inert
Were roused, and lively natures rapt away!
They who had fed their childhood upon dreams,
The playfellows of fancy, who had made
All powers of swiftness, subtility, and strength
Their ministers—who in lordly wise had stirred
Among the grandest objects of the sense,
And dealt with whatsoever they found there
As if they had within some lurking right
To wield it;—they, too, who, of gentle mood,
Had watched all gentle motions, and to these
Had fitted their own thoughts, schemers more
    mild,
And in the region of their peaceful selves;—
Now was it that both found, the meek and lofty
Did both find, helpers to their heart's desire,
And stuff at hand, plastic as they could wish;
Were called upon to exercise their skill,
Not in Utopia, subterranean fields,
Or some secreted island, Heaven knows where!
But in the very world, which is the world
Of all of us,—the place where in the end
We find our happiness, or not at all!

(**Note:** It is rightly said about Shakespeare that no historian could ever describe the situation and events as they prevailed or took place in Rome as described by Shakespeare in Julius Caesar. Likewise, it is perhaps true of Wordsworth that no historian could describe in so few words "The French Revolution" as described by Wordsworth in his poem of the same name).

In one of the most famous of his poems "Tintern Abbey" Wordsworth calls nature :

"The anchor of my purest thoughts, the nurse,
The guide, the guardian of my heart, and soul
Of all my moral being."

Here are the last lines of the celebrated poem :

    Nor perchance,
If I were not thus taught, should I the more
Suffer my genial spirits to decay:
For thou art with me here upon the banks
Of this fair river; thou my dearest Friend,
My dear, dear Friend; and in thy voice I catch
The language of my former heart, and read
My former pleasures in the shooting lights
Of thy wild eyes. Oh! yet a little while

May I behold in thee what I was once,
My dear, dear Sister! and this prayer I make,
Knowing that Nature never did betray
The heart that loved her; 'tis her privilege,
Through all the years of this our life, to lead
From joy to joy: for she can so inform
The mind that is within us, so impress
With quietness and beauty, and so feed
With lofty thoughts, that neither evil tongues,
Rash judgements, nor the sneers of selfish men,
Nor greetings where no kindness is, nor all
The dreary intercourse of daily life,
Shall e'er prevail against us, or disturb
Our cheerful faith, that all which we behold
Is full of blessings. Therefore let the moon
Shine on thee in thy solitary walk;
And let the misty mountain-winds be free
To blow against thee: and, in after years,
When these wild ecstasies shall be matured
Into a sober pleasure, when thy mind
Shall be a mansion for all lovely forms,
Thy memory be as a dwelling-place
For all sweet sounds and harmonies; oh! then
If solitude, or fear, or pain, or grief,
Should be thy portion, with what healing
    thoughts
Of tender joy wilt thou remember me,
And these my exhortations! Nor, perchance—
If I should be where I no more can hear
Thy voice, nor catch from thy wild eyes these
    gleams
Of past existence—wilt thou then forget
That on the banks of this delightful stream
We stood together; and that I, so long
A worshipper of Nature, hither came
Unwearied in that service: rather say
With warmer love—oh! with far deeper zeal
Oh holier love. Nor wilt thou then forget
That after many wanderings, many years
Of absence, these steep woods and lofty cliffs,
And this green pastoral landscape, were to me
More dear, both for themselves and for thy sake!

Even if we do not find that level of loftiness and excellence in his "To The Cuckoo" as we find in his "Ode on Intimations of Immortality," yet the poem deserves appreciation : Here are the first five stanzas:

### To The Cuckoo

O Blithe Newcomer! I have heard,
I hear thee and rejoice.
O Cuckoo! shall I call thee Bird,
Or but a wandering Voice?

While I am lying on the grass
Thy twofold shout I hear;
From hill to hill it seems to pass
At once far off and near.

Though babbling only to the Vale,
Of sunshine and of flowers,
Thou bringest unto me a tale
Of visionary hours.

Thrice welcome, darling of the Spring!
Even yet-thou art to me
No bird, but an invisible thing,
A voice, a mystery;

Wordsworth is also renowned for his sonnets, not only for their structural perfection, but also for introduction in them of the element of nature, humanity, concern for common man, simplicity, countryside, pantheism, love for God and his creatures, genuine description, high ethical sense, etc. Here is an example:

### It is a Beauteous Evening

It is a beauteous evening, calm and free,
The holy time is quiet at a Nun
Breathless with adoration; the broad sun
Is sinking down in its tranquillity;
The gentleness of heaven broods o'er the Sea:
Listen! the mighty Being is awake,
And doth with his eternal motion make
A sound like thunder—everlastingly.
Dear Child! dear Girl! that walkest with me here,
If thou appear untouched by solemn thought,
Thy nature is not therefore less divine:
Thou liest in Abraham's bosom all the year;
And worshipp'st at the Temple's inner shrine,
God being with thee when we know it not.

Given below are the first eight lines (the octave) of one of his most famous sonnets :

### The World is Too Much With us

The world is too much with us; late and soon,
Getting and spending, we lay waste our powers:
Little we see in Nature that is ours;
We have given our hearts away, a sordid boon!
This Sea that bares her bosom to the moon;
The winds that will be howling at all hours,
And are up-gathered now like sleeping flowers;
For this, for everything, we are out of tune;

Here are some extracts from his most powerful work "The Prelude" which has been so enthusiastically hailed by Hudson:

### *(i)* One Summer Evening

One summer evening (led by her)[1] I found
A little boat tied to a willow tree
Within a rocky cave, its usual home.
Straight I unloosed her chain, and stepping in
Pushed from the shore. It was an act of stealth
And troubled pleasure, nor without the voice
Of mountain-echoes did my boat move on;
Leaving behind her still, on either side,
Small circles glittering idly in the moon
Until they melted all into one track
Of sparkling light. But now, like one who rows,
Proud of his skill, to reach a chosen point
With an unswerving line, I fixed my view
Upon the summit of a craggy ridge,
The horizon's utmost boundary; for above
Was nothing but the stars and the grey sky.
She was an elfin pinnace; lustily
I dipped my oars into the silent lake,
And, as I rose upon the stroke, my boat
Went heaving through the water like a swan;
When, from behind that craggy steep, till then,
The horizon's bound, a huge peak, black and huge,
As if with voluntary power instinct.
Upreared its head. I struck and struck again,
And, growing still in stature, the grim shape
Towered up between me and the stars, and still,
For so it seemed with purpose of its own
And measured motion like a living thing,
Strode after me. With trembling oars I turned,
And through the silent water stole my way
Back to the covert of the willow tree;
There in her mooring-place I left my bark,—
And through the meadows homeward went, in
   grave

And serious mood; but after I had seen
That spectacle, for many days, my brain
Worked with a dim and undetermined sense
Of unknown modes of being; o'er my thoughts
There hung a darkness, call it solitude
Or blank desertion. No familiar shapes
Remained, no pleasant images of trees,
Of sea or sky, no colours of green fields;
But huge and mighty forms, that do not live
Like living men, moved slowly through the mind
By day, and were a trouble to my dreams.
(Prelude, i, II, 357-49)

1. her = Nature

### Winander Lake

There was a Boy: ye knew him well, ye cliffs
And islands of Winander!—many a time
At evening, when the earliest stars began
To move along the edges of the hills,
Rising or setting, would he stand alone
Beneath the trees or by the glimmering lake,
And there, with fingers interwoven, both hands
Pressed closely palm to palm, and to his mouth
Uplifted, he, as through an instrument,
Blew mimic hootings to the silent owls,
That they might answer him; and they would
    shout
Across the watery vale, and shout again,
Responsive to his call, with quivering peals,
And long halloos and screams, and echoes loud,
Redoubled and redoubled, concourse wild
Of jocund din; and, when a lengthened pause
Of silence came and baffled his best skill,
Then sometimes, in that silence while he hung
Listening, a gentle shock of mild surprise
Has carried far into his heart the voice
Of mountain torrents; or the visible scene
Would enter unawares into his mind,
With all its solemn imagery, its rocks,
Its woods, and that uncertain heaven, received
Into the bosom of the steady lake.
(Prelude, v, II, 364-88)

(**Note :** Given below are three of his most famous
poems :
  (*i*)  The Solitary Reaper
  (*ii*)  The Tintern Abbey
  (*iii*)  The Ode on Intimations of Immortality.)

### The Solitary Reaper

Behold her, single in the field,
You solitary Highland Lass!
Reaping and singing by herself;
Stop here, or gently pass!
Alone she cuts and binds the grain,
And sings a melancholy strain;
O listen! for the Vale profound
Is overflowing with the sound.

No Nightingale did ever chaunt
More welcome notes to weary bands
Of travellers in some shady haunt,
Among Arabian sands:
A voice so thrilling ne'er was heard
In spring-time from the Cuckoo-bird,
Breaking the silence of the seas
Among the farthest Hebrides.

Will no one tell me what she sings?—
Perhaps the plaintive numbers flow
For old, unhappy, far-off things,
And battles long ago:
Or is it some more humble lay,
Familiar matter of to-day?
Some natural sorrow, loss, or pain,
That has been, and may be again?

Whate'er the theme, the Maiden sang
As if her song could have no ending;
I saw her singing at her work,
And o'er the sickle bending;—
I listened, motionless and still;
And, as I mounted up the hill,
The music in my heart I bore,
Long after it was heard no more.

### Lines Composed A Few Miles Above Tintern Abbey

Five years have passed; five summers, with the length
Of five long winters! and again I hear
These waters, rolling from their mountain-springs
With a soft inland murmur.—Once again
Do I behold these steep and lofty cliffs,
That on a wild secluded scene impress—
Thoughts of more deep seclusion; and connect
The landscape with the quiet of the sky.
The day is come when I again repose
Here, under this dark sycamore, and view

These plots of cottage-ground, these orchard-tufts,
Which at this season, with their unripe fruits,
Are clad in one green hue, and lose themselves
'Mid groves and copses. Once again I see
These hedge-rows, hardly hedge-rows, little lines
Of sportive wood run wild; these pastoral farms,
Green to the very door; and wreaths of smoke
Sent up, in silence, from among the trees!
With some uncertain notice, as might seem
Of vagrant dwellers in the houseless woods,
Or of some Hermit's cave, where by his fire
The hermit sits alone.
    These beauteous forms,
Through a long absence, have not been to me
As is a landscape to a blind man's eye:
But oft, in lonely rooms, and 'mid the din
Of towns and cities, I have owed to them,
In hours of weariness, sensations sweet,
Felt in the blood, and felt along the heart;
And passing even into my purer mind,
With tranquil restoration:—feelings too
Of unremembered pleasure: such, perhaps,
As have no slight or trivial influence
On that best portion of a good man's life,
His little, nameless, unremembered, acts
Of kindness and of love, Nor less, I trust,
To them I may have owed another gift,
Of aspect more sublime; that blessed mood
In which the burthen of the mystery,
In which the heavy and the weary weight
Of all this unintelligible world,
Is lightened:—that serene and blessed mood,
In which the affections gently lead us on,—
Until, the breath of this corporeal frame
And even the motion of our human blood
Almost suspended, we are laid asleep
In body, and become a living soul:
While with an eye made quiet by the power
Of harmony, and the deep power of joy,
We seen into the life of things.
                    If this
Be but a vain belief, yet, oh! how oft—
In darkness and amid the many shapes
Of joyless daylight; when the fretful stir
Unprofitable, and the fever of the world,
Have hung upon the beatings of my heart—
How oft, in spirit, have I turned to thee,

O sylvan Wye! thou wanderer thro' the woods,
How often has my spirit turned to thee!
And now, with gleams of half-extinguished thought,
With many recognitions dim and faint,
And somewhat of a sad perplexity,
The picture of the mind revives again:
While here I stand not only with the sense
Of present pleasure, but with pleasing thoughts
That in this moment there is life and food
For future years. And so I dare to hope,
Though changed, no doubt, from what I was when
    first
I came among these hills; when like a roe
I bounded o'er the mountains, by the sides
Of the deep rivers, and the lonely streams,
Wherever nature led : more like a man
Flying from something that he dreads than one
Who sought the thing he loved. For nature then
(The coarser pleasures of my boyish days,
And their glad animal movements all gone by)
To me was all in all.—I cannot paint
What then I was. The sounding cataract
Haunted me like a passion: the tall rock,
The mountain, and the deep and gloomy wood
Their colours and their forms, were then to me
An appetite; a feeling and a love,
That had no need of a remoter charm,
By thought supplied, nor any interest
Unborrowed from the eye.—That time is past
And all its aching joys are now no more,
And all its dizzy raptures. Not for this
Faint I, nor mourn nor murmur; other gifts
Have followed; for such loss, I would believe,
Abundant recompense. For I have learned
To look on nature, not as in the hour
Of thoughtless youth; but hearing oftentimes
The still, sad music of humanity,
Nor harsh nor grating, though of ample power
To chasten and subdue. And I have felt
A presence that disturbs me with the joy
Of elevated thoughts; a sense sublime
Of something far more deeply interfused,
Whose dwelling is the light of setting suns,
The dreary intercourse of daily life,
Shall e'er prevail aganst us, or disturb
Our cheerful faith, that all which we behold

Is full of blessings. Therefore let the moon
Shine on thee in thy solitary walk;
And let the misty mountain-winds be free
To blow against thee: and, in after years,
When these wild ecstasies shall be matured
Into a sober pleasure; when thy mind
Shall be a mansion for all lovely forms,
Thy memory be as a dwelling-place
For all sweet sounds and harmonies; oh! then,
If solitude, or fear, or pain, or grief,
Should be thy portion, with what healing thoughts
Of tender joy wilt thou remember me,
And these my exhortations! Nor, perchance—
If I should be where I no more can hear
Thy voice, nor catch from thy wild eyes these gleams
Of past existence—wilt thou then forget
That on the banks of this delightful stream
We stood together; and that I, so long
A worshipper of Nature, hither came
Unwearied in that service: rather say
With warmer love—oh! with far deeper zeal
Of holier love. Nor wilt thou then forget
That after many wanderings, many years
Of absence, these steep woods and lofty cliffs,
And this green pastoral landscape, were to me
More dear, both for themselves and for thy sake!

### Intimations of Immortality from
### Recollections of Early Childhood

#### I

There was a time when meadow, grove, and stream,
The earth, and every common sight,
    To me did seem
  Apparell'd in celestial light,
The glory and the freshness of a dream.
It is not now as it hath been of yore;—
    Turn wheresoe'er I may,
      By night or day,
The things which I have seen I now can see no more.

#### II

    The Rainbow comes and goes,
    And lovely is the Rose;
    The Moon doth with delight
Look round her when the heaven are bare,
    Waters on a starry night
    Are beautiful and fair;
    The sunshine is a glorious birth;

  But yet I know, where'er I go,
That there hath past away a glory from the earth.

#### III

Now, while the birds thus sing a joyous song,
    And while the young lambs bound
      As to the tabor's sound,
To me alone there came a thought of grief:
A timely utterance gave that thought relief,
      And I again am strong:
The cataracts blow their trumpets from the steep;
No more shall grief of mine the season wrong;
I hear the Echoes through the mountains throng,
The Winds come to me from the fields of sleep,
    And all the earth is gay;
      Land and sea
    Give themselves up to jollity,
      And with the heart of May
    Doth every beast keep holiday;—
      Thou Child of Joy
Shout round me, let me hear thy shouts, thou happy
    Shapherd-boy!

#### IV

Ye blessed Creatures, I have heard the call
    Ye to each other make; I see
The heavens laugh with you in your jubilee;
    My heart is at your festival,
      My head hath its coronal,
The fullness of your bliss, I feel—I feel it all.
      O evil day! if I were sullen
      While Earth herself is adorning,
        This sweet May-morning,
      And the Children are culling
      On every side,
    In a thousand valleys far and wide,
    Fresh flowers; while the sun shines warm,
And the Babe leaps up on his Mother's arm:—
    I hear, I hear, with joy I hear!
    —But there's a Tree, of many, one,
A single Field which I have look'd upon,
Both of them speak of something that is gone:
    The Pansy at my feet
    Doth the same tale repeat:
Whither is fled the visionary gleam?
Where is it now, the glory and the dream?

### V

Our birth is but a sleep and a forgetting:
The Soul that rises with us, our life's Star,
    Hath had elsewhere its setting,
        And cometh from afar:
    Not in entire forgetfulness,
    And not in utter nakedness,
But trailing clouds of glory do we come
    From God, who is our home:
Heaven lies about us in our infancy!
Shades of the prison-house begin to close
    Upon the growing Boy
But He beholds the light, and whence it flows,
    He sees it in his joy;
The Youth, who daily farther from the east
    Must travel, still is Nature's Priest,
    And by the vision splendid
    Is on his way attended;
At length the Man perceives it die away,
And fade into the light of common day.

### VI

Earth fills her lap with pleasures of her own;
Yearnings she hath in her own natural kind,
And, even with something of a Mother's mind,
    And no unworthy aim,
    The homely Nurse doth all she can
To make her Foster-child, her Inmate Man,
    Forget the glories he hath known,
And that imperial palace whence he came.

### VII

Behold the Child among his new-born blisses,
A six years' Darling of a pigmy size!
See, where 'mid work of his own hand he lies,
Fretted by sallies of his mother's kisses,
With light upon him from his father's eyes!
See, at his feet, some little plan or chart,
Some fragment from his dream of human life,
Shaped by himself with newly-learned art;
    A wedding or a festival,
    A mourning or a funeral;
        And this hath now his heart,
    And unto this he frames his song:
        Then will he fit his tongue

To dialogues of business, love, or strife;

But it will not be long
    Ere this be thrown aside,
    And with new joy and pride

The little Actor cons another part;
Filling from time to time his 'humorous stage'
With all the Persons, down to palsied Age,
That Life brings with her in her equipage;
    As if his whole vocation
    Were endless imitation.

### VIII

Thou, whose exterior semblance doth belie
    Thy Soul's immensity;
Thou best Philosopher, who yet dost keep
Thy heritage, thou Eye among the blind,
That, deaf and silent, read'st the eternal deep,
Haunted for ever by the enternal mind,—
    Mighty Prophet! Seer blest!
    On whom those truths do rest,
Which we are toiling all our lives to find,
In darkness lost, the darkness of the grave;
Thou, over whom thy Immortality
Broods like the Day, a Master o'er a Slave,
A presence which is not to be put by;
Thou little Child, yet glorious in the might
Of heaven-born freedom on thy being's height,
Why with such earnest pains dost thou provoke
The years to bring the inevitable yoke,
Thus blindly with thy blessedness at strife?
Full soon thy Soul shall have her earthly freight,
And custom lie upon thee with a weight,
Heavy as frost, and deep almost as life!

### IX

    O joy! that in our embers
    Is something that doth live,
    That nature yet remembers
    What was so fugitive!
The thought of our past years in me doth breed
Perpetual benediction: not indeed
For that which is most worthy to be blest;
Delight and liberty, the simple creed
Of Childhood, whether busy or at rest,
With new-fledged hope still fluttering in his
breast:—
    Not for these I raise
    The song of thanks and praise;

But for those obstinate questionings
Of sense and outward things,
Fallings from us, vanishings;
Blank misgivings of a Creature
Moving about in worlds not realized,
High instincts before which our mortal Nature
Did tremble like a guilty Thing surprised:
  But for those first affections,
  Those shadowy recollections,
 Which, be they what they may,
Are yet the fountain-light of all our day,
Are yet a master-light of all our seeing;
 Uphold us, cherish, and have power to make
Our noisy years seem moments in the being
Of the eternal Silence: truths that wake,
 To perish never:
Which neither listlessness, nor mad endeavour,
 Nor Man nor Boy,
Nor all that is at enmity with joy,
Can utterly abolish or destroy!
 Hence in a season of calm weather
  Though inland far we be,
Our Souls have sight of that immortal sea
  Which brought us hither,
 Can in a moment travel thither,
And see the Children sport upon the shore,
And hear the mighty waters rolling evermore,

X

Then sing, ye Birds, sing, sing a joyous song!
 And let the young Lambs bound
 As to the tabor's sound!
We in thought will join your throng,
 Ye that pipe and ye that play,
 Ye that through your hearts to-day
 Feel the gladness of the May!
What though the radiance which was once so bright
Be now for ever taken from my sight,
 Though nothing can bring back the hour
Of splendour in the grass, of glory in the flower;
  We will grieve not, rather find
  Strength in what remains behind;
  In the primal sympathy
  Which having been must ever be;
  In the soothing thoughts that spring
  Out of human suffering;

  In the faith that looks through death,
In years that bring the philosophic mind.

XI

And O, ye Fountains, Meadows, Hills, and Groves,
Forebode not any severing of our loves l
Yet in my heart of hearts I feel your might;
I only have relinquished one delight
To live beneath your more habitual sway.
I love the Brooks which down their channels fret,
Even more than when I tripped lightly as they;
The innocent brightness of a new-born Day
 Is lovely yet;
The Clouds that gather round the setting sun
Do take a sober colouring from an eye
That hath kept watch o'er man's mortality;
Another race hath been, and other palms are won.
Thanks to the human heart by which we live,
Thanks to its tenderness, its joys, and fears,
To me the meanest flower that blows can give
Thoughts that do often lie too deep for tears.

—William Wordsworth

## JOHN KEATS (1795-1821)

**Life**

1. He was born in London in 1795.

2. His father was a hostler and stable keeper.

3. Both his parents died before he was fifteen.

4. It is said that his guardians cheated him and his brothers and sisters.

5. At first, he started the profession of a surgeon but later abandoned it.

6. He was greatly impressed by Spenser, particularly his Faerie Queene which he read most fervently.

7. Byron and some other critics and literary men held, the view that savage criticism of Keats' "Endymion" in the Blackwood Magazine shortened the life of this young poet, but Matthew Arnold does not subscribe to this view.

8. Since he was suffering from tuberculosis and could not tolerate the severity and coldness of the British climate, he left for Italy, where in Rome, he settled with his friend Severn, but soon he breathed his last in February, 1821.

**Works**

1.  His first work was 'Endymion' which although immature and imperfect, has flashes of beautiful and charming lines in it.

2.  Odes : Keats is most famous for his odes, some of which are named below:

*(i)* Ode to a Nightingale

*(ii)* Ode on a Grecian Urn

*(iii)* Ode of Psyche

*(iv)* Ode to Autumn

*(v)* Ode of Indolence

(**Note :** He is undeniably the greatest ode writer in English literature.)

**Last Work**

1.  His last volume which was composed in 1820, comprised the following poems :

*(i)* Lamia

*(ii)* Isabella

*(iii)* The Eve of St. Agnes, etc.

2. *(i)* Keats left his stupendously planned work: "Hyperion" a mere fragment.

*(ii)* The poem was to be a wonderful epic on a grand scale but were never completed.

*(iii)* It is in this work that the following celebrated line occurs :

"For it's the eternal law that the first in beauty shall be the first in might."

(**Note:** 1. Keats considered by many the greatest romanticist, had always been a lover of beauty. Thus, we have—

2.  'A thing of beauty is a joy for ever.'

*—Endymion*

3.  'Beauty is truth, truth beauty,
That is all ye know on earth
and all ye need to know."

*—Ode on a Grecian Urn*

4.  One of his most famous poems is :
"La Belle Dame Sans Merci":
"O what can ail thee, knight -ate arms,
Alone and palely loitering?
The sedge is withered on the lake,
And no birds sing."

As a Sonneteer: Keats did not live to write many sonnets, but the few sonnets he wrote, are some of the best in English literature. Some of them are :

1.  When I have fears that I may cease to be
2.  Human Seasons
3.  On Looking Into Chapman's Homer
4.  Bright Star! .....

### (1) The Eve of St. Agnes

#### I

St. Agnes' Eve—Ah, bitter chill it was!
The owl, for all his feathers, was a-cold;
The hare limp'd trembling through the frozen grass,
And silent was the flock in woolly fold:
Numb were the Beadsman's fingers, while he told
His rosary, and while his frosted breath,
Like pious incense from a censor old,
Seem'd taking flight for heaven, without a death,
Past the sweet Virgin's picture, while his prayer he saith.

#### II

His prayer he saith, this patient, holy man;
Then takes his lamp, and riseth from his knees,
And back returneth, meagre, barefoot, wan,
Along the chapel aisle by slow degrees:
The sculptur'd dead, on each side, seem to freeze,
Emprison'd in black, purgatorial rails:
Knights, ladies, praying in dumb orat'ries.
He passeth by; and his weak spirit fails
To think how they may ache in icy hoods and mails.

#### III

Northward the turneth through a little door,
And scarce three steps, ere Music's golden tongue
Flatter'd to tears this aged man and poor
But no—already had his deathbell rung:
The joys of all his life were said and sung:
His was harsh penance on St. Agnes' Eve:
Another way he went, and soon among
Rough ashes sat he for his soul's reprieve,
And all night kept awake, for sinner's sake to grieve.

Undoubtedly, the given lines corroborate a deft hand behind them: and a brain which is master of the arts of narration, plastic description and portrayal with all the delicacy and appropriateness of language. Had the terms impressionism, expressionism, imagism, Freudianism, surrealism, etc. existed in Keat's time, the critics would have surely included him into one or more of these folds. The real warmth of love, however, comes later in Madeline's room when we leave the coldness of the natural world and the Beadsman's Chapel.

### (2) Ode on a Grecian Urn

#### I

Thou still unravish'd bride of quietness!
Thou foster-child of Silence and slow Time,
Sylvan historian, who canst thus express
A flowery tale more sweetly than our rhyme:
What leaf-fringed legend haunts about thy shape
Of deities of mortals, or of both,
In Tempe or the dales of Arcady?
What men or gods are these? What maidens loth?
What mad pursuit? What struggle to escape?
What pipes and timbrels? What wild ecstasy?

#### II

Heard melodies are sweet, but those unheard
Are sweeter; therefore, ye soft pipes, play on;
Not to the sensual ear, but, more endear'd
Pipe to the spirit ditties of no tone:
Fair youth, beneath the trees, thou canst not leave
Thy song, nor ever can those trees be bare;
Bold Lover, never, never canst thou kiss,
Though winning near the goal—yet, do not grieve;
She cannot fade, though thou hast not thy bliss,
For ever wilt thou love, and she be fair!

The poem is, undoubtedly, the triumph of art over the transcience of human life and is comparable to Yeats Lapis Lazily :

Every discoloration of the stone,
Every accidental crack of dent,
Seems a water-course or an avalanche,
Or lofty slope where it still snows
Though doubtless plum or cherry-branch
Sweetens the little half-way house
Those Chinamen climb towards, and I
Delight to imagine them seated there,
There, on the mountain and the sky,
On all the tragic scene they stare.
One asks for mournful melodies;
Accomplished fingers begin to play.
Their eyes mid many wrinkles, their eyes,
Their ancient, glittering eyes, are gay.

In both the poems, immortality of human life has been achieved through art, through same have found fault with the last two lines of Keat's poem:

"'Beauty is truth, truth beauty'—that is all
Ye know on earth, and all ye need to know,"

### (3) Ode to Psyche

O brightest! though too late for antique vows,
Too, too late for the fond believing lyre,
When holy were the haunted forest boughs.
Holy the air, the water, and the fire;
Yet even in these days so far retired
From happy pieties, thy lucent fans,
Fluttering among the faint Olympians,
I see, and sing, by my own eyes inspired.
So let me be thy choir, and make a moan
Upon the midnight hours!

Keat's love of the Greek mythology which fits squarely in his Romantic moorings, is clearly brought home in these lines. His love of the mysterious, the haunted, the natural phenomenon, the religions (without being religious) is also brought out vividly.

### (4) Ode to a Nightingale

#### VII

Thou wast not born for death, immortal Bird!
No hungry generations tread thee down;
The voice I hear this passing night was heard
In ancient days by emperor and clown :
Perhaps the self-same song that found a path
Through the sad heart of Ruth, when, sick for home,
She stood in tears amid the alien corn;
The same that oft-times hath
Charm'd magic casements, opening on the foam
Of perilious seas, in faery lands forlorn.

#### VIII

Foriorn! the very word is like a bell
To toll me back from thee to my sole self!
Adieu! the fancy cannot cheat so well
As she is fam'd to do, deceiving elf.
Adieu! adieu! thy plaintive anthem fades
Past the near meadows, over the still stream,
Up the hill-side; and now 'tis buried deep
In the next valley-glades:
Was it a vision, or a waking dream?
Fled is that music:—Do I wake or sleep?

We again find Keat's affinity with Yeats. After all, magic and dreams are unreal and short lived and both the poets had to go in for real life, as Keats went to Hyperion at last, in an epic way, though still in the form of a dream!

### (5) Prologue to the Second Hyperion

Fanatics have their dreams, wherewith they weave
A paradise for a sect; the savage, too,
From forth the loftiest fashion of his sleep
Guesses at Heaven! Pity these have not
Traced upon vellum or wild Indian leaf
The shadows of melodious utterance.
But bare of laurel they live, dream and die;
For poesy alone can tell her dreams,—
With the fine spell of words alone can save
Imagination from the sable chain
And dumb enchantment.

### (6) The Second Hyperion

Thou art a dreaming thing;
A fever of thyself: think of the earth:
What bliss, even in hope, is there for thee?
What haven? every creature hath its home,
Every sole man hath days of joy and pain,
Whether his labours be sublime of low—
The pain alone, the joy alone, distinct:
Only the dreamer venoms are his days,
Being more we than all his sins deserve."

Actually, Keats is interested in finding human life and realising its both beauty and misery through poetry which may even he dreaming.

But, he does want—
a nober life
Where I may find the agonies, the strife
Of human hearts.

**(7)** From : "Bards of Passion and Mirth." and full poems—

   *(i)* Ode to Autumn, and
   *(ii)* When I Have Fears That I May Cease To Be (Sonnet)
   *(iii)* La Belle Dame Sans Merci.

### Bards of Passion and Mirth

Bards of Passion and of Mirth,
Ye have left your souls on earth!
Have ye souls in heaven too,
Double lived in regions new?
Yes, and those of heaven commune
With the spheres of sun and moon;
With the noise of fountains wond'rous,
And the parle of voices thund'rous;
With the whisper of heaven's trees
And one another, in soft ease

Seated on Elysian lawns
Brows'd by none but Dian's fawns;
Underneath large blue-shells tented,
Where the daisies are rose-scented,
And the rose herself has got
Perfume which on earth is not;
Where the nightingale doth sing
Not a senseless, tranced thing,
But divine melodious truth;
Philosophic numbers smooth;
Tales and golden histories
Of heaven and its mysteries.

Thus ye live on high, and then
On the earth ye live again;
And the souls ye left behind you
Teach us, here, the way to find you,
Where your other souls are joying,
Never slumber'd, never cloying.
Here, your earth-born souls still speak
To mortals, of their little week;
Of their sorrows and delights;
Of their passions and their spites;

........................................................

### Ode To Autumn

Season of mists and mellow fruitfulness,
   Close bosom-friend of the maturing sun;
Conspiring with him how to load and bless
  With fruit the vines that round the thatch-eaves run;
To bend with apples the moss'd cottage-trees,
  And fill all fruit with ripeness to the core;
  To swell the gourd, and plump the hazel shells
  With a sweet kernel; to set budding more,
And still more, later flowers for the bees,
Until they think warm days will never cease,
  For Summer has o'er-brimm'd their clammy cells.

Who hath not seen Thee oft amid thy store?
  Sometimes whoever seeks abroad may find
Thee sitting careless on a granary floor,
  Thy hair soft-lifted by the winnowing wind;
Or on a half-reap'd furrow sound asleep,
  Drows'd with the fume of poppies, while thy hook

Spares the next swath and all its twined flowers;
    And sometimes like a gleaner thou dost keep
Steady thy laden head across a brook;
Or by a cider-press, with patient look,
    Thou watchest the last oozings, hours by hours.

Where are the songs of Spring? Ay, where are
    they?
    Think not of them, thou hast thy music too,
While barred clouds bloom the soft-dying day,
    And touch the stubble-plains with rosy hue;
Then in a wailful choir the small gnats mourn
    Among the river-sallows, borne aloft
Or sinking as the light wind lives or dies;
And full-grown lambs loud bleat from hilly
    bourn;
    Hedge-crickets sing; and now with treble soft
    The red-breast whistles from a garden-croft;
        And gathering swallows twitter in the skies.

## When I Have Fear That I May Cease To Be

When I have fears that I may cease to be
    Before my pen has glean'd my teeming brain,
Before high-piled books, in charactery,
    Hold like rich garners the full ripen'd grain;
When I behold, upon the night's starr'd face,
    Huge cloudy symbols of a high romance,
And think that I may never live to trace
    Their shadows, with the magic hand of
chance;
    And when I feel, fair creature of an hour,
    That I shall never look upon thee more,
Never have relish in the faery power
    Of unreflecting love;—then on the shore
Of the wide world I stand alone, and think
Till love and fame to nothingness do sink.

### La Belle Dame Sans Merci

O, what can ail thee, knight-at-arms,
    Alone and palely loitering?
The sedge is wither'd from the lake,
    And no birds sing.
O, what can ail thee, knight-at-arms,
    So haggard and so woe-begone?
The squirrel's granary is full,
    And the harvest's done.

I see a lily on thy brow,
    With anguish moist and fever-dew;
And on thy cheek a fading rose
    Fast withereth too.

I met a lady in the meads,
    Full beautiful—a faery's child,
Her hair was long, her foot was light,
    And her eyes were wild.

I made a garland for her head,
    And bracelets too, and fragrant zone;
She look'd at me as she did love,
    And made sweet moan.

I set her on my pacing steed,
    And nothing else saw all day long;
For sidelong would she bend, and sing
    A faery's song.

She found me roots of relish sweet,
    And honey wild, and manna dew,
And sure in language strange she said—
    'I love thee true.'

She took me to her elfin grot,
    And there she wept and sigh'd full sore,
And there I shut her wild eyes
    With kisses four.

And there she lulled me asleep
    And there I dream'd—Ah! woe betide!
The latest dream I ever dream'd
    On the cold hill side.

I saw pale kings and princes too,
    Pale warriors, death-pale were they all;
They cried—"La Belle Dame sans Merci
    Hath thee in thrall!'

I saw their starved lips in the gloam,
    With horrid warning gaped wide,
And I awoke and found me here,
    On the cold hill's side.

And this is why I sojourn here
    Along and palely loitering,
Though the sedge has wither'd from the lake,
    And no birds sing.

*John Keats*

## SAMUEL TAYLER COLERIDGE (1772-1834)

### Life

1. Coleridge was born in Devonshire in 1772.

2. His father Rev. John Coleridge was a vicar and incharge of a primary school. He was an honest, sincere, religiously minded man who left the indelible mark of his personality on his children, including S.T. Coleridge.

3. Coleridge, was a precocious child who could read at three and recite from memory a great part of the Bible and the Arabian Nights.

4. It was at the Charity School of Christ's Hospital where he was sent when he was ten and where he made friendship with Lamb.

5. As a boy, he was largely poor and neglected but he was a great dreamer.

6. In 1791, he joined Cambridge as a charity student but left in 1794 without taking a degree.

7. Now, he met the youthful Southey with whom he planned to establish Pantisocracy (an ideal society), on the banks of the Susquehanna.

8. The plan regarding Pantisocracy failed and Coleridge went to Germany to study.

9. Thereafter, he went to Rome.

10. He started a paper "The Friend" which was devoted to truth and also started lectures on poetry and fine arts; he gained a good success, but since he was not regular in his engagements, his audiences ultimately dwindled.

### Early works

Among his early poems, we have:

(i) A Day Dream

(ii) The Devil's Thoughts

(iii) The Suicide's Arguments

(iv) The Wanderings of Cain.

### Later works

His later works which have made him immortal are:

#### 1. Kubla Khan

It is just a fragment. It is commonly known that he composed the poem in a dream which he remembered and started writing as he woke up but was interrupted and forgot beyond what he had written (54 lines).

#### 2. Christabel

(i) This poem is also a fragment.

(ii) Here, the heroine, Geraldine, is a German woman who, in fact, is a pure young girl who has fallen under the spell of a sorcerer.

(iii) The poem contains:

(a) exquisitely poetic lines.

(b) grotesque musical tones.

(c) element of supernaturalism.

(d) an atmosphere of awfulness.

#### 3. The Rime of the Ancient Mariner

(i) It is Coleridge's most famous poem and as Long points out, "one of the world's masterpieces."

(ii) It was a part of the Lyrical Ballads which appeared in 1798.

(iii) The story is too well-known to be recounted.

(iv) Some of the important elements in the poem are:

(a) supernaturalism

(b) wonderful narration

(c) triumph of story-telling art

(d) exquisite poetry

(e) sweet, luscious music

(f) triumph of simplicity over complexity

(g) wonderfully smooth sailing lines

(h) a well-knit plot and anecdotes

(i) an element of suspense

(j) a true vindication of the moral purpose

(k) a queer atmosphere

(l) exact geographical positions

(m) gorgeous scenery, as if painted.

(n) deep pathos

(o) value of repentance

(p) futility of boastful human endeavours.

(q) final predominance of fate and mysterious divine power ruling over mankind and all creatures.

(r) a true account of the life on the sea during Coleridge's days.

(s) freedom from obscurity of any sort despite the element of mystery and suspense.

(t) vindication of the "willing suspension of disbelief, etc. etc.

**Coleridge's Shorter poems**

Some of such poems are

1. Ode on Dejection
2. Frost at Midnight
3. Fears in Solitude
4. Love Poems
5. Hymn Before Sunrise in the Vale of Chamouni
6. Work without Hope
7. Religious Musing, etc.

**Prose works**

1. His most well-known prose-work is Biographia Literaria, or Sketches of My Literary Life and Opinions (1817).

2. His other prose works are :

   (i) Aids to Reflection (1815)

   (ii) Lectures on Shakespeare (1849)

**As a Philosopher**

As such, he was greatly influenced by the German idealistic philosophy which he introduced into England.

**As a Music lover and critic**

It is well-known that he loved music and was a keen, constructive critic of it.

Some extracts from his poems are given below :

**(from the Rime of the Ancient Mariner)**

(i) I took the oars: the Pilot's boy,
Who now doth crazy go,
Laughed loud and long, and all the while
His eyes went to and fro,
"Ha! ha!" quoth he, "full plain I see,
The Devil knows how to row."
And now, all in my own countree,
I stood on the firm land!
The Hermit stepped forth from the boat,
And scarcely he could stand.
"O shrieve me, shrieve me, holy man!"
The Hermit crossed his brow.
"Say quick," quoth he, "I bid thee say—
What manner of man art thou?"
Forthwith this frame of mine was wrenched
With a woful agony,
Which forced me to begin my tale;
And then it left me free.
Since then, at an uncertain hour,

That agony returns:
And till my ghastly tale is told,
This heart within me burns,
I pass, like night, from land to land;
I have strange power of speech;
That moment that his face I see,
I know the man that must hear me;
To him my tale I teach.
What loud uproar bursts from the door!
The wedding-guests are there:
But in the garden-bower the bride
And hark the little vesper bell,
Which biddeth me to prayer!
O Wedding-Guest! this sould hath been
Alone on a wide wide sea:
So lonely 'twas, that God himself
Scarce seemed there to be.

(ii) O sweeter than the marriage-feast,
'Tis sweeter far to me,
To walk together to the kirk
With a goodly company!—
To walk together to the kirk,
And all together pray,
While each to his great Father bends,
Old men, and babes, and loving friends
And youths and maidens gay!
Farewell, farewell! but this I tell
To thee, thou Wedding-Guest!
He prayeth well, who loveth well
Both man and bird and beast.
He prayeth best, who loveth best
All things both great and small;
For the dear God who loveth us,
He made and loveth all.'
The Mariner, whose eye is bright,
Whose beard with age is hoar,
Is gone: and now the Wedding-Guest
Turned from the bridegroom's door.
He went like one that hath been stunned,
And is of sense forlorn:
A sadder and a wiser man,
He rose the morrow morn.

(**Note :** Given below are :

(i) Kubla Khan a fragment (full poem)

(ii) Love (extract)

*(iii)* Reflections on Having Left A Place of Retirement :

### From Kubla Khan

In Xanadu did Kubla Khan
A stately pleasure-dome decree:
Where Alph, the sacred river, ran
Through caverns measureless to man
Down to a sunless sea.
So twice five miles of fertile ground
With walls and towers were girdled round:
And there were gardens bright with sinuous rills,
Where blossomed many an incense-bearing tree;
And here were forests ancient as the hills,
Enfolding sunny spots of greenery.

But oh! that deep romantic chasm which slanted
Down the green hill athwart a cedarn cover!
A savage place! as holy and enchanted
As e'er beneath a waning moon was haunted
By woman wailing for her demon-lover!
And from this chasm, with ceaseless turmoil seething,
As if this earth in fast thick pants were breathing,
A mighty fountain momently was forced :
Amid whose swft half-intermitted burst
Huge fragments vaulted like rebounding hail,
Or chaffy grain beneath the thresher's flail;
And 'mid these dancing rocks at once and ever
It flung up momently the sacred river.
Five miles meandering with a mazy motion
Through wood and dale the sacred river ran,
Then reached the caverns measureless to man,
And sank in tumult to a lifeless ocean :
And 'mid this tumult Kubla heard from far
Ancestral voices prophesying war!
    The shadow of the dome of pleasure
      Floated midway on the waves;
    Where was heard the mingled measure
      From the fountain and the caves.
It was a miracle of rare device,
A sunny pleasure-dome with caves of ice!
    A damsel with a dulcimer
    In a vision once I saw:
    It was an Abyssinian maid,
    And on her dulcimer she played,
    Singing of Mount Abora,

Could I revive within me
   Her symphony and song,
    To such a deep delight 'twould win me,
That with music loud and long,
I would build that dome in air,
That sunny dome! those caves of ice!
And all who heard should see them there,
And all should cry, Beware! Beware!
His flashing eyes, his floating hair!
Weave a circle round him thrice,
And close your eyes with holy dread,
For he on honey-dew hath fed,
And drunk the milk of Paradise.

### Love

All thoughts, all passions, all delights,
Whatever stirs this mortal frame,
All are but ministers of Love,
    And feed his sacred flame.
Oft in my waking dreams do I
Live o'er again that happy hour,
When midway on the mount I lay,
    Beside the ruined tower.
The moonshine, stealing o'er the scene,
Had blended with the lights of eve;
And she was there, my hope, my joy,
    My own dear Genevieve!

### *Reflections on Having Left a Place of Retirement*

Low was our pretty Cot: our tallest Rose
Peeped at the chamber-window. We could hear
At silent noon, and eve, and early morn,
The sea's faint murmur. In the open air
Our Myrtles blossom'd; and across the porch
Thick Jasmines twined: the little landscape round
Was green and woody, and refreshed the eye,
It was a spot which you might aptly call
The Valley of Seclusion! Once I saw
(Hallowing his Sabbath-day by quietness)
A wealthy son of Commerce saunter by,
Bristowa's citizen : methought, it calmed
His thirst of idle gold, and made him muse
With wiser feelings; for the paused, and looked
With a pleased sadness, and gazed all around,
Then eyed our Cottage, and gazed round again,
And sighed, and said, it was Blessed Place.
And we *were* blessed. Oft with patient ear

Long-listening to the viewless skylark's note
(Viewless, or haply for a moment seen
Gleaming on sunny wings) in whispered tones
I've said to my beloved, "Such, sweet Girl!
The inobtrusive song of Happiness,
Unearthly minstrelsy! then only heard
When the Soul seeks to hear; when all is hush'd
And the Heart listens!"

(**Note :** It is clear that Coleridge is the master of :

*(i)* Creating supernatural atmosphere

*(ii)* Clear, simple, highly impressive musical lines

*(iii)* A certain philosophical tone pervading as backdrop.

## NATHARIEL HAWTHORNE (1804-64)

1. He regarded himself as a romancer rather than a novelist.

2. He chiefly employed the device of symbolism in his novels.

3. He is a great novelist and allegorist.

4. He is constantly preoccupied with the themes of sin and evil, believing pride to be the principal sin.

5. Some of his works are :

*(i)* The Scarlet Letter (1850)

*(ii)* The House of Seven Gables (1851)

*(iii)* The Blithedale Romance (1852)

*(iv)* The Marble Faun (1860)

6. *(i)* He had already produced a juvenile novel; and a few short stories which were later on published "Twice Told Tales" in 1837.

*(ii)* Some of these stories had earlier appeared in the "The Token."

*(iii)* Some of the popular stories were :

*(a)* An Old Woman's Tale

*(b)* My Kinsman, Major Molinex (1832)

*(c)* The Gray Champion (1832)

*(d)* Young Goodman Brown (1835)

*(e)* Wakefield (1835), etc.

7. In 1846, his collection of 25 short stories, historical sketches and histories was published under the caption "Moses From an Old Mouse."

8. In 1884, he produced a history book for children under the caption: "Grandfather's Chair."

**Certain Characteristics of Hawthorne**

1. He is a great symbolist and allegorist.

2. He is fond of writing romances.

3. He is interested in the study of the Puritan conscience and the Calvinistic idea of the damnation of Man.

4. His chief theme is the impact of sin on the human soul.

5. He tries to introduce the supernatural element in his works, as, for instance, in The Scarlet Letter.

6. Henry James has complained of a lack of intricacy in the rendering of human reality in his novels.

7. Another complaint against him is the tightness of structure (as in the Scarlet Letter) which sometimes encroaches upon his otherwise imaginative and suggestive poetic style.

8. A deep psychoanalytic approach is writ large on almost every page of his novels.

9. The intention to destroy the human soul is something unpardonable in his view.

10. The social, economic, religious and political aspects emerge in one sweep in his novels.

11. His novels present suggestive comments on such themes as :

*(i)* Puritanism in general.

*(ii)* Human relations on all planes such as:

*(a)* sexual

*(b)* conjugal

*(c)* filial, etc.

*(iii)* mystery of life.

*(iv)* Characteristics of sin.

*(v)* value of repentance and redemption.

*(vi)* relationship with the past.

*(vii)* unexplored human psyche.

*(viii)* deviation of best intentions from their path.

*(ix)* Calvinistic Puritanism which enshrines chiefly:

*(a)* depravity of man

*(b)* Pre-destined nature of punishment for sinfulness.

*(c)* Not all are saved.

*(d)* God's grace has its own independent way of working.

*(e)* Those saved have to surrender their will to God.

12. Nature (as in the Forest Scene in The Scarlet Letter) as the representative of the Immanent Spirit.

13. The divine spark in man himself, (as in Pearl's elfin beauty).

Significance of intuition and imagination, as per transcendental doctrine, *vis-a-vis* the English eighteenth century stress correctness and refinement. (This may not be so marked in Hawthorne as in the main Transcendentalists like Emerson and Thoreau).

14. The intrinsic coherence of symbols despite their apparent incoherence, etc., etc.

## ERNEST HEMINGWAY (1899-1961)

1. His novels and stories portray the real events honestly, where toughness and courage are the rule rather than the exception and emotion of often held in abeyance—a method reminiscent of Ezra Pound by whom he was influenced immensely.

2. Some of his works are :

(i) The Sun Also Rises (1926)

(ii) A Farewell To Arms (1929)

(iii) To Have and Have Not (1937)

(iv) For Whom the Bell Tolls (1940)

(v) The Old Man and The Sea (1952)

(This novelette won him the Nobel Prize in 1954)

3. He committed suicide in 1961.

4. He wrote several other books on :

(i) fiction

(ii) bull fighting

(iii) big game hunting in Africa, etc.

(iv) stories

5. Among his works which appeared posthumously, there are a number of poems also.

## EMILY DICKINSON (1830-86)

1. She led a secluded life during the last 25 years of her life.

2. During this period, she cut herself up from all worldly contact except with some intimate friends.

3. (i) In her life she wrote more than one thousand lyrics, but she never cared to get them published during her lifetime.

(ii) During her life, only six of her poems were published.

4. Her poems often are about :

(i) life and death.

(ii) the mystery of death.

(iii) some mystic experiences.

(iv) visions.

(v) sound comments on various aspects of human life and destiny.

(vi) a sympathetic attitude to pathos of life.

(vii) expression of a poignant wit.

5. They contain :

(i) economy of expression.

(ii) novelty of expression.

(iii) new experiments even in simple old metres.

(iv) an aphoristic tone at places.

(v) mystic obscurity or ambiguity at other places.

6. After her death, her poems were published in a number of volumes.

Some of her well-known poems are mentioned below :

1. Success is counted Sweetest:
"Success is counted sweetest
By those who ne'er succeed.
To comprehend a nectar
Requires sorest need."

2. This is my Letter to The World.

3. I Never Saw a Moor

4. I Had Been Hungry

5. Hope is The Thing With Feathers

6. A Bird Came Down The Walk

7. The Sky is Low, the Clouds are Mean

8. A Light Exists in Spring

9. Before I God My Eye Put Out

10. The Heart Asks Pleasure First

11. The Brain Is Wider Than the Sky

12. I Taste A Liquor Never Brewed

13. A Narrow Fellow in the Grass

14. I Heard a Buzz when I Died

15. I Years Had Been from Home

16. A Bird Came Down the Walk
17. I Felt A Funeral in My Brain
18. Safe In Their Alabaster Chambers
19. Much Madness is Divinest Sense
20. The Soul Selects Her Own Society, etc.

Here are some extracts from her works :

1. Because I could not stop for Death,
   He kindly stopped for me;
   The carriage held but just ourselves
   And Immortality.　　　　　　*—The Chariot*

2. How dreary to be somebody!
   How public, like a frog
   To tell your name the livelong day
   To an admiring bog!　　　　　　　*—Life*

3. I never saw a moor,
   I never saw the sea;
   Yet know I how the heather looks,
   And what a wave must be.
   　　　　　　　　　*—Time and Eternity*

4. My life closed twice before its, close;
   It yet remains to see
   It Immortality unveil
   A third event to me.　　　　　　*—Parting*

5. How much can come
   And much can go,
   And yet abide the world!
   　　　　　　　*—There Came a Wind*

6. Parting is all we know of heaven,
   And all we need of hell.
   　　　　　　　　　　　*—Parting*

## G.B. SHAW
## (1856-1950)

### Life

1. He was born in Dublin, Ireland in a Protestant middle-class family.

2. His parents were, however, originally of English stock.

3. As Long points out, "Of music he knew a little, of art or drama nothing; but he had a naturally keen intellect, a vast conceit and what the Irish call a 'gift of gab'".

4. At first, he became a journalist living by his poem, a drama critic and only later a dramatist proper.

5. Before becoming a dramatist, he tried his hand at the novel, but all his novels flopped, *e.g.*
   (i) The Irrational Knot
   (ii) Love Among the Artists
   (iii) An Unsocial Socialist, etc.

### Works

1. (i) "Widowers' Houses" staged in 1893 was his first comedy.
   (ii) It gave him some popularity and, surely, a new type of prose drama was on its way.

2. Then appeared his following dramas included in "Plays Pleasant and Unpleasant" (1898)
   (i) The Philanderer
   (ii) Mrs. Warren's Profession
   (iii) Arms and the Man
   (iv) Candida
   (v) The Man of Destiny
   (vi) You Never Can Tell

3. Thereafter appeared the following plays which were included in "Three Plays for Puritans, (1901):
   (i) The Devil's Disciple
   (ii) Caesar and Cleopatra
   (iii) Captain Brassbound's Conversion

4. 'Man and Superman' appeared in 1903.

5. Thereafter appeared the following plays :
   (i) John Bull's Other Island
   (ii) Major Barbara
   (iii) How he lied to her husband
   (iv) The Doctor's Dilemma
   (v) Getting Married
   (vi) The Showing-up of Blanco Posnet
   (vii) Misalliance
   (viii) Fanny's First Play
   (ix) Androcles and the Lion
   (x) Pygmalion

6. Still later appeared in 1917:
   (i) The Inca of Peruslam
   (ii) Augustus does his Bit
   (iii) Heartbreak House
   (iv) Back to Methuselah (1920)
   (v) Saint Joan (1923)
       (For this, he received the Nobel Prize in 1925)
   (vi) The Apple Cart (1929)
   (vii) Too True to be Good (1932)

*(viii)* Geneva 1939

*(ix)* In Good King Charles's Golden Days (1939)

(**Note :** As stated above, Shaw received the Nobel Prize for literature on Saint Joan in 1925. Though Man and Superman is perhaps his most popular play, many regard Saint Joan as his best play. Given below are extracts from the Preface to the play and from the play itself :

## Extracts from Preface to "Saint Joan" by G.B. Shaw

### Joan and Socrates

If Joan had been malicious, selfish, cowardly, or stupid, she would have been one of the most odious persons known to history instead of one of the most attractive. If she had been old enough to know the effect she was producing on the men whom she humiliated by being right when they were wrong, and had learned to flatter and manage them, she might have lived as long as Queen Elizabeth. But she was too young and rustical and inexperienced to have any such arts. When she was thwarted by men whom she thought fools, she made no secret of her opinion of them or her impatience with their folly; and she was naive enough to expect them to be obliged to her for setting them right and keeping them out of mischief. Now it is always hard for superior wits to understand the fury roused by their exposures of the stupidities of comparative dollords. Even Socrates for all his age and experience, did not defend himself at his trial like a man who understood the long accumulated fury that had burst on him, and was clamouring for his death. His accuser, if born 2300 years later, might have been picked out of any first class carriage on a suburban railway during the evening or morning rush from or to the City; for he had really nothing to say except that he and his like could not endure being shewn up as idiots every time Socrates opened his mouth. Socrates, unconscious of this, was paralyzed by his sense that somehow he was missing the point of the attack. He petered out after he had established the fact that he was an old soldier and a man of honorable life, and that his accuser was a silly snob. He had no suspicion of the extent to which his mental superiority had roused fear and hatred against him in the hearts of men towards whom he was conscious of nothing but good will and good service.

### Contrast with Napoleon

If Socrates was as innocent as this at the age of seventy, it may be imagined how innocent Joan was at the age of seventeen. Now Socrates was a man of argument, operating slowly and peacefully on men's minds, whereas Joan was a woman of action, operating with impetuous violence on thier bodies. That, no doubt, is why the contemporaries of Socrates endured him so long, and why Joan was destroyed before she was fully grown. But both of them combined terrifying ability with a frankness, personal modesty and benevolence which made the furious dislike to which they fell victims absolutely unreasonable, and therefore inapprehensible by themselves. Napoleon, also possessed of terrifying ability, but neither frank nor disinterested, had no illusions as to the nature of his popularity. When he was asked how the world would take his death he said it would give a gasp of relief. But it is not so easy for mental giants who neither hate nor intend to injure their fellows to realize that nevertheless their fellows hate mental giants and would like to destroy them, not only enviously because the juxtaposition of a superior wounds their vanity, but quite humbly and honestly because it frightens them. Fear will drive men to any extreme; and the fear inspired by a superior being is a mystery which cannot be reasoned away. Being immeasurable it is unbearable when there is no presumption or guarantee of its benevolence and moral responsibility: in other words, when it has no official status. The legal and conventional superiority of Herod and Pilate, and of Annas and Caiaphas, inspires fear; but the fear, being a reasonable fear of measurable and avoidable consequences which seem salutary and protective, is bearable; whilst the strange superiority of Christ and the fear it inspires elicit a shriek of Crucify Him from all who cannot divine its benevolence. Socrates has to drink the hemlock, Christ to hang on the cross, and Joan to burn at the stake, whilst Napoleon, though he ends in St. Helena, at least dies in his bed there; and many terrifying but quite comprehensible official scoundrels die natural deaths in all the glory of the kingdoms of this world, proving that it is far more dangerous to be a saint than to be a conqueror. Those who have been both, like Mahomet and Joan, have found that it is the conqueror who must save the saint, and that defeat and capture mean martyrdom. Joan was burnt without a hand lifted on her own side to save her. The comrades she had led to victory and the enemies she had disgraced and defeated, the French king she had crowned and the English king whose crown she had kicked into the Loire, were equally glad to be rid of her.

### Was Joan Innocent or Guilty?

As this result could have been produced by a crapulous inferiority as well as by a sublime supriority, the question which of the two was operative in Joan's case has to be faced. It was decided against her by her contemporaries after a very careful and conscientious trial; and the reversal of the verdict twenty-five years later, in form a rehabilitation of Joan, was really only a confirmation of the validity of the coronation of Charles VII. It is the more impressive reversal by a unanimous Posterity, culminating in her canonization, that has quashed the original proceedings, and put her judges on their trial, which so far, has been much more unfair than their trial of her. Nevertheless the rehabilitation of 1456, corrupt job as it was, really did produce evidence enough to satisfy all reasonable critics that Joan was not a common termagant, not a harlot, not a with, not a blasphemer no more an idolater than the Pope himself...."

### Joan's Voices and Visions

Joan's voices and visions have played many tricks with her reputation. They have been held to prove that she was mad, that she was a liar and impostor, that she was a sorceress (she was burned for this), and finally that she was a saint....... Socrates, Luther, Swedenborg, Blake saw visions and heard voices just as Saint Francis and Saint Joan did.... Gravitation, being a reasoned hypothesis which fitted remarkably well into the Copernicus version of the observed physical facts of the universe, established Newton's reputation for extraordinary intelligence, and would have done so no matter how fantastically he had arrived at it. Yet his theory of gravitation is not so impressive a mental feat as his astounding chronology, which establishes him as the king of mental conjurors, but a Bedlamite king whose authority no one now accepts. On the subject of the eleventh horn of the beast seen by the prophet Daniel he was more fantastic than Joan, because his imagination was not dramatic but mathematical and therefore extraordinarily susceptible to numbers: indeed if all his works were lost except his chronology we should say that he was as mad as a hatter. As it is, who dares diagnose Newton as a madman?

In the same way Joan must be judged a sane woman in spite of her voices because they never gave her any advice that might not have come to her from her mother wit exactly as gravitation came to Newton. We can all see now, especially since the late war threw so many of our women into military life, that Joan's compaigning could not have been carried on in petticoats. This was not only because she did a man's work, but because it was morally necessary that sex should be left out of the question as between her and her comrades-in-arms. She gave this reason herself when she was pressed on the subject; and the fact that this entirely reasonable necessity came to her imagination first as an order from God delivered through the mouth of Saint Catherine does not prove that she was mad. The soundness of the order proves that she was usually sane; but its form proves that her dramatic imagination played tricks with her senses. Her policy was also quite sound: nobody dipsutes that the relief of Orleans, followed up by the coronation at Rheims of the Dauphin as a counterblow to the suspicions then current of his legitimacy and consequently of his title, were military and political masterstrokes that saved France. They might have been planned by Napoleon or any other illusionproof genius. They came to Joan as an instruction from her Counsel, as she called her visionary saints; but she was none the less an able leader of men for imagining her ideas in this way.

### The Evolutionary Appetite

What then is the modern view of Joan's voices and visions and messages from God? The nineteenth century said that they were delusions, but that as she was a pretty girl, and has been abominably ill-treated and finally done to death by a superstitious rabble of medieval priests hounded on by a corrupt political bishop, it must be assumed that she was the innocent dupe of these delusions. The twentieth century finds this explanation too vapidly common-place and demands something more mystic. I think the twentieth century is right, because an explanation which amounts to Joan being mentally defective instead of, as she obviously was, mentally excessive, will not wash. I cannot believe, nor, if I could, could I expect all my readers to believe, as Joan did, that three ocularly visible well dressed persons, named respectively Saint Catherine, Saint Margaret, and Saint Michael, came down from heaven and gave her certain instructions with which they were charged by God for her. Not that such a belief would be more improbable or fantastic than some modern beliefs which we all swallow; but there are fashions and family habits in belief, and it happens that, my fashion being Victorian and my family habit Protestant, I find myself unable to attach any such obective validity to the form of Joan's visions.

But that there are forces at work which use individuals for purposes far transcending the purpose of keeping these individuals alive and prosperous and respectable and safe and happy in the middle station in life, which is all any good bourgeois can reasonably require, is established by the fact that men will, in the pursuit of knowledge and of social readjustments for which they will not be penny the better, and are indeed often many pence the worse, face poverty, infamy, exile, imprisonment, dreadful hardship, and death. Even the selfish pursuit of personal power does not nerve men to efforts and sacrifies which are eagerly made in pursuit of extensions of our power over nature, though these extensions may not touch the personal life of the seeker at any point. There is no more mystery about this appetite for knowledge and power than about the appetite for food: both are known as facts and as facts only, the difference between them being that the appetite for food is necessary to the life of the hungry man and is therefore a personal appetite, whereas the other is an appetite for evolution; and therefore a superpersonal need.

The diverse manner in which our imaginations dramatize the approach of the superpersonal forces is a problem for the psychologist, not for the historian. Only, the historian must understand that visionaries are neither impostors nor lunatics. It is one thing to say that the figure Joan recognized as St. Catherine was not really St. Catherine, but the dramatization by Joan's imagination of that pressure upon her of the driving force that is behind evolution which I have just called the evolutionary appetite. It is quite another to class her visions with the vision of two moons seen by a drunken person, or with Brocken spectres, echoes and the like. Saint Catherine's instructions were far too cogent for that; and the simplest French peasant who believes in apparitions of celestial personages to favored mortals is nearer to the scientific truth about Joan than the Rationalist and Materialist historians and essayists..... If Joan was mad, all Christendom was mad too...."

**A Void in The Elizabethan Drama**

I have, however, one advantage over the Elizabethans. I write in full view of the Middle Ages, which may be said to have been rediscovered in the middle of the nineteenth century after an eclipse of about four hundred and fifty years. The Renascence of antique literature and art in the sixteenth century, and the lusty growth of Capitalism, between them buried the Middle Ages; and the resurrection is a second Renascence. Now there is not a breath of medieval atmosphere in Shakespeare's histories. His John of Gaun is like a study of the old age of Drake. Although he was a Catholic by family tradition, his figures are all intensely Protestant, indvidualist, sceptical, self-centred in everything but their love affairs and completely personal and selfish even in them. His kings are not statesmen: his cardinals have no religion: a novice can read his plays from one end to the other without learning that the world finally governed by forces expressing themselves in religions and laws which make epochs rather than by vulgarly ambitious individuals who make rows. The divinity which shapes our ends, rough hew them how we will, is mentioned fatalistically only to be forgotten immediately like a passing vague apprehension. To Shakespeare as to Mark Twain, Cauchon would have been a tyrant and bully instead of a Catholic, and the Inquisitor Lemaitre would have been a Sadist instead of a lawyer. Warwick would have had not more feudal quality than his successor the King Maker has in the play of Henry VI. We should have seen them all completely satisfied that if they would only to their own selves be true they could not then be false to any man (a precept which represents the reaction against medievalism at its interest) as if they were being in the air, without public responsibilities of any kind. All Shakespare's characters are so: that is why they seem natural to our middle classes, who are comfortable and irresponsible at other people's expense, and are neither ashamed of the condition nor even conscious of it. Nature abhors this vacuum in Shakespeare; and I have taken care to let the medieval atmosphere blow through my play freely. Those who see it performed will not mistake the starting event it records for a mere personal accident. They will have before them not only the visible and human puppets, but the Church, the Inquisition, the Feudal System, with divine inspiration always beating against their too inelastic limits: all more terrible in their dramatic force than any of the little mortal figures clanking about in plate armor or moving silently in the frocks and hoods of the order of St Dominic.

### Tragedy, not Melodrama

There are no villains in the piece. Crime, like disease, is not interesting: it is something to be done away with by general consent, and that is all about it. It is what men do at their best, with good intentions, and what normal men and women find that they must and will do in spite of their intentions, that really concern us. The rascally bishop and the cruel inquisitor of Mark Twain and Andrew Lang are as dull as pickpockets; and they reduce Joan to the level of the even less interesting person whose pocket is picked. I have represented both of them as capable and eloquent exponents of The Church Militant and The ChurchLitigant, because only by doing so can I maintain my drama on the level of high tragedy and save it from becoming a mere police court sensation. A villain in a play can never be anything more than *a diabolus ex machina*, possibly a more exciting expedient than *a deus ex machina*, but both equally mechanical, and therefore interesting only as mechanism. It is, I repeat, what normally innocent people do that concerns us; and if Joan had not been burnt by normally innocent people in the energy of their righteousness her death at their hands would have no more significance than Tokyo earthquake, which burnt a great many maidens. The tragedy of such murders is that they are not committed by murderers. They are judicial murders; pious murders; and this contradiction at once brings an element of comedy into the tragedy: the angels may weep at the murder, but the gods laugh at the murderers.

### Extracts from Saint Joan

Here are some extracts from the play :

Joan [*trenchant and masterful*] Blethers! We are all like that to begin with. I shall put courage into thee.

*Charles:* But I don't want to have courage put into me. I want to sleep in a comfortable bed, and not live in continual terror of being killed or wounded. Put courage into the others, and let them have their bellyful of fighting; but let me alone.

*Joan:* It's no use, Charlie: thou must face what God puts on thee. If thou fail to make thyself king, thoult be a beggar: what else art fit for? Come! Let me see thee sitting on the throne. I have looked forward to that.

*Charles:* What is the good of sitting on the throne when the other fellows give all the orders? However! [*he sits enthroned, a piteous figure*] here is the king for you! Look your fill at the poor devil.

*Joan:* Thourt not king yet, lad: thourt but Dauphin. Be not led away by them around thee. Dressing up don't fill empty noddle. I know the people: the real people that make thy bread for thee; and I tell thee they count no man king of France until the holy oil has been poured on his hair, and himself consecrated and crowned in Rheims Cathedral. And thou needs new clothes, Charlie. Why does not Queen look after thee properly?

*Charles:* We're too poor. She wants all the money we can spare to put on her own back. Besides, I like to see her beautifully dressed; and I don't care what I wear myself: I should look ugly anyhow.

*Joan:* There is some good in thee, Charlie; but it is not yet a king's good.

*Charles:* We shall see I am not such a fool as I look. I have my eyes open; and I can tell you that one good treaty is worth ten good fights. These fighting fellows lose all on the treaties that they gain on the fights. If we can only have a treaty, the english are sure to have the worst of it, because they are better at fighting than at thinking.

*Joan:* If the English win, it is they that will make the treaty: and then God help poor France! Thou must fight, Charlie, whether thou will or no. I will go first to hearten thee. We must take our courage in both hands : aye, and pray for it with both hands too.

*Charles: [descending from his throne and again crossing the room to escape from her dominating urgency]* Oh do stop talking about God and praying. I cant bear people who are always praying. Isnt it bad enough to have to do it at the proper times?

*Joan: [pitying him]* Thou poor child, thou hast never prayed in the life. I must teach thee from the beginning.

*Charles:* I am not a child: I am a grown man and a father; and I will not be taught any more.

*Joan:* Aye, you have a little son. He that will be Louis the Elventh when you die. Would you not fight for him?

*Charles:* No: a horrid boy. He hates me. He hates everybody, selfish little beast! I dont want to be bothered with children. I dont want to be a father; and I don't want to be a son: especially a son of St Louis. I don't want to be any of these fine things you all have your heads full of: I want to be Just what I am. Why cant you mind your own business. and let me mind mine?

*Joan: [again contemptuous]* Minding your own business is like minding your own body; it's the shortest way to make yourself sick. What is my business? Helping mother at home. What is thine? Petting lapdogs and sucking sugar-sticks. I call that muck. I tell thee it is God's business we are here to do: not our own. I have a message to thee from God; and though must listen to it, though thy heart break with the terror of it.

*Charles:* I don't want a message; but can you tell me any secrets? Can you do any cures? Can you turn lead into gold, or anything of that sort?

*Joan:* I can turn thee into a king, in Rheims Cathedral; and that is a miracle that will take some doing, it seems.

*Charles:* If we go to Rheims, and have a coronation, Anne will want new dresses. We can't afford them. I am all right as I am.

*Joan:* In God's name, then, let us cross the bridge, and fall on them.

*Dunois:* It seems simple; but it cannot be done.

*Joan:* Who says so?

*Dunois:* I say so; and older and wiser heads than mind are of the same opinion.

*Joan: [roundly]* Then your older and wiser heads are fatheads: they have made a fool of you; and now they want to make a fool of me too, bringing me to the wrong side of the river. Do you not know that I bring you better help than ever came to any general or any town?

*Dunois: [smiling patiently]* Your own?

*Joan:* No: the help and counsel of the King of Heaven. Which is the way to the bridge?

*Dunois:* You are impatient, Maid.

*Joan:* Is this a time for patience? Our enemy is at our gates; and here we stand doing nothing. Oh, why are you not fighting? Listen to me: I will deliver you from fear. I—

*Dunois: [laughing heartily, and waving her off]* No, no, my girl: if you delivered me from fear I should be a good knight for a story book, but a very bad commander of the army. Come! let me begin to make a soldier of you. *[He takes her to the water's edge].* Do you see those two forts at this end of the bridge? the big ones?

*Joan:* Yes. Are they ours or the goddams'?

*Dunois:* Be quiet, and listen to me. If I were in either of those forts with only ten men I could hold it against an army. The English have more than ten times ten goddams in those forts to hold them against us.

*Joan:* They cannot hold them against God. God did not give them the land under those forts: they stole it from Him. He gave it to us. I will take those forts.

*Dunois:* Single-handed?

*Joan:* Our men will take them. I will lead them.

*Dunois:* Not a man will follow you.

*Joan:* I will not look back to see whether anyone is following me.

*Dunois: [recognizing her mettle, and clapping her heartily on the shoulder]* Good. You have the makings of a soldier in you. You are in love with war.

*Joan:* [*startled*] Oh! And the Archbishop said I was in love with religion.

*Dunois:* I, God forgive me, am a little in love with war myself, the ugly devil! I am like a man with two wives. Do you want to be like a woman with two husbands?

*Joan:* [*matter-of-fact*] I will never take a husband. A man in Toul took an action against me for a breach of promise; but I never promised him. I am soldier: I do not want to be thought of as a woman. I will not dress as a woman. I do not care for the things women care for. They dream of lovers, and of money. I dream of leading a charge, and of placing the big guns. You soldiers do not know how to use the big guns: you think you can win battles with a great noise and smoke.

*Dunois:* [*with a shrug*] True. Half the time artillery is more trouble than it is worth.

*Joan:* Aye, lad; but you cannot fight stone walls with horses: you must have guns, and much bigger guns too.

*Dunois:* [*grinning at her familiarity, and echoing it*] Aye, lass; but a good heart and a stout ladder will get over the stoniest wall.

*Joan:* I will be first up the ladder when we reach the fort, Bastard. I dare you to follow me.

*Dunois:* You must not dare a staff officer, Joan: only company officers are allowed to indulge in displays of personal courage, Besides, you must know that I welcome you as a saint, not as a soldier. I have daredevils enough at my calls, if they could help me.

*Joan:* I am not a daredevil: I am a servant of God. My sword is sacred: I found it behind the altar in the church of St. Catherine, where God hid it for me; and I may not strike a blow with it. My heart is full of courage, not of anger. I will lead; and your men will follow: that is all I can do. But I must do it: you shall not stop me.

**ROBERT FROST**
**(1874-1963)**

1. He could not get good response from the American publishers in the beginning.

2. (*i*) His first volume of poems: "*A Boy's Will*" was published in 1913 by an English publisher.

(*ii*) His second volume "*North of Boston*" was published by the same publisher in 1914.

(*iii*) His first poem "The Butterfly" had already appeared in "The Independent" (New York) in 1894.

3. When he lived in Beaconsfield, England, most of his friends were Georgian poets.

4. Some of his other works which appeared later were :

(*i*) Mountain Interval (1916)
(*ii*) New Hampshire.... (1923)
(*iii*) West-Running Brook (1928)
(*iv*) A Further Range (1936)
(*v*) A Witness Tree (1942)
(*vi*) Steeple Bush (1947)

5. His "Complete Poems" appeared in 1949, at the end of which were placed two of his verse dramas:

(*i*) A Masque of Reason (1945) and
(*ii*) A Masque of Mercy (1947)

6. In his life, Frost received four Pulitzer Prizes, Poet Laureateship of New England and several other honours.

7. Before his death, he had become a national poet.

8. In his "The Figure a Poem Makes" (1949) which is a kind of Preface to his "Collected Poems," he gave his comments on a poem :

(*i*) "(A poem) begins in delight and ends in wisdom.... it runs a course of lucky events, and ends in a clarification of life...."

(*ii*) "The artist.... matches a thing from some previous order in time and space into a new order."

9. Some of the more famous poems of Frost are :

(*i*) Neither Out Far Nor in Deep
(*ii*) Birches
(*iii*) The Onset
(*iv*) The Pasture
(*v*) Provide, Provide
(*vi*) Mending Wall
(*vii*) The Road Not Taken
(*viii*) After Apple-Picking
(*ix*) Two Tramps in Mud Time
(*x*) Stopping By Woods on a Snowy Evening
(*xi*) Directive

*(xii)* Meetting and Passing
*(xiii)* The Gift Outright
*(xiv)* A Considerable Speck
*(xv)* The Death of a Hired Man
*(xvi)* West, Running Brook
*(xvii)* Home Burial
*(xviii)* Departmental
*(xix)* Snow
*(xx)* The Tuft of Flowers
*(xxi)* Mowing
*(xxii)* Acquainted with the Night
*(xxiii)* The Need of Being Versed in County Things
*(xxiv)* I Will Sing You One—O
*(xxv)* Blueberries, etc.

10. Frost is studied on several levels:

*(i)* As an American poet
*(ii)* As a poet of nature
*(iii)* As a poet of New England
*(iv)* As a Rural poet
*(v)* As a Modern poet
*(vi)* As a poet of Truth
*(vii)* As a poet of known for new type or techniques, etc.
*(viii)* As a poet of New England/of New Hampshire, in particular.

10. He was invited by President John F. Kennedy to recite his patriotic poem "The Gift Outright" at the inaugural ceremony.

Given below are extracts from some of his poems :

1. *From After Apple-Picking*

"I feel the ladder sway as the boughs bend.
And I keep hearing from the cellar bin
The rumbling sound
Of load on load of apples coming in.
For I have had too much
Of apple-picking: I am overtired
Of the great harvest I myself desired."

The lines show, *inter alia*, the truth of life: man gets tired of the excess of a thing he previously so much longed for.

2. *From Design*

"Like the ingredients of a witches' broth—
A snow-drop spider, a flower like froth,

..............................

The wayside blue and the innocent heal-all?
What brought the kindred spider to that height,

Then steered the white moth thither in the night?
What but design of darkness to appall?
If design govern govern a thing so small."

Sometimes, Frost is censured for lack of depth. But the lines given here direct human attention to the great puzzle whether there is any design in objects of nature, big and small.

3. *From Fire and Ice*

Some say the world will end in fire,
Some say in ice,
From what I've tasted of desire
I hold with those who favour fire,
But if I had to perish twice,
I think I know enough of hate
To say that for destruction ice
Is also great
And would suffice.

The lines clearly show Frost's appeal to mankind to give up hatred and excessive desire and have a faith in mutual co-operation, goodwill and love. This is what seems implied in the poem.

4. *From Mending Wall*

In this famous poem, there is clear appeal for good neighbourliness, brotherhood and mutual cooperation.

"Something there is that doesn't love a wall,

..............................................

There where it is we do not need the wall:
He is all pine and I am apple orchard
My apple trees will never get across
And eat the cones under his pines.
I tell him.
He only says, "Good fences make good neighbours.'

..............................................

**Frost's Later Poetry**

A number of critics have condemned Frost's later poetry as being cold, unsympathetic, unemotional and the like. Rendall Jarrell is one of them. This is what he says about his later poetry:

"I never dared be radical when young for fear it would make me conservative when old" is truthful and his conservatism affected his poetry to a considerable extent. In the later poetry of Frost, one gets a self-made man's political editorial, full of cracker-box, philosophizing, almanac joke-cracking—of a snake oil statesman's mysticism, one gets sentimentality and whimsicality, an arch complacency, a complacent archness, and one gets Homely Wisdom till the cows come home. Often the later Frost makes demands on himself that are minimum; he uses a little wit and an observation and a little sentiment to stuff, not very tight—a little sonnet, and it's not bad, but not good enough to matter either. The extremely rare, extremely wonderful, dramatic and narrative element that is more important than anything else in his early poetry almost disappears from his later poetry; in his later work the best poems are usually special-case, rather than all out; full-scale affairs. The youngest Frost is surrounded by his characters, living being he has known or created; the older Frost is alone. But it is loneliness that is responsible for the cold finality of poems like "Neither Out Far Nor in Deep" or "Design". Frost's latest books deserve little more than a footnote, since they have had few of his virtues, most of vices, and all of his tricks, the heathen who would be converted to Frost by them is hard to construct...."

Frost's later poetry has also been condemned by Yuvor Winters:

....Frost, the rustic realist of North of Boston, appears in his old age as a standard exemplar of irresponsible Romantic irony, of the kind of irony that has degenerated steadily from the moderately low level of Laforgue, through Pound, Eliot, Cummings and their younger imitators."

Cowley also has said a lot about his later poems as compared to earlier poems which he greatly praises as under:

"It is a pleasure to name over the poems of youth and age that become more vivid in one's memory with each new reading: the dramatic dialogues like "The Death of the Hired Man" and "The Witch of Coos." Besides half a dozen others almost equally good, the descriptions or narrations that turn imperceptibly into Aesop's fables, like "The Grindstone" and "Cow in Apple Time," and best of all the short lyrics like "The Pasture," "Now Close the Windows," "The Sound of the Trees," "Fire and Ice," "Stopping by Woods on a Snowy Evening" (always a favourite with anthologists). "To Earthward," "Tree at My Window," "Acquainted with the Night," "Neither out Far Nor in Deep," "Beech," "Wilful Homing," "Come In "and I could easily add to the list."

**Frost's Faults:** Frost has been taken to account by several critics on several counts some of which are mentioned below :

**1. Lack of profundity and Defective Style**
Yuvor Winters says :

"The result in the didactic poems is the perversity and incoherence of thought, the result in the narrative poem is either slightness of subject or a flat and uninteresting apprehension of the subject, the result in the symbolic lyrics is a disturbing location between the descriptive surface, which is frequently lovely, and the ultimate meaning, which is usually sentimental and unacceptable. The result in nearly all the poems is a measure of carelessness in the style, sometimes small and sometimes great, but usually evident; the conversational manner will naturally suit a poet who takes all experience so casually, and it is only natural that the conversational manner should often become very conversational indeed."

**2. Lack of Intensity of Language :** According to Leonard Unqer and William Van O'Connor :

"There are marked limitations to the tonal range within which Frost works and his successes. One does not find intensity of language in Frost's poetry. Intensity is not characteristic of the Yankee manner. It is not produced by understatement, whimsey and casualness. But while Frost does not commit himself to intensity, he can achieve concentration of meaning."

**3. Lack of Dramatic and narrative element :**
Randall Jarrell opines, in his later poetry:

"The extremely rare, the extremely wonderful, dramatic and narrative element that is more important than anything else in his early poetry almost disappears from his later poetry."

**4. Defective Social Philosophy :**
See Short Essays

Given below are some important dates in the life of Frost :

1874      Born in San Francisco, California, March 26. Son of William Prescott Frost. Jr. and Isabelle Moodie Frost.

| | |
|---|---|
| 1874-85 | Boyhood in San Francisco. |
| 1885 | Moves to Lawrence, Massachusetts, with his mother and sister, after the death of his father. |
| 1885-95 | School years and young manhood in Lawrence, Massachusetts. |
| 1892 | Graduates from Lawrence High School. Co-valedictorian with Elinor Miriam White. Attends Dartmouth College for few months. |
| 1894 | "My Butterfly" published in the *independent*, November. |
| 1895 | Marries Elinor Miriam White. |
| 1895 | Birth of first child, Eliot. |
| 1897-99 | Attends Harward as an undergraduate. |
| 1899 | Birth of daughter, Lesley. |
| 1900-10 | maintains Farms (near West Derry), writes poetry, and teaches school (Pinkerton Academy, Derry Village) in New Hampshire. |
| 1900 | Birth of son, Carol. |
| 1903 | Birth of daughter, Irma. |
| 1905 | Birth of daughter, Marjorie. |
| 1907 | Birth of daughter, Elinor Bettina, who dies in infancy. |
| 1911-12 | Teaches psychology at New Hampshire State Normal School, Plymouth, New Hampshire. |
| 1912-15 | Goes to England with wife and four children. Writes and maintains farms in Buckinghamshire and Herefordshire. |
| 1913 | *A Boy's Will.* |
| 1914 | *North of Boston.* |
| 1915 | Returns to America from England. Settles on a farm, Franconia, New Hampshire. |
| 1916 | *Mountain Interval.* Elected to National Institute of Arts and Letters. |
| 1917-20 | Professor of English Amherst College. |
| 1919 | Moves to new farm, South Shaftesbury, Vermont. |
| 1920 | Co-founder, Bread Loaf School of English, Middlebury College. |
| 1921-23 | Poet in Residence, University of Michigan. |
| 1923 | *Selected Poems. New Hampshire.* |
| 1923-25 | Professor of English, Amherst College. |
| 1924 | Pulitzer Prize for *New Hampshire*. |
| 1925-26 | Fellow in Letters, University of Michigan. |
| 1926-38 | Professor of English, Amherst College. John Woodruff Simpson Foundation. |
| 1928 | *West-Running Book.* |
| 1930 | A Way Out (One-act play, first printed in 1917; produced at Amherst College, Northampton Academy of Music, February 24, 1919). *Collected Poems.* |
| 1931 | Pulitzer Prize for *Collected Poems*. |
| 1934 | Death of Marjorie Frost Fraser. |
| 1936 | *A Further Range*, Charles Eliot Norton, Professor of Poetry, Harvard University. |
| 1937 | Pulitzer Prize for *A Further Range*. |
| 1938 | Death of Elinor White Frost. |
| 1939 | *Collected Poems.* |
| 1939-42 | Ralph Waldo Emerson Fellow in Poetry. Harvard University. |
| 1940 | Death of Card Frost. |
| 1942 | *A Witness Tree.* |
| 1943 | Pulitzer Prize for *A Witness Tree*. |
| 1943-49 | Ticknor Fellow in the Humanities, Dartmouth College. |
| 1945 | A Masque of Reason. |
| 1947 | *Steeple Bush. A Masque of Mercy.* |
| 1949 | *Complete Poems.* |
| 1957 | Litt. D.S. at Oxford and Cambridge Universities and National University of Ireland. |
| 1958 | Consultant in Poetry to Library of Congress. |
| 1959 | Eighty-fifth Birthday Anniversary. |
| 1961 | Reads "The Gift Outright" at Presidential Inauguration, January 20. |
| 1962 | *In the Clearing* appeared. |
| 1963 | Died on January 22. |

## ARTHUR MILLER (1915-)

1.   Whereas O'Neill was the pioneer of American drama in the pre-First World War period, Miller and Tennessee Williams were the only two

important American dramatists during the post war period.

2. *(i)* He got admission in the University of Michigan in 1934.

*(ii)* There he won the first Avery Hopwood Prize for the play: "The Grass Still Grows."

3. Some of his important works are :

*(i)* *Situation Normal (1944):* It is a volume of sketches pertaining to life in the army.

*(ii)* *The Man Who Had All the Luck:* It is his first novelistic play.

*(iii)* *Focus (1945):* It is his successful novel.

*(iv)* *All My Sons (1947):* It is his first highly successful play.

*(v)* *Death of a Salesman (1949):* It is generally considered his masterpiece.

*(vi)* *The Crucible (1953):* This play is a kind of modern parable.

*(vii)* *(a)* A Memory of Two Mondays (1955)

*(b)* A View From the Bridge (1955)
In these two plays, Miller's main focus is on the common man.

*(viii)* *Misfits:* In this play, the central theme is the effect of maladjustment in a matrimonial alliance.

*(ix)* *After the Fall (1964):* This emotional play is modelled on the stream of consciousness technique.

*(x)* *Incident at Vichy (1964):* It is a long one-act play based on the theme of individual gilt.

*(xi)* *The Prince (1968):* This play depicts a family feud between two brothers.

---

### ANITA DESAI
### (1937-)

1. She is a renowned novelist and short story writer.

2. Some of her famous novels are :

*(i)* Cry, the Peacock (1963)

*(ii)* Voices in the City (1965)

*(iii)* Bye-Bye, Blackbird (1971)

*(iv)* Fire on the Mountain (1977)

*(v)* Clear Light of Day (1980)

3. Her collection of short stories is captioned "Games at Twilight" (1978)

---

### NISSIN EZEKIEL
### (1924-)

(A) 1. He is a famous Bombayite who has written on all aspects of the mega-city.

2. He worked as an editor of the Quest and Poetry India and later became President of PEN (India).

3. He is also a poetry and an art critic. He is, however better known as a poet.

4. Some of his works are :

*(i)* A Time to Change (1952)

*(ii)* Sixty Poems (1953)

*(iii)* The Third (1959)

*(iv)* The Unfinished Man (1960)

*(v)* The Exact Name (1969)

*(vi)* The Sleepwalkers (1969)

*(vii)* Snakeskin and Other Poems (1974)

*(viii)* Hymns in Darkness (1976)

*(ix)* Latter Day Psalms (1982).

5. He won the Sahitya Akademi Award in 1983.

6. He had worked as a good samaritan collecting funds from Israel for the poor Bombay Jews children before he had to be hospitalised for Alzhmeir's Disease.

(B) Some of his most famous poems are :

1. Night of the Scorpion.

2. Poet, Lover, Birdwatcher.

In one of his interviews, he said, "A winter needs a national or cultural identity, without that you become a series of limitations, echoes, responses, but you do not develop because there is nothing at the core to develop."

(Interview with N.E. : Indian Literary Review Vol. 1, No 10, Feb. 1979, Bombay).

---

### K. N. DARUWALLA
### (1937-)

1. He wrote short stories and his critical work has also often appeared in journals, but he is known more for his poetry.

2. He is one of the judges who decide the poetic works at competitions held by the All-India (English) Poetry Society and Sahitya Akademi, New Delhi.

3. He won the Sahitya Akademi Award for Poetry in 1984.

4. In his poetry, he is virtually a social protester, but he is known for his vivid imagery and accuracy of description.

5. He is one of the most famous living Indian English poets, who says about himself, "I am not an urban writer and my poems are rooted in the rural landscape. My poetry is earthy, and I like to consciously keep it that way..."

6. In all, he has published nine collections of poems so far (Dec. 2002).

Some of them are :
 (i) Under Orion (1970)
 (ii) Apparition in April (1971)
 (iii) Crossing of Rivers (1976)
 (iv) Winter Poems (1980)
 (v) The Keeper of the Dead (1982)
 (vi) Landscapes (1987)
 (vii) The Map-Maker (Pub. by Ravi Dayal) (2002)

7. His poems have appeared in :
 (i) Opinion
 (ii) Poetry Australia, Sydney
 (iii) Transatlantic Review, London
 (iv) Triquarterly—Illinois

8. Some of his well-known poems are :
 (i) The Epileptic
 (ii) The Ghaghra in Spate
 (iii) Rumination
 (iv) Death of a Bird
 (v) Fire-Hymn
 (vi) Routine
 (vii) Old Sailor (The opening poem of "The Map Maker")
 (viii) The Birth of Maya ⎫ included in "The
 (ix) Draupadi ⎬ Map Maker"

9. The famous collection of his short stories is entitled : "Sword and Abyss."

10. Some of the qualities of his poetry are :
 (i) faithful depiction of north Indian landscape.
 (ii) element of social protest.
 (iii) a bitter, satiric tone.
 (iv) concrete statuesque imagery.
 (v) complete surrender of self to the poetic art.
 (vi) crude earthiness.
 (vii) mainly a rural atmosphere.

(viii) bringing into full poetic display of his experience in the police department :
"A crowd senses a mishap before it sees one."

11. Here are some extracts from his poems :
 1. "The nights move on; you go by other signs:
 it is not dreams I wish to talk about,
 The body speaks of its premositions:
 and you must always hear the body out..."
 from "Old Sailor."
 2. "The travails of Draupadi are never-ending.
 It seems some people have it
 in their bleeding stars.
 First exploited by the Pandavas,
 five to one,
 then by the Kauravas,
 hundred to one
 and now by the feminists in million."
 3. "There was nothing, neither air nor substance, "Draupadi"
 Not energy, nor ether,
 Not thought nor dream....."
 —*"The Birth of Maya"*

## R.K. NARAYAN (1906-2001)

1. Of the three great novelists, Narayan, Anand and Rao, it is Narayan who has won the maximum accolade both in India and abroad.

2. One of his great achievements is his creation of the famous town of Malgudi like Hardy's Wessex.

3. Narayan is the true master of humour, irony, realism, romance and artistry.

4. Most of his novels and stories depict the life of people of South India.

5. It is sometimes held that Narayan lacks true pathos, genuine depth of feeling, realistic description of poverty and misery, the elements which go in for making a novelist a great one.

6. However, he has earned much popularity as a novelist, and within the range of his own art, he cannot be taken except with due regard and attention.

Some of his famous novels are :
 1. Swami and Friends (1935)
 2. Bachelor of Arts
 3. The English Teacher
 4. The Financial Expert

5. Mr. Sampath (1949)
6. The Guide (1958)
7. The Man-eater of Malgudi
8. The Dark Room (1939)
9. Waiting for the Mahatma
10. The Vendor of Sweets
11. The Painter of Signs (1976)

(He won the Sahitya Akademi Award for 'Guide' in 1961)

### R. K. Narayan
### as a short story writer

1. Some of his stories have appeared in the following collections:

*(i)* Malgudi Days
*(ii)* Dodu and Other Stories
*(iii)* Cyclone and Other Stories
*(iv)* Gods, Demons and Others

Narayan has written a few hundred stories, most of them quite interesting and highly readable:

Some of his famous short stories are :

1. The Golden
2. A Career
3. The Snake Song
4. Man Hunt
5. A Willing Slave
6. An Astrologer's Day
7. The Doctor's word
8. God of Troubles, etc.

## MULK RAJ ANAND

1. He was greatly influenced by Premchand on the one hand and Tagore on the other.

2. According to Jack Lindsay, "And so there are in his work elements of nature poetry, breath of compassion, irony and serenity; a wealth of varying planes of perception, which Premchand could not encompass."

3. Anand is often known as the mouthpiece of the underdog.

4. According to Srinivas Iyengar, "...he is enough of an artist to save his excellent novels from the stigma of mere propaganda. And hence his characters.... at any rate, his Indian characters are almost as a rule recognizably human beings, not automats or formulae."

5. *(i)* His novels are surrealistic in structure.

*(ii)* Hence his plots lack the complexity which is the hallmark of more popular and artistic novels in the world.

6. Some of his novels lack organic unity, *e.g.* "Coolie" in spite of having won the Sahitya Akademi Award (in 1972) is at best a picaresque attempt, a loose tying up of detached episodes which may be called epical, but not quite artistic.

7. His women are not so lively and they are often subservient to the will of men.

**Works**

Some of his famous novels are :

1. The Village (1939)
2. Across the Black waters (1940)
3. The Sword and the sickle (1942)
4. Untouchable (1933) (his first novel)
5. Seven summers (1951)
6. Private Life of an Indian Prince (1953)
7. The Big Heart (1945)
8. Coolie (1936) (It was recast in seventies)
9. Two Leaves and a Bud (1937)
10. The Old Woman and the Cow (1960)
11. The Road (1961)
12. Death of a Hero (1963)
13. Confession of a Lover (1976)
14. Morning Face (1968)

**Anand as a short story writer**

1. Mr. Anand is also known as a great short story writer.

2. His stories appeared in a number of volumes.

*(i)* The Barber's Trade Union and Other Stories (1944).
*(ii)* The Tractor and The Corn Goddess (1947).
*(iii)* Reflections on the Golden Bed and Other Stories (1955-59).
*(iv)* Lajwanti and Other Stories (1966)
*(v)* The Lost child and Other Stories (1934)
*(vi)* Lament on the Death of a Master of Arts (1968)
*(vii)* Between Tears and Laughter (1973)
*(viii)* Power of Darkeness, and Other Stories (1959)

3. Mr. Anand has written realistic stories of all kinds which are often full of humour, pathos, irony and satire. According to V.S. Pritchett, "Mr Anand's picture is real, comprehensive and subtle, and his gifts

in all moods from farce to comedy, from pathos to tragedy, from the realistic to the poetic, are remarkable."

**Some of his well-known short stories are :**
- *(i)* A Pair of Mustachios
- *(ii)* On the Border
- *(iii)* The Cobbler and the Machine
- *(iv)* A Promoter of Quarrels
- *(v)* A Dark Night
- *(vi)* A Rumour
- *(vii)* Lullaby
- *(viii)* Barber's Trade Union
- *(ix)* The Parrot in the Cage
- *(x)* The Liar
- *(xi)* Mahadev and Parvati
- *(xii)* The Lost Child

### KHUSWANT SINGH

1. He is known for his novels :
- *(i)* Train to Pakistan (his masterpiece)
- *(ii)* I Shall Not Hear the Nightingale (1959). (It describes the social life of a Sikh family during the pre-Independence period).

2. "The Mark of Vishnu" is another of his well-known works.

3. Some of his known stories
- *(a)* Karma
- *(b)* When Sikh Meets Sikh
- *(c)* The Rape, etc.

4. He is also known for his:
- *(i)* A History of the Sikhs
- *(ii)* Translation of Japji Sahib, etc.

5. His regular columns appear weekly in some dailies, *e.g.* :
- *(i)* 'With Malice Towards One And All'—The Hindustan Times.
- *(ii)* 'This Above All'—The Tribune.

6. Mulk Raj Anand is stated to have said that Khushwant Singh's "Train to Pakistan" is likely to last, while about his other creative literary work, one may have some doubts.

7. Among his latest work is "Truth, Love and Little Malice."

# OBJECTIVE MULTIPLE CHOICE QUESTIONS

1. Who wrote Don Juan?
   - *(a)* Shakespeare
   - *(b)* Tennyson
   - *(c)* Byron
   - *(d)* T.S. Eliot

2. Who wrote The Life of Johnson?
   - *(a)* Boswell
   - *(b)* Macaulay
   - *(c)* Churchill
   - *(d)* Sir Walter Raleigh

3. Priest's Nun's Tale was written by
   - *(a)* Spenser
   - *(b)* Charles Lamb
   - *(c)* Tennyson
   - *(d)* Chaucer

4. Malvolio is a character in
   - *(a)* Macbeth
   - *(b)* Hamlet
   - *(c)* Twelfth Night
   - *(d)* Much Ado About Nothing

5. Pip is a character in
   - *(a)* Much Ado About Nothing
   - *(b)* Great Expectations
   - *(c)* Mrs. Dalloway
   - *(d)* A Passage to India

6. In which poem does the following line occur :

"Our sweetest songs are those that tell of saddest thought"
   - *(a)* Ulysses
   - *(b)* Faery Queene
   - *(c)* Ode to Skylark
   - *(d)* The Wasteland

7. Who is said to have first used the term "Metaphysics"?
   - *(a)* Matthew Arnold
   - *(b)* Sidney
   - *(c)* Donne
   - *(d)* Dr. Johnson

8. The writer of Volpone is
   - *(a)* Johnson
   - *(b)* Milton
   - *(c)* Jonson
   - *(d)* Shelley

9. Which is the correct chronological sequence
   - *(a)* Spenser—Chaucer—Milton—Donne
   - *(b)* Spenser—Wordsworth—Tennyson—T.S. Eliot
   - *(c)* Milton—Shakespeare—Philip Larkin—Keats
   - *(d)* Auden—Eliot—Shelley—Keats

10. Pilgrim's Progress was written by
   - *(a)* Milton
   - *(b)* Shelley
   - *(c)* Swinburne
   - *(d)* John Bunyan

**11.** The writer of the line : "Stone walls do not a prison make" is
(a) Lovelace        (b) Milton
(c) W.B. Yeats      (d) T.S. Eliot

**12.** "Monkey's Paw" is a
(a) Poem         (b) Drama
(c) Short story      (d) Novel

**13.** Lyrical Ballads appeared in
(a) 1690         (b) 1798
(c) 1802         (d) 1800

**14.** The writer of 'A Pair of Blue Eyes' is
(a) Thackeray      (b) Dickens
(c) George Eliot    (d) Thomas Hardy

**15.** Hard Times was written by
(a) Thackeray      (b) Dickens
(c) Trollope       (d) Marquese

**16.** Elizabeth Bennet is a character in
(a) Emma
(b) The Mill on the Floss
(c) Pride and Prejudice
(d) Herzog

**17.** Ariel is a character in
(a) Tempest
(b) Paradise Lost
(c) In Memoriam
(d) Murder in the Cathedral

**18.** Which of the following poets was most impressed by the German philosophy?
(a) Chaucer       (b) Wordsworth
(c) Coleridge      (d) Southey

**19.** The two cities referred to in "A Tale of Two Cities" are
(a) London and Paris
(b) London and Rome
(c) Rome and Paris
(d) Moscow and Rome

**20.** The Peasant's Bread is a story by
(a) Maupassant    (b) Tagore
(c) R.K. Narayan   (d) Tolstoy

**21.** The Financial Express was written by
(a) Raja Rao      (b) R.K. Narayan
(c) Tagore        (d) Mulk Raj Anand

**22.** "Negative Capability" is a term associated with
(a) Tagore        (b) Shelley
(c) Keats         (d) Coleridge

**23.** The most impressive treatment of "imagination" has been given by
(a) Coleridge      (b) Shelley
(c) Eliot          (d) Yeats

**24.** Maggie is a character in
(a) The Middlemarch
(b) The Vanity Fair
(c) The Mill on the Floss
(d) None of these

**25.** Who said about poetry "Emotion recollected in tranquillity"
(a) Wordsworth    (b) Eliot
(c) Shelley       (d) Arnold

**26.** Lady Chatterley's Lover was banned because it was considered
(a) obscene      (b) revolutionary
(c) obscurantist   (d) None of these

**27.** For Whom The Bell Tolls was written by
(a) Marquese     (b) Hemingway
(c) Hawthorne    (d) None of these

**28.** Who said: "I awoke one morning and found myself famous"
(a) Byron        (b) Tennyson
(c) Eliot         (d) Keats

**29.** Paradise Lost comprises
(a) 10 books     (b) 12 books
(c) 6 books      (d) 8 books

**30.** Who used the expression "unaging monuments of intellect"?
(a) Yeats        (b) Shakespeare
(c) Whitman     (d) Auden

**31.** Which poet was invited by John F. Kennedy to his inauguration ceremony?
(a) Whitman     (b) Frost
(c) Eliot         (d) Masefield

**32.** The writer of : "A Pair of Mustachios" is
(a) Anand       (b) Tagore
(c) Raja Rao     (d) Anita Desai

**33.** Estella is a character in
(a) Joseph Andrews
(b) Great Expectations
(c) A Tale of Two Cities
(d) Old Man and the Sea

**34.** The writer of Scarlet Letter is
(a) Henry James   (b) James Joyce
(c) Hawthorne    (d) None of these

**35.** In which poem does the following line occur:
"To strive, to seek, to find and not to yield"
  (a) Morte de Arthur
  (b) Ulysses
  (c) Maud
  (d) Ode to the West Wind

**36.** Rousseau is associated with
  (a) French Revolution
  (b) American War of Independence
  (c) Russian (Bolshevik) Revolution
  (d) None of these

**37.** Which of the following novelists got the Nobel Prize?
  (a) Virginia Woolf  (b) James Joyce
  (c) Hemingway  (d) Conrad

**38.** Which of the following statesmen got the Nobel Prize?
  (a) M.K. Gandhi  (b) Stalin
  (c) Churchill  (d) Saddam Hussein

**39.** Who wrote 'Train to Pakistan'
  (a) Narayan
  (b) Manohar Malgaon
  (c) Khushwant Singh
  (d) Anand

**40.** Henchard is the hero of
  (a) Jude the Obscure
  (b) The Return of the Native
  (c) The Mayor of Casterbridge
  (d) Far From the Madding Crowd

**41.** Who is the writer of Azadi?
  (a) R.K. Narayan  (b) Khushwant Singh
  (c) Tagore  (d) Chaman Nahal

**42.** "The God of Small Things" is written by
  (a) R.K. Narayan  (b) Hemingway
  (c) Graham Greene  (d) Arundhati Roy

**43.** Who wrote the poem "Listeners"?
  (a) Tennyson  (b) Thomas Hood
  (c) Goldsmith  (d) Walter de la Mare

**44.** In writing "Canterbury Tales" Chaucer was influenced by
  (a) Decameron
  (b) The Divine Comedy
  (c) The Holy Bible
  (d) None of these

**45.** Which poem starts with "Behold her single in the field...."
  (a) Lucy Gray
  (b) The Solitary Reaper
  (c) Hymn to Intellectual Beauty
  (d) Dover Beach

**46.** 'Animal Farm' was written by
  (a) James Joyce
  (b) Virginia Woolf
  (c) George Orwell
  (d) Hemingway

**47.** Shobha De is a
  (a) poet  (b) dramatist
  (c) novelist  (d) an actress

**48.** Dunciad was written by
  (a) Dryden  (b) Pope
  (c) Tennyson  (d) Shelley

**49.** King Magnus is a character in
  (a) Apple Cart
  (b) Man and Superman
  (c) Pygmalion
  (d) Saint Joan

**50.** Bernard Shaw got the Nobel Prize for
  (a) Pygmalion
  (b) Man and Superman
  (c) Saint Joan
  (d) None of these

**51.** The Victorian Period is marked by
  (a) Great political upheavals
  (b) Great social security
  (c) Great wars
  (d) Economic deprivation

**52.** In which play the hero demanded more food from the authorities
  (a) Great Expectations
  (b) David Copperfield
  (c) Pickwick Papers
  (d) Oliver Twist

**53.** Swift is known mainly as
  (a) an essayist  (b) a poet
  (c) a satirist  (d) a short story writer

**54.** Who wrote the line :
"Slow rises worth by poverty depressed"?
  (a) Shakespeare  (b) Wordsworth
  (c) Dr. Johnson  (d) Matthew Arnold

**55.** Who is the writer of the novel "The Village"

(a) Khushwant Singh    (b) Anita Desai
(c) Mulk Raj Anand    (d) R.K. Narayan

**56.** The most famous writer of the heroic couplet is
(a) Dryden    (b) Chaucer
(c) Spenser    (d) Pope

**57.** Who wrote: "Heard melodies are sweet but those unheard are sweeter"?
(a) Shelley    (b) Keats
(c) Pope    (d) Wordsworth

**58.** Who used the term "Egotistical sublime" for Wordsworth's poetry?
(a) Keats    (b) Shelley
(c) Coleridge    (d) Tennyson

**59.** Into how many acts did Marlowe originally divide his "Dr. Faustus"
(a) five    (b) two
(c) four    (d) one (no division)

**60.** Shakespeare died in
(a) 1620    (b) 1616
(c) 1606    (d) 1610

**61.** Macflecknoe is a poem written by
(a) Dryden    (b) Pope
(c) Tennyson    (d) Yeats

**62.** Who wrote 'Everyman in His Humour'
(a) Shakespeare    (b) Jonson
(c) Milton    (d) Keats

**63.** 'Indian Jugglers' is an essay by
(a) De Quincey    (b) Gardiner
(c) Hazlitt    (d) Lamb

**64.** In which poem did Tennyson say "Ring out the old, ring in the new"
(a) Mand    (b) Ulysses
(c) In Memoriam    (d) The Brook

**65.** Who wrote 'The Gropes of Wrath'
(a) Pearl Buck    (b) Hemingway
(c) Virginia Woolf    (d) John Steinbeck

**66.** Who rendered into English the ancient Greek tragedy "Atlanta in Calydon"
(a) Swinburne    (b) Shelley
(c) Tennyson    (d) Arthur Hugh Clough

**67.** The Deserted Village was written by
(a) Cowper    (b) Goldsmith
(c) Keats    (d) Johnson

**68.** 'Savitri' is an epic written by

(a) Tagore
(b) Prem Chand
(c) Aurobindo
(d) Bankim Chandra Chatterjee

**69.** The anthem "Vande Mataram" occurs in
(a) Godan    (b) Anand Math
(c) Gora    (d) Train to Pakistan

**70.** 'All Fool's Day' is an essay written by
(a) Charles Lamb    (b) Hazlitt
(c) A.G. Gardiner    (d) R.C. Stevenson

**71.** The drama Tamburlaine is written by
(a) Shakespeare    (b) Marlowe
(c) Lyly    (d) Green

**72.** The book "Appreciations" was written by
(a) Morris    (b) Arnold
(c) Walter Pater    (d) Christina Rossetti

**73.** "Strife" describes the strike by
(a) factory workers    (b) office workers
(c) teachers    (d) students

**74.** "The Admirable Crichton" was written by
(a) Steinbeck    (b) T.S. Eliot
(c) Trollope    (d) James Barrie

**75.** "The Death of a Salesman" was written by
(a) James Barrie    (b) Eugene O'Neill
(c) Arthur Miller    (d) None of these

**76.** Which king of England was beheaded
(a) James I    (b) James II
(c) Charles I    (d) Charles II

**77.** The Restoration period is said to have started from
(a) 1660    (b) 1676
(c) 1625    (d) 1645

**78.** Who gave up writing poetry for a long period for the sake of struggle for democracy
(a) Shakespeare    (b) Donne
(c) Milton    (d) Yeats

**79.** Who wrote "The Lady's Not for Burning"
(a) Barrie    (b) Christopher Fry
(c) Robert Bridges    (d) T.S. Eliot

**80.** Who wrote the poem "Brahma"
(a) T.S Eliot    (b) Emerson
(c) Whitman    (d) Frost

**81.** The writer of Walden is
(a) Tennyson    (b) Whitman
(c) Thoreau    (d) Frost

**82.** In 'Sons and Lovers' Lawrence has depicted the life of
  (a) factory workers    (b) miners
  (c) farmers    (d) animals

**83.** Who wrote Kim?
  (a) Kipling    (b) Tagore
  (c) Lawrence    (d) Narayan

**84.** 'The Hairy Ape' is a famous play by
  (a) Barrie    (b) Eugene O'Neill
  (c) Christopher Fry    (d) T.S. Eliot

**85.** Who at the time of his death asked a friend of his to pay his debt (a cock) after his death?
  (a) Plato    (b) Aristotle
  (c) Socrates    (d) Alexander

**86.** Who is the writer of Frankenstein
  (a) George Eliot    (b) Jane Austen
  (c) Mary Shelley    (d) Emile Bronte

**87.** Which poem was conceived in a dream?
  (a) Ode to the West Wind
  (b) Kubla Khan
  (c) Ode to a Nightingale
  (d) Lucy Gray

**88.** Lines from a poem by which poet were found written on the writing pad of Jawaharlal Nehru after his death?
  (a) Whitman    (b) Tagore
  (c) Sarojini Naidu    (d) Frost

**89.** Who wrote his own epitaph: "Here lies the one whose name is writ in water?"
  (a) Byron    (b) Southey
  (c) Keats    (d) Yeats

**90.** Who wrote the 'Cries of Children'
  (a) Robert Browning    (b) Elizabeth Barrett
  (c) Thomas Hood    (d) Cowper

**91.** Which poet is known as poet's poet?
  (a) Shakespeare    (b) Milton
  (c) Spenser    (d) Shelley

**92.** Bohemia is a place in the drama
  (a) Macbeth
  (b) Everyman in His Humour
  (c) The Winter's Tale
  (d) Tempest

**93.** Caliban is a character in
  (a) Hamlet
  (b) Merchant of Venice
  (c) The Admirable Crichton
  (d) Tempest

**94.** Who wrote the maximum number of sonnets
  (a) Shakespeare    (b) Milton
  (c) Sidney    (d) Wordsworth

**95.** Which character in 'The Merchant of Venice' said, "The quality of mercy is not strained,"
  (a) Bassanio    (b) Portia
  (c) Jessica    (d) Antonio

**96.** Adonais is the eulogy written on the death of
  (a) Coleridge    (b) Byron
  (c) Keats    (d) Wordsworth

**97.** Oedipus Complex is expressed most strongly in
  (a) David Copperfield
  (b) Great Expectations
  (c) Pride and Prejudice
  (d) Sons and Lovers

**98.** Who was addicted to opium taking
  (a) Keats    (b) Wordsworth
  (c) Coleridge    (d) T.S. Eliot

**99.** Who wrote Mother
  (a) Tolstoy    (b) Maxim Gorky
  (c) Chekhov    (d) Hardy

**100.** Who is associated with Malgudi
  (a) Narayan
  (b) Anand
  (c) Manohar Malgonkar
  (d) Anita Desai

**101.** The author of Beowulf is
  (a) Bede    (b) Cynewulf
  (c) Chaucer    (d) Unknown

**102.** The Anglo-Saxon period is often said to be from 450 to ......
  (a) 900    (b) 1000
  (c) 1050    (d) 1100

**103.** The name of the monster in Beowulf is
  (a) Gomanzo    (b) Grendel
  (c) Frankenstein    (d) Mephistophilis

**104.** Who says "Life, life, eternal life"?
  (a) Christian    (b) Maggie
  (c) Henchard    (d) Chaucer's Parson

**105.** Beatrice was the woman whose love inspired a man to write an immortal poem. Who was that man?
  (a) Shelley    (b) Shakespeare
  (c) Homer    (d) Dante

**106.** Charles I was executed in
    *(a)* 1648      *(b)* 1645
    *(c)* 1649      *(d)* 1650

**107.** Alexander Pope died in
    *(a)* 1740      *(b)* 1742
    *(c)* 1744      *(d)* 1743

**108.** Burns was born in
    *(a)* England      *(b)* Ireland
    *(c)* Scotland      *(d)* France

**109.** "To a Mountain Daisy" is a poem by
    *(a)* Wordsworth      *(b)* Shelley
    *(c)* Keats      *(d)* Burns

**110.** Who wrote: "The Devil's Disciple"?
    *(a)* Galsworthy      *(b)* Barrie
    *(c)* Shaw      *(d)* Fry

**111.** George Eliot believed in
    *(a)* A moral law
    *(b)* Promiscuity of sex
    *(c)* Violent Revolution
    *(d)* Indiscriminate fate

**112.** "A foundling" is a part of the name of the novel
    *(a)* Amelia
    *(b)* David Copperfield
    *(c)* Oliver Twist      *(d)* Tom Jones

**113.** Who wrote "The Decline and Fall of the Roman Empire"?
    *(a)* Walter Raleigh      *(b)* Trollope
    *(c)* Smollett      *(d)* Edward Gibbon

**114.** Richard Hooker was a prose writer of the
    *(a)* Victorian period
    *(b)* Romantic period
    *(c)* Elizabethan period
    *(d)* Chaucerian age

**115.** Sir Walter Raleigh died in
    *(a)* 1622      *(b)* 1621
    *(c)* 1618      *(d)* 1623

**116.** D' Artagnan is a character in
    *(a)* The Three Musketeers
    *(b)* Don Quixote
    *(c)* Alice in Wonderland
    *(d)* War and Peace

**117.** Alexander Dumas was
    *(a)* an English writer    *(b)* an American writer
    *(c)* a French writer      *(d)* a German writer

**118.** Who said about Wordsworth, "He uttered nothing base"
    *(a)* Keats      *(b)* Coleridge
    *(c)* Byron      *(d)* Tennyson

**119.** Which one was not one of the Lake poets?
    *(a)* Shelley      *(b)* Wordsworth
    *(c)* Southey      *(d)* Coleridge

**120.** Emma appeared in
    *(a)* 1816      *(b)* 1815
    *(c)* 1817      *(d)* 1820

**121.** Mrs. Browning's book "Sonnets from the Portuguese" is an inspiring book of
    *(a)* nature poems
    *(b)* metaphysical poems
    *(c)* love poems
    *(d)* didactic poems

**122.** D.G. Rossetti was the son of
    *(a)* An Italian painter
    *(b)* A German poet
    *(c)* French nobleman
    *(d)* An English peasant

**123.** The translation of Goethe's "Wilhelm Meister" appeared in
    *(a)* 1822      *(b)* 1820
    *(c)* 1832      *(d)* 1824

**124.** In 'The Doctor's Dilemma' Shaw makes fun of
    *(a)* teachers      *(b)* physicians
    *(c)* painters      *(d)* politicians

**125.** The Theory of Catharsis is associated with
    *(a)* Plato      *(b)* Dryden
    *(c)* Aristotle      *(d)* Sidney

**126.** Who wrote 'In Defence of Poetry'?
    *(a)* T.S. Eliot      *(b)* Yeats
    *(c)* Keats      *(d)* Shelley

**127.** 'The Playboy of the Western World' is a play by
    *(a)* Barrie      *(b)* Synge
    *(c)* Fry      *(d)* Eliot

**128.** For the best condensation of a novel Arnold Bennet won a prize of
    *(a)* £ 100      *(b)* £ 50
    *(c)* £ 25      *(d)* £ 20

**129.** Who wrote :
"The year's at the spring.
And day's at the morn."
    *(a)* Tennyson      *(b)* Robert Browning
    *(c)* Keats      *(d)* Swinburne

**130.** The Ring and the Book contains how many more lines than the Iliad?

(a) about three thousand
(b) about two thousand
(c) about four thousand
(d) about five thousand

**131.** In which poem do the following lines occur?
"...Do not all charms fly
At the mere touch of cold philosophy?"
(a) Ode To A Grecian Urn
(b) The Eve of St. Agnes
(c) Lamia
(d) Hyperion

**132.** Boswell was born in
(a) 1732      (b) 1740
(c) 1735      (d) 1742

**133.** 'Silent Woman' is a play by
(a) Marlowe      (b) Shakespeare
(c) Ben Jonson      (d) Lyly

**134.** The Duchess of Malfi was published in
(a) 1632      (b) 1635
(c) 1625      (d) 1623

**135.** The Scene of Beowulf is laid in
(a) England      (b) France
(c) Spain      (d) None of these

**136.** Pap is a character in
(a) Great Expectations
(b) Hucklebery Finn
(c) Silas Mariner
(d) The Mocking Bird

**137.** A Mad Tea-Party takes place in
(a) Don Quixote
(b) The Three Musketeers
(c) Robinson Crusoe
(d) Alice in Wonderland

**138.** What was the name of the girl whom Kalidas loved?
(a) Shakuntala      (b) Nagini
(c) Kamini      (d) Savitri

**139.** "Kidnapped" was written by
(a) Dickens      (b) Thackeray
(c) Hardy      (d) R.L. Stevenson

**140.** Mr. Collins is a character in
(a) Sense and Sensibility
(b) Pride and Prejudice
(c) Emma
(d) Hard Times

**141.** 'The Prisoner of Zenda' was written by
(a) Sterne      (b) Trollope
(c) Anthony Hope      (d) George Eliot

**142.** What was the full name of Cervantes
(a) Jim Cervantes
(b) John Cervantes
(c) Miguel de Cervantes
(d) Sir Roger Cervantes

**143.** The letter referred to in 'The Scarlet Letter' is
(a) A      (b) B
(c) L      (d) M

**144.** Robert Frost lived for sometime in
(a) France      (b) Germany
(c) England      (d) Italy

**145.** Besides being a poet, Chaucer was
(a) a trader      (b) a manufacturer
(c) a teacher      (d) a diplomat

**146.** Bacon's essays were influenced by
(a) Montesque      (b) Montaigne
(c) Boccaccio      (d) Pascal

**147.** Charles Lamb worked as a
(a) clerk      (b) seaman
(c) teacher      (d) mechanic

**148.** Who wrote: "Keep right on to the end of the road."
(a) Shakespeare      (b) Milton
(c) Sir Harry Lauder      (d) Chaucer

**149.** Who said: "Two men look out through the same bars:
One sees the mud, and the one the stars."
(a) Chaucer
(b) Keats
(c) Milton
(d) Frederick Langbridge

**150.** In which book does the following line appear : "What a falling off was there."
(a) King Lear
(b) Othello
(c) Hamlet
(d) Antony and Cleopatra

**151.** The meaning of "widsith" in old English is
(a) width      (b) widely
(c) wise      (d) wanderer

**152.** The name of William Golding's first novel is
(a) The Inheritors      (b) Lord of the Flies
(c) Pincher Martin      (d) The Pyramid

**153.** In his "Progress and Poverty", Henry George is influenced by
    *(a)* The American War of Independence
    *(b)* The French Revolution
    *(c)* The Marxian System
    *(d)* None of these

**154.** The author of Erewhon is
    *(a)* Hardy     *(b)* Marquese
    *(c)* Samuel Butler     *(d)* Cervantes

**155.** Which of the following is a Comedy of Manners?
    *(a)* The Way of the World
    *(b)* The Duchess of Malfi
    *(c)* The Lady's Not for Burning
    *(d)* The Hairy Ape

**156.** Which one among the following is not a pessimist?
    *(a)* Gissing     *(b)* Browning
    *(c)* Hardy     *(d)* Thomson

**157.** Charles Reade's drama "Drink" was adapted from a work of
    *(a)* Goethe     *(b)* Zola
    *(c)* Mallarwe     *(d)* Tennyson

**158.** James Mill was born in
    *(a)* France     *(b)* Ireland
    *(c)* Scotland     *(d)* Italy

**159.** The classical theory of rent was advocated by
    *(a)* Bentham     *(b)* Ricardo
    *(c)* James Mill     *(d)* Marx

**160.** Which one among the following was not a utilitarian?
    *(a)* Rousseau     *(b)* James Mill
    *(c)* Ricardo     *(d)* Bentham

**161.** Kipling was born in
    *(a)* 1872     *(b)* 1865
    *(c)* 1870     *(d)* 1864

**162.** The monk Augustine came to England in
    *(a)* 590     *(b)* 587
    *(c)* 597     *(d)* 591

**163.** The Battle of Maldon was fought in
    *(a)* 993     *(b)* 990
    *(c)* 975     *(d)* 980

**164.** To whom are the following lines ascribed?
    "When Adam delved and Eve span,
    Who was then the gentleman?"
    *(a)* Gower     *(b)* John Ball
    *(c)* Wat Tayler     *(d)* Chaucer

**165.** 'The Praise of Folly' was written by
    *(a)* Walter Raleigh     *(b)* Thomas Moore
    *(c)* Charles Lamb     *(d)* Ruskin

**166.** Who wrote: "In Praise of Idleness"?
    *(a)* Bertrand Russell     *(b)* Thomas More
    *(c)* Charles Lamb     *(d)* Hazlitt

**167.** Which one of the following comprises one accented syllable followed by one unaccented syllable
    *(a)* A Dactyl     *(b)* An Anapaest
    *(c)* A trochee     *(d)* An iambus

**168.** In which work does the following line occur: "That with no middle flight intends to soar."
    *(a)* L'Allegro     *(b)* Il Penseroso
    *(c)* Paradise Lost     *(d)* Lycidas

**169.** The trial scene in 'The Merchant of Venice' was presided over by
    *(a)* Portia     *(b)* Antonio
    *(c)* Dr. Bellario     *(d)* The Duke

**170.** The real name of Saki is
    *(a)* H.H. Munro     *(b)* Samuel Butler
    *(c)* George Orwell     *(d)* The Duke

**171.** Who started: "The Tatler"?
    *(a)* Addison     *(b)* Swift
    *(c)* Steele     *(d)* Stevenson

**172.** The poem 'The Song of the Shirt' was written by
    *(a)* Mrs. Browning     *(b)* Pope
    *(c)* Shelley     *(d)* Thomas Hood

**173.** Sir Roger was originally the creation of
    *(a)* Addison     *(b)* Dryden
    *(c)* Steele     *(d)* Milton

**174.** Who wrote: "Areopagitica"?
    *(a)* Charles Lamb     *(b)* Hazlitt
    *(c)* De Quincey     *(d)* Milton

**175.** Mary Lamb killed her
    *(a)* mother     *(b)* father
    *(c)* sister     *(d)* brother

**176.** 'The Selfish Giant' is a story written by
    *(a)* Tagore     *(b)* Oscar Wilde
    *(c)* Maupassant     *(d)* Tolstoy

**177.** Which one of the following is not a part of the proverbial "Three Unities"

(a) Unity of Purpose   (b) Unity of Time
(c) Unity of Place   (d) Unity of Action

**178.** Which one of the following letters is most often not pronounced before a consonant?
(a) p    (b) r
(c) n    (d) s

**179.** The setting of Walpole's novel "The Castle of Otranto" is
(a) ancient England   (b) medieval France
(c) medieval Italy   (d) ancient Ireland

**180.** Who wrote : "Four Quartets"?
(a) T.S. Eliot   (b) W.B. Yeats
(c) W.H. Auden   (d) Philip Larkins

**181.** Who wrote : "Look Back in Anger"?
(a) Steinbeck   (b) Christopher Fry
(c) John Osborne   (d) Barrie

**182.** Who wrote : "The Devils of Loundun"?
(a) Bertrand Russell   (b) Aldous Huxley
(c) J.B. Priestley   (d) Hazlitt

**183.** Iris Murdoch was born in
(a) 1921    (b) 1923
(c) 1930    (d) 1919

**184.** In the 'Heart of Darkness' Conrad has explored
(a) Ceylon   (b) India
(c) Congo   (d) Brazil

**185.** Virginia Woolf died in
(a) 1941    (b) 1940
(c) 1943    (d) 1935

**186.** In which one of the following words 'b' is not silent
(a) plumber   (b) comb
(c) lumbago   (d) lamb

**187.** Who wrote : "Principles of Human Knowledge"
(a) Milton   (b) John Bunyan
(c) Nash   (d) George Berkeley

**188.** Who wrote : "Liber Amoris"
(a) Lamb   (b) Hazlitt
(c) Byron   (d) Wordsworth

**189.** Fielding wrote Joseph Andrews in reaction against
(a) Pamela
(b) Robinson Crusoe
(c) Jane Eyre
(d) Roderick Random

**190.** Fielding was a

(a) Romanticist
(b) Supernaturalist
(c) Realist
(d) Science fiction writer

**191.** "A Railway Clerk" is a poem by
(a) Keki N. Daruwallah
(b) Nissim Ezekiel
(c) Shiv K. Kumar
(d) Jayanta Mahapatra

**192.** Raju is the hero of
(a) Guide
(b) The Mark of Vishnu
(c) Azadi
(d) The God of Small Things

**193.** The Indian novelist who won the Booker Prize in 1997 was
(a) Vikram Seth   (b) Salman Rushdie
(c) R.K. Narayan   (d) Arundhati Roy

**194.** Who won The Booker of Bookers
(a) Arundhati Roy   (b) Khushwant Singh
(c) Mulk Raj Anand   (d) Salman Rushdie

**195.** Who among the following is not a pre-Romantic poet
(a) William Mason   (b) Beattie
(c) Bowles   (d) Byron

**196.** Disraeli was influenced by
(a) Carlyle   (b) Burke
(c) Benthem   (d) Godwin

**197.** Dickens died in
(a) 1870    (b) 1865
(c) 1868    (d) 1872

**198.** Who is not a novelist besides being a poet
(a) Jayanta Mahapatra   (b) Shiv K. Kumar
(c) Kamala Das   (d) Tagore

**199.** The favourite poet of Jawaharlal Nehru was
(a) Whitman   (b) Frost
(c) Eliot   (d) Yeats

**200.** Who wrote: "The Battle of Books"
(a) Bacon   (b) Hazlitt
(c) Swift   (d) None of these

**201.** Which of the following sounds is not a guttural
(a) k    (b) ng
(c) g    (d) p

**202.** Which of the following consonants is not considered redundant

(a) c
(b) q
(c) r
(d) x

**203.** In which metre is Shelley's 'Ode to the West Wind' written
(a) Terza Rima
(b) Ottava Rima
(c) Spenserian Stanza
(d) Blank Verse

**204.** Who wrote the following lines:
"'Tis sweet to hear the watch dog's honest bark
Bay deep mouthed welcome as we near our home."
(a) Shakespeare
(b) Byron
(c) Pope
(d) Robert Bridges

**205.** Who wrote the following lines :
"The cock's shrill clarion, and the echoing horn,
No more shall rouse than from their lowly bed."
(a) Milton
(b) Donne
(c) Gray
(d) Cowper

**206.** In which class should we place Spenser's 'Shepherd's Calendar'?
(a) Pastoral
(b) Romance
(c) Epic
(d) Eulogy

**207.** In which book do the following lines occur :
"Here is thy footstool and there rest thy feet where live the poorest, and lowliest, and lost."
(a) Ramcharitmanas
(b) The Rig Veda
(c) The Gitanjali
(d) None of these

**208.** Who among the following was the contemporary of Tennyson
(a) Auden
(b) Robert Browning
(c) Cowper
(d) Day Lewis

**209.** Who wrote the following line:
"God made the country and man made the town".
(a) Blake
(b) Cowper
(c) Wordsworth
(d) Shelley

**210.** Which one among the following is the correct chronological order
(a) Faerie Queene—Paradise Lost—Lamia—Prospice
(b) Macbeth—Canterbury Tales—In Memoriam—Waste Land
(c) Faustus—The Duchess of Malfi—The Eve of St. Agnes—Ulysses
(d) Hamlet—Prelude—Hyperion—Comus

**211.** Who wrote: "Nectar in a Sieve"?
(a) Mulk Raj Anand
(b) Manohar Malgonkar
(c) Kamala Markandaya
(d) Pearl S. Buck

**212.** 'The Good Earth' was written by
(a) Raja Rao
(b) R.K. Narayan
(c) Pearl S. Buck
(d) Kamala Markandaya

**213.** The writer of 'The Dove Found No Rest' is
(a) Pearl S Buck
(b) Hemingway
(c) Raja Rao
(d) Dennis Stoll

**214.** Who wrote: "So Many Hungers"?
(a) Bhabani Bhattacharya
(b) Kamala Markandaya
(c) Manohar Malgonkar
(d) Chaman Nahal

**215.** The main theme of 'So Many Hungers' is
(a) necessity of a revolution
(b) degradation of humanity
(c) description of nature
(d) vision of India as a developed country

**216.** Who said about Shaw:
"He studied every known theory of socialism"
(a) Hudson
(b) Hugh Walker
(c) Henderson
(d) Legouis

**217.** Who is the writer of "The Middleman and Other Stories "?
(a) Mulk Raj Anand
(b) Bharati Mukherjee
(c) Tagore
(d) Prem Chand

**218.** Which one of the following is not an example of "fine writing" according to Prof. Terry Eagleton of St. Catherine College, University of Oxford
(a) Lamb
(b) Macaulay
(c) Mill
(d) Darwin

**219.** Which one among the following cannot be considered an early Indian English poet
(a) Henry Derozio
(b) Toru Dutt
(c) Manmohan Ghosh
(d) Kamala Das

**220.** Who declared that he would "sing the song" of his "experience."
(a) Shiv K. Kumar

    *(b)* Nissim Ezekiel
    *(c)* Keki N. Daruwalla
    *(d)* Jayanta Mahapatra

**221.** Who said, "I only know how to work at one poem at a time, stitch by stitch"
    *(a)* Nissim Ezekiel     *(b)* A.K. Ramanujan
    *(c)* Shiv K. Kumar     *(d)* Arun Kolatkar

**222.** Cicero was a Roman
    *(a)* philologist     *(b)* physician
    *(c)* orator     *(d)* None of these

**223.** Who is the writer of "Gita Rahasya"?
    *(a)* Tulsi Das     *(b)* Vivekananda
    *(c)* Shivananda     *(d)* B.G. Tilak

**224.** In Arnold's 'The Scholar Gipsy,' the great modern melancholy is spiritualised into a symbol of
    *(a)* the advent of a new age
    *(b)* mystery and dreams
    *(c)* a source of poetic inspiration
    *(d)* an expectation of some divine dispensation.

**225.** 'The Rubaiyat of Omar Khayyam' was translated into English by
    *(a)* Robert Browning     *(b)* Tennyson
    *(c)* Fitz Gerald     *(d)* Hopkins

**226.** Mayakovsky was the famous poet of
    *(a)* France     *(b)* Italy
    *(c)* Austria     *(d)* Russia

**227.** Marquese originally wrote his "One Hundred Years of Solitude" in
    *(a)* French     *(b)* German
    *(c)* Spanish     *(d)* Italian

**228.** The word 'Dialogue' is derived from "dialogos" which is a
    *(a)* German word     *(b)* Latin word
    *(c)* French word     *(d)* Greek word

**229.** The word 'strength' is derived from 'strengthu' which is
    *(a)* A French word
    *(b)* A Latin word
    *(c)* An Old English word
    *(d)* An Italian word

**230.** Who said, "Poets are the unacknowledged legislators of the world"?
    *(a)* Shelley     *(b)* Keats
    *(c)* Byron     *(d)* Coleridge

**231.** In which of Shakespeare's plays does Lancelott Gobbo appear
    *(a)* Tempest
    *(b)* The Merchant of Venice
    *(c)* Winter's Tale
    *(d)* Cymbeline

**232.** In which year did Tagore receive the Nobel Prize?
    *(a)* 1912     *(b)* 1913
    *(c)* 1914     *(d)* 1915

**233.** In which year did the Bolshevik Revolution take place?
    *(a)* 1918     *(b)* 1920
    *(c)* 1921     *(d)* 1917

**234.** From the poem of which poet did E.M. Forster take the name of his novel "A Passage to India"?
    *(a)* Frost     *(b)* Sandburg
    *(c)* Whitman     *(d)* Yeats

**235.** Identify Emile Bronte's novel in the following
    *(a)* Persuasion
    *(b)* Wuthering Heights
    *(c)* Jane Eyre
    *(d)* Middlemarch

**236.** Which one is believed to be the first English tragedy
    *(a)* Gorboduc
    *(b)* The Spanish Tragedy
    *(c)* Dr. Faustus
    *(d)* The Jew of Malta

**237.** Which of the following works is not by Milton
    *(a)* Paradise Lost     *(b)* Il Penseroso
    *(c)* Lycidas     *(d)* Maud

**238.** 'Music At Night' is a book of essays by
    *(a)* A.G. Gardiner     *(b)* Bertrand Russell
    *(c)* Aldous Huxley     *(d)* Chesterton

**239.** The character of Sherlock Holmes was created by
    *(a)* Arthur Conan Doyle
    *(b)* Hazlitt
    *(c)* I.A. Richards
    *(d)* Agatha Christie

**240.** Who pruned the draft of the 'Waste Land' to about one third of its original length?
    *(a)* I.A. Richards     *(b)* W.B. Yeats
    *(c)* Ezra Pound     *(d)* Virginia Woolf

**241.** Who wrote the Preface to the Gitanjali
    *(a)* W.B. Yeats      *(b)* T.S. Eliot
    *(c)* Auden      *(d)* Philip Larkin

**242.** What can be said to be the tragic flaw in Hamlet?
    *(a)* Revenge      *(b)* Indecisiveness
    *(c)* Hastiness      *(d)* Suspicion

**243.** Who said the following words:
"There is Providence even in the fall of a sparrow"
    *(a)* Tennyson      *(b)* Shelley
    *(c)* Keats      *(d)* Eliot

**244.** Who wrote 'The Spanish Tragedy'
    *(a)* Shakespeare      *(b)* Thomas Kyd
    *(c)* Marlowe      *(d)* Lyly

**245.** Name the author of "1984"
    *(a)* George Orwell      *(b)* Graham Greene
    *(c)* Naipaul      *(d)* James Joyce

**246.** Who is the creator of Wessex
    *(a)* Dickens      *(b)* Smollett
    *(c)* Meredith      *(d)* Hardy

**247.** Columbus discovered America in
    *(a)* 1490      *(b)* 1492
    *(c)* 1482      *(d)* 1488

**248.** Who said of Keats that he was "snuffed out by an article"
    *(a)* Shelley      *(b)* Wordsworth
    *(c)* Browning      *(d)* Byron

**249.** Who said, "Poetry is the spontaneous overflow of powerful feelings".
    *(a)* Herrick      *(b)* Lovelace
    *(c)* Wordsworth      *(d)* Thomas Nash

**250.** Who said that democracy was like a balloon
    *(a)* Galsworthy      *(b)* Shaw
    *(c)* Hardy      *(d)* I.A. Richards

**251.** In which poem the following lines occur:
"Grow old along with me,
The best is yet to be."
    *(a)* The Last Ride Together
    *(b)* Rabbi Ben Ezra
    *(c)* Prospice
    *(d)* Sordello

**252.** Which of Browning's poems did Tennyson complain that it was unintelligible to him except for the first and the last lines both of which were wrong?

    *(a)* The Grammarian's Funeral
    *(b)* The Last Ride Together
    *(c)* Sordello
    *(d)* Prospice

**253.** Which of the following writers did not get the Nobel Prize?
    *(a)* Octavio Paz      *(b)* R.N. Tagore
    *(c)* Aurobindo      *(d)* W.B. Yeats

**254.** Who wrote the following lines :
"The wind disentangles itself from your frenzied body as hurricanes of dreams follow me."
    *(a)* Nissim Ezekiel      *(b)* R. Parthasarthy
    *(c)* Jayanta Mahapatra      *(d)* Pritish Nandy

**255.** Which one of the following is not Gurdial Singh's novel
    *(a)* Addh Chanini Rat (Night of the Half-Moon)
    *(b)* Parsa
    *(c)* Godan
    *(d)* Marhi Da Deeva (The Last Flicker)

**256.** Who made the sensational pronouncement of "end of ideology" in 1960
    *(a)* David Bell      *(b)* Graham Greene
    *(c)* Mulk Raj Anand      *(d)* Octavio Paz

**257.** Gurdial Singh was born in
    *(a)* 1930      *(b)* 1931
    *(c)* 1932      *(d)* 1933

**258.** Which novel of Sarat Chandra Chattopadhyaya has caught the imagination of the Indians the most, so much so that even another film bearing this name has been made?
    *(a)* Ses Prasna      *(b)* Grih Daha
    *(c)* Devdas      *(d)* Chritraheen

**259.** Whose rendering into English (as given below) are the following lines by Tagore:
"What voice is that I hear
From the land of dawn,
'Fear not! Fear not!
Who will give up his life
Retaining nothing
Will never end, never perish!'"
    *(a)* Khushwant Singh
    *(b)* Sir Jadunath Sircar
    *(c)* Tagore himself
    *(d)* Sister Nivedita

**260.** When was the famous Hindi poet Kumar Vikal born
    *(a)* 1939          *(b)* 1930
    *(c)* 1932          *(d)* 1935

**261.** Whose novel "The Foundation Pit?" was discovered only a few years ago?
    *(a)* Andrey Platanov
    *(b)* Cherneshevysky
    *(c)* Jane Austen
    *(d)* George Eliot

**262.** The novel "We" was written by
    *(a)* Andrey Platanov     *(b)* Tolstoy
    *(c)* Maxim Gorky      *(d)* Zamayatin

**263.** Name the writer of "What Is To Be Done"
    *(a)* Zamayatin       *(b)* Gorky
    *(c)* Cherneshevysky   *(d)* Chekhov

**264.** Who in 'Paradise Lost' tells Adam:
"Be lowly wise
Dream not of other worlds."
    *(a)* Satan           *(b)* Angel Gabriel
    *(c)* Mammon        *(d)* Mephistophilis

**265.** Name the writer of the novel "Les Miserables"
    *(a)* Virginia Woolf    *(b)* Mrs. Radcliffe
    *(c)* Victor Hugo      *(d)* James Joyce

**266.** Who wrote the following lines:
"Hurrah for revolution,
Let the cannon shoot."
    *(a)* Eliot            *(b)* Stephen Spender
    *(c)* Auden          *(d)* Yeats

**267.** Who was the renowned English novelist who became the first great foreign writer to show a keen interest in R.K. Narayan's fiction which finally made the latter so famous
    *(a)* E.M. Forster     *(b)* D.H. Lawrence
    *(c)* Graham Greene   *(d)* Virginia Woolf

**268.** R.K. Narayan was a
    *(a)* Tamilian       *(b)* Bengali
    *(c)* Gujarati       *(d)* Maharashtrian

**269.** Which of the following novels is not by Salman Rushdie?
    *(a)* Midnight's Children
    *(b)* Grimus
    *(c)* The Moor's Last Sigh
    *(d)* The Lighthouse

**270.** Which novel of Salman Rushdie was adjudged the best one to have won the Booker Prize in its first 25 years
    *(a)* Grimus
    *(b)* Midnight's Children
    *(c)* The Satanic Verses
    *(d)* Shame

**271.** When was Rushdie awarded the Austrian State Prize for European Literature
    *(a)* 1993          *(b)* 1990
    *(c)* 1991          *(d)* 1995

**272.** When was Ted Hughes made the poet laureate of England?
    *(a)* 1980          *(b)* 1982
    *c)* 1981          *(d)* 1984

**273.** In which year between 1921 and 1940 no Nobel Prize for Literature was awarded
    *(a)* 1925          *(b)* 1930
    *(c)* 1935          *(d)* 1939

**274.** In which year did Galsworthy receive the Nobel Prize
    *(a)* 1930          *(b)* 1934
    *(c)* 1931          *(d)* 1932

**275.** In which year did Dylan Thomas die?
    *(a)* 1951          *(b)* 1950
    *(c)* 1955          *(d)* 1953

**276.** Aurobindo's Savitri is
    *(a)* en epic
    *(b)* a long narrative poem
    *(c)* a dramatic monologue
    *(d)* a historical work

**277.** Lamb's essays are full of
    *(a)* irony and satire
    *(b)* humour and pathos
    *(c)* sarcasm
    *(d)* None of these

**278.** Shelley's genius was basically
    *(a)* dramatic       *(b)* narrative
    *(c)* lyrical          *(d)* descriptive

**279.** A sonnet comprises
    *(a)* 16 lines       *(b)* 14 lines
    *(c)* 12 lines       *(d)* 20 lines

**270.** Civil war in England was fought in ........ century
    *(a)* fifteenth      *(b)* sixteenth
    *(c)* seventeenth    *(d)* fourteenth

**281.** The soldiers of Cromwell were known as
*(a)* Dark heads      *(b)* Round heads
*(c)* Large heads      *(d)* Brave heads

**282.** Who is renowned for his outstanding work "Holy Sonnets"
*(a)* Donne      *(b)* Herrick
*(c)* Milton      *(d)* Pope

**283.** When did Frederic Mistral of France and Jose Eizaguirre of Spain jointly win the Nobel Prize in Literature?
*(a)* 1910      *(b)* 1920
*(c)* 1902      *(d)* 1904

**284.** Name the Russian who won the Nobel Prize for literature in 1933
*(a)* Mayakovsky      *(b)* Ivan Bunin
*(c)* Checkov      *(d)* Stalin

**285.** In what field did Churchill win the Nobel Prize?
*(a)* Peace      *(b)* Literature
*(c)* Economics      *(d)* Medicine

**286.** From which book are the following lines taken :
"And Moses stretched out his hand over the sea; and the Lord caused the sea to go back by a strong east wind all that night, ........"
*(a)* The Holy Bible      *(b)* Paradise Lost
*(c)* Pilgrim's Progress      *(d)* None of these

**287.** In which book do the following lines occur:
"Heavens lights for ever shine,
Earth's shadows fly."
*(a)* The Holy Bible      *(b)* Adonais
*(c)* Paradise Lost      *(d)* Pilgrim's Progress

**288.** Who wrote the Latin "History of the Britons"
*(a)* Henry I
*(b)* Geoffrey of Monmouth
*(c)* Wycliffe
*(d)* Walter Giffart

**289.** When was the final result of slow transformation of Anglo-Saxon into modern English felt?
*(a)* In the fourteenth century
*(b)* In the fifteenth century
*(c)* In the sixteenth century
*(d)* In the seventeenth century

**280.** Normandy was lost by John Lackland in

*(a)* 1205      *(b)* 1204
*(c)* 1201      *(d)* 1203

**291.** Until about the middle of the 14th century English literature was mostly
*(a)* romantic
*(b)* revolutionary
*(c)* metaphysical
*(d)* religious and didactic

**292.** The book "Ormulum" comprised forty gospels translated and paraphrased by the monk named
*(a)* Augustine      *(b)* Cynewulf
*(c)* Orm      *(d)* John

**293.** Thomas Henry Huxley associates
*(a)* science with daily life
*(b)* God and man
*(c)* man and nature
*(d)* man and society

**294.** Brave New World was published in
*(a)* 1930      *(b)* 1928
*(c)* 1935      *(d)* 1932

**295.** Which of the following is not written by Hugo Charteris
*(a)* Pictures in the wall
*(b)* A Piece of String
*(c)* The Old Boys
*(d)* The Boarding House

**296.** Cecil Day Lewis's 'The Poetic Image' appeared in
*(a)* 1938      *(b)* 1945
*(c)* 1946      *(d)* 1947

**297.** Ann Jellicoe became famous in 1958
*(a)* with the production of a play
*(b)* by writing a novel
*(c)* by getting a poem published
*(d)* by getting a short story telecast over the T.V.

**298.** Which of the following statements is not true:
*(a)* Shelley was a cricketer
*(b)* Byron was a cricketer
*(c)* Keats had been a physician
*(d)* Lamb was a clerk

**299.** Which of the following statements is true :
*(a)* Shakespeare died by falling from a horse
*(b)* Dr. Johnson was a contemporary of Shakespeare

(c) Richardson's Pamela was written in the form of letters

(d) Shelley did not like revolutionary ideas.

**300.** Which of the following works is by H.G. Wells
(a) All in a Garden Fair
(b) The Invisible Man
(c) A Child of the Jago
(d) Point Counter Point

**301.** Who wrote : "The Ideal of a Christian Church"
(a) John Keble
(b) Newman
(c) Nash
(d) William George Ward

**302.** Which of the following is not the off-shoot of Romanticism
(a) Aesthetic Theory
(b) Pre-Raphaelitism
(c) Classicism
(d) Super-naturalism

**303.** The greatest worshipper of beauty among the Romantic poets was
(a) Keats
(b) Shelley
(c) Byron
(d) Wordsworth

**304.** Humanism is most pronounced in
(a) Romanticism
(b) Renascence
(c) Classicism
(d) Pre-Raphaelitism

**305.** When was Hazlitt born
(a) 1782
(b) 1780
(c) 1778
(d) 1785

**306.** Which of the following odes is not by Keats
(a) Ode on Intimations of Immortality
(b) Ode to a Nightingale
(c) Ode on a Grecian Urn
(d) Ode to Autumn

**307.** Which of the following is not a Romantic characteristic?
(a) An atmosphere of wonder
(b) An impression of strangeness
(c) A conscious adherence to set rules
(d) Spontaneousness

**308.** In which country was Romanticism associated with an innovatory aesthetic creed
(a) England
(b) France
(c) Italy
(d) Germany

**309.** English Romanticism from 1790 to 1830 being a native development, was partly influenced by

(a) Germany
(b) France
(c) Spain
(d) Italy

**310.** Crabbe was mainly a ......... poet.
(a) Romantic
(b) Realistic
(c) Metaphysical
(d) None of these

**311.** Which characteristic among the following is not contained in "The Monk" by Lewis
(a) Lack of moral depth
(b) Highly religious atmosphere
(c) A sense of unreality
(d) Melodramaticism

**312.** Which of the following works is not that of David Hume
(a) Treatise of Human Nature
(b) The Rise and Fall of the Roman Empire
(c) Political Discourses
(d) History of Great Britain

**313.** In Tristram Shandy, the hero is born in
(a) the second book
(b) the fourth book
(c) the third book
(d) the fifth book

**314.** Don Quixote basically presents
(a) the romantic nature of man
(b) the contrasting glory and misery of mankind
(c) the greedy nature of man
(d) the foolish instincts inherent in man's nature

**315.** In writing Tristram Shandy, Sterne was mainly influenced by
(a) Shakespeare
(b) Chaucer
(c) Cervantes
(d) Lamb

**316.** Tristram Shandy is primarily a ......... novel
(a) sentimental
(b) romantic
(c) comical
(d) intellectual

**317.** In the 'Vicar of Wakefield' Goldsmith mainly offers a ............. figure
(a) romantic
(b) moral
(c) carefree
(d) extremely worried

**318.** What is A.C. Bradley mainly known for
(a) Shakespearean comedy
(b) Historical plays of Shakespeare
(c) Shakespearean tragedy
(d) Shakespeare's romances

**319.** Who is the writer of 'The School for Scandal'
(a) Ben Jonson
(b) R.B. Sheridan
(c) Congreve
(d) Webster

**320.** Raymond Williams is primarily a
(a) Dramatist (b) Novelist
(c) Essayist (d) Critic

**321.** Who is the writer of the poem "The Canonization"
(a) Milton (b) Dryden
(c) Donne (d) Chaucer

**322.** Name the writer of the poem "Wind Hour"
(a) Hopkins (b) Eliot
(c) Dryden (d) Yeats

**323.** Who is the writer of the poem "Adam's Course"
(a) Eliot (b) Tagore
(c) Yeats (d) Shelley

**324.** Who wrote the poem: "Lay Your Sleeping Head".
(a) Auden (b) Yeats
(c) Stephen Spender (d) Ted Hughes

**325.** The play "The Birthday Party" is written by
(a) G.B. Shaw (b) Galsworthy
(c) Harold Pinter (d) Osborne

**326.** Who is believed to be the writer of "On the Sublime"
(a) Aristotle (b) Longinus
(c) Plato (d) M. Arnold

**327.** Name the author of "An Essay on Dramatic Poesie"
(a) Dryden (b) Sidney
(c) Shelley (d) Arnold

**328.** Who is the writer of "Culture and Society"
(a) Cleanth Brooks
(b) Eliot
(c) Bertrand Russell
(d) Raymond Williams

**329.** The writer of the 'Mirror and the Lamp' is
(a) Hume (b) Lionel Trilling
(c) M.H. Abrams (d) Sean Lucy

**330.** The writer of "Provide Provide" is
(a) Whitman (b) Frost
(c) Yeats (d) Auden

**331.** In whose essays the idea of the "oversoul" pervades...........
(a) Thoreau (b) Emerson
(c) Whitman (d) Mark Twain

**332.** Who wrote "Desire Under the Elms"
(a) Arthur Miller (b) Osborne
(c) Eugene O'Neill (d) Shaw

**333.** Who is the writer of "A Severed Head"
(a) Iris Murdoch (b) Paul Scott
(c) Goldwing (d) Huxley

**334.** 'Das Kapital' is written by
(a) Engel (b) Freud
(c) Marx (d) Lawrence

**335.** "Waiting for Godot" is written by
(a) Samuel Beckett (b) Ibsen
(c) Brecht (d) Chekhov

**336.** Who is the writer of "A House for Mr. Biswas"?
(a) Salman Rushdie (b) V.S. Naipaul
(c) Vikram Seth (d) R.K. Narayan

**337.** Name which is not the work of Marlowe
(a) Richard I (b) Tambarlaine
(c) The Jew of Malta (d) Dr. Faustus

**338.** Name the writer of the poem "The Weary Blues"
(a) Longfellow (b) Whitman
(c) Frost (d) Langston Hughes

**339.** Which of the following poems is not written by Robert Lowell
(a) In the Cage (b) Dolphin
(c) Good Morning (d) The Old Flame

**340.** Which of the following poems is written by Wallace Stevens
(a) Red Sun Blues (b) Sunday Morning
(c) From Survivor (d) "Going"

**341.** Which of the following poems is not written by Philip Larkin
(a) Art Grass (b) Sad Steps
(c) Traveller (d) Church going

**342.** Oedipus Rex was written by
(a) Sophocles (b) Homer
(c) Seneca (d) Aeschylus

**343.** Flaubert's famous work is
(a) Odysseus (b) Madame Bovary
(c) The Trial (d) The Outsider

**344.** Northrop Fry is basically a
(a) Dramatist (b) Novelist
(c) Poet (d) Critic

**345.** The writer of "The Beauty in a State" is
(a) Raja Rao
(b) Tagore
(c) Shelley
(d) Ananda Coomaraswami

**346.** The most important work of K.R. Srinivas Iyengar is
(a) Indian Way of Writing
(b) Indians Under the Foreign Rule
(c) Indian Writing in English
(d) Indian Literary Scene

**347.** The writer of "The Swan and the Eagle" is
(a) M.K. Naik      (b) C   .   D   . Narasimhaiah
(c) Bruce King      (d) V.K. Gokak

**348.** Name the writer of the book "Introducing Applied Linguistics" (Penguin)
(a) Allen      (b) Mac Arthur
(c) G.A. Leech      (d) S. Pittcorder

**349.** Danglars is a character in
(a) The Treasure Island (b) Monte Cristo
(c) Oliver Twist      (d) Huckleberry Finn

**350.** "A sleepless hour or more has its strange value only in the middle."
Name the writer of the lines given above
(a) Kamala Das      (b) Daruwalla
(c) Dilip Chitre      (d) Nissim Ezekiel

**351.** Who said about Virginia Woolf "She had no taste for rough diamonds"
(a) A.D. Moody      (b) E. Albert
(c) H.V. Routh      (d) W. Allen

**352.** The name of Virginia Woolf's father was
(a) Stephen Woolf      (b) John Woolf
(c) James Woolf      (d) Robert Woolf

**353.** In which work does the following line appear : "Her sympathy seemed to fly back into her face, like a bramble spring."
(a) Mrs. Dalloway
(b) Lord Jim
(c) To The Lighthouse
(d) David Copperfield

**354.** Identify the last line of Whitman's "Passage to India"
(a) Passage to more than India
(b) O farther, farther, farther sail!
(c) O brave soul!
(d) Away O soul! Lost instantly the anchor!

**355.** The generally accepted date of the death of Plato is
(a) 342 BC      (b) 341 BC
(c) 348 BC      (d) 340 BC

**356.** It is generally believed that Aristotle was born in
(a) 380 BC      (b) 384 BC
(c) 390 BC      (d) 391 BC

**357.** Aristotle was engaged as tutor to
(a) King Philip      (b) King of Persia
(c) Alexander      (d) Princess of Turkey

**358.** What was the most revolutionary deed done by Aristotle, regarding human rights and freedom, which he did before his death?
(a) He wrote Poetics
(b) He inverted most of Plato's theories
(c) He liberated all his slaves through his will
(d) He noted down everything that he studied at Plato's Academy

**359.** Which critic is most associated with the view that "Poetry is criticism of life."
(a) Dryden      (b) Eliot
(c) Wordsworth      (d) Matthew Arnold

**360.** What did Byron die of
(a) heart failure      (b) fever
(c) dysentery      (d) gouts

**361.** Which among the following critics did not believe in the authority of ancient classics
(a) Dryden      (b) Jonson
(c) Wordsworth      (d) Pope

**362.** Which of the following poets made a fortune by translating Homer
(a) Shelley      (b) Dryden
(c) Spenser      (d) Pope

**363.** Who is believed to have said : "That which does not concern the common man, is of no significance."
(a) Voltaire      (b) Rousseau
(c) Locke      (d) Southey

**364.** Who is stated to have said "Criticism is the art of interpreting art."
(a) Dryden      (b) Arnold
(c) Walter Pater      (d) Eliot

**365.** Who wrote the poem: "The Lake Isle of Innisfree"
(a) Yeats      (b) Eliot
(c) Spender      (d) Auden

**366.** Who is primarily associated with the term "Objective Correlative"

*(a)* Shelley      *(b)* Sandburg
*(c)* Eliot      *(d)* Hardy

**367.** Who is stated to have said, "What criticism undertakes is the profitable discussion of literature."
*(a)* Eliot      *(b)* F.R. Leavis
*(c)* Middleton Murry    *(d)* Chatterton

**368.** Who wrote : "The Lives of the Poets"
*(a)* Boswell      *(b)* Hazlitt
*(c)* Macaulay      *(d)* Dr. Johnson

**369.** Who is said to have used the term "high seriousness"
*(a)* Dryden      *(b)* Sidney
*(c)* M. Arnold      *(d)* Eliot

**370.** Who used the term "high disdain"
*(a)* Shakespeare      *(b)* Milton
*(c)* Yeats      *(d)* Darwin

**371.** Who wrote: "The Interpretation of Dreams"
*(a)* Marx      *(b)* Jung
*(c)* Freud      *(d)* Darwin

**372.** Who wrote : "Principles of Literary Criticism" (in 1924)
*(a)* T.R. Leavis      *(b)* Kenneth Brooke
*(c)* I.A. Richards      *(d)* A.G. Gardiner

**373.** Who said : "Poetry is not a turning loose of emotion, but an escape from emotion"
*(a)* Wordsworth      *(b)* T.S. Eliot
*(c)* I.A. Richards      *(d)* Wilson Knight

**374.** Who said : "Language may be defined as the expression of thought by means of speech sounds."
*(a)* Sapir      *(b)* R.H. Robins
*(c)* Henry Sweet      *(d)* A.H. Gardiner

**375.** In what respect among the following do the human beings and animals have at least partly identical station in the matter of language as a means of communication?
*(a)* acquired      *(b)* instinctive
*(c)* grammaticality      *(d)* behaviourial

**376.** Who said: "So, Here I am......
Twenty years largely wasted.....
Trying to use word......."
*(a)* Yeats      *(b)* T.S. Eliot
*(c)* Wordsworth      *(d)* Hardy

**377.** Who said: "Style is the skin and the mere coat."

*(a)* Shelley      *(b)* Pater
*(c)* Carlyle      *(d)* Quillar Couch

**378.** When did Trubetzkoy's "Principles of Phonology", appear
*(a)* 1942      *(b)* 1931
*(c)* 1930      *(d)* 1939

**379.** Whose book "Language" (1933) is considered "The Bible of American Linguistics"
*(a)* Robert A. Hall      *(b)* Bloomfield
*(c)* Bernard Bloch      *(d)* Edward Sapir

**380.** Who said: Language is "primarily an auditory system of symbols."
*(a)* Franz Boas      *(b)* Bloch
*(c)* Sapir      *(d)* Whitney

**381.** Which of the following poems is not by Frost.
*(a)* Design      *(b)* Birches
*(c)* Reluctance      *(d)* Michael

**382.** What does the term "Deus ex machina" mean?
*(a)* God out of the machine
*(b)* devil out of the machine
*(c)* man out of the machine
*(d)* beast out of the machine

**383.** The famous soliloquy "To be or not to be" occurs in
*(a)* Macbeth      *(b)* King Lear
*(c)* Hamlet      *(d)* Othello

**384.** Who wrote : "Flower in the crammied well
..................................
Little flower but if I could understand what you are ..........................
I should know what God and Man is."
*(a)* Wordsworth      *(b)* Shelley
*(c)* Yeats      *(d)* Tennyson

**385.** Which is the 'odd man out' in the following
*(a)* Paradise Lost      *(b)* The Ramayana
*(c)* Essay on Man      *(d)* Iliad

**386.** Which Italian poet is most famous for his sonnets
*(a)* Petrarch      *(b)* Dante
*(c)* Ovid      *(d)* None of these

**387.** Who wrote the following line :
"Blow, blow, thou winter wind"
*(a)* Milton      *(b)* Tennyson
*(c)* Shakespeare      *(d)* Browning

**388.** In which of the following word the adverb form is made by simply applying "ly" at the end

(a) Present      (b) Incident

(c) Accident      (d) Occasion

**389.** Tetra metre comprises a line with...........iambus

(a) Two      (b) Three

(c) Four      (d) Five

**390.** What figure of speech has been used in the following line:

"Milton! thou shouldnt be living with us at this hour."

—Wordsworth

(a) Hyperbole      (b) Simile

(c) Metaphor      (d) Apostrophe

**391.** Under which category should Dryden's Mac flecknoe be placed

(a) Satire      (b) Epic

(c) Ode      (d) Lyric

**392.** Which figure of speech has been used in the term : "immemorial elms"

(a) Allegory      (b) Rhyme

(c) Alliteration      (d) Oxymoron

**393.** Who is the writer of the following line : "Busy old fool, unruly sun"

(a) Shelley      (b) Milton

(c) Clough      (d) Donne

**394.** What is the name of the central figure in Tagore's play "Muktadhara"

(a) King Vivajit      (b) King Ranajit

(c) Prince Abhijit      (d) Amba

**395.** Which play of Shaw is also sometimes called "The Chocolate Soldier"

(a) Arms and the Man      (b) Candida

(c) Pygmalion      (d) Saint Joan

**396.** In which episode of "The Merchant of Venice" did the Prince of Arragon make the choice of the silver casket

(a) The Bond Episode

(b) The Casket Episode

(c) The Trial Scene

(d) The Ring Episode

**397.** Which one among the following was not the demand of the Chartists in 19th century in England.

(a) annual parliaments

(b) pensions to all widows

(c) vote by ballot

(d) universal manhood suffrage

**398.** In which category among novelists should Mrs. Gaskell be placed

(a) humanitarian      (b) determinist

(c) picaresque      (d) revolutionary

**399.** Which one among the following cannot be deemed to be a writer of the "Problem Play"

(a) G.B. Shaw

(b) Galsworthy

(c) Harley Granville-Barker

(d) Eliot

**400.** In which decade of the twentieth century did the group of novelists commonly known as "Angry Young Men" appear?

(a) Thirties      (b) Forties

(c) Fifties      (d) Sixties

**401.** In which year was Magna Carta signed

(a) 1205      (b) 1212

(c) 1215      (d) 1220

**402.** To which King of England did Pope give the title 'Defender of the Faith'

(a) Henry VII      (b) Henry VIII

(c) James I      (d) Charles I

**403.** When did Mandeville's 'Travels' appear

(a) 1500      (b) 1501

(c) 1496      (d) 1490

**404.** Who is the writer of "Metamorphoses"

(a) Ovid      (b) Dante

(c) Petrarch      (d) Virgil

**405.** When is Wyclif believed to have died?

(a) 1380      (b) 1382

(c) 1383      (d) 1384

**406.** East India Company was set up in

(a) 1604      (b) 1603

(c) 1600      (d) 1605

**407.** G.M. Trevelyan was primarily a

(a) historian      (b) dramatist

(c) poet      (d) novelist

**408.** In which book does the following line appear: "A god is not so glorious as a king." — Marlowe

(a) Dr. Faustus      (b) The Jew of Malta

(c) Tamburlaine      (d) Edward II

**409.** The book "Euphues" was written by

(a) Greene      (b) Jonson

(c) Dryden      (d) John Lyly

**410.** Bacon's essays are the finest example of

*(a)* wit and humour     *(b)* practical wisdom
*(c)* pathos            *(d)* irony

**411.** Tamberlaine is basically an expression of the spirit of ......... in full measure
*(a)* Renaissance     *(b)* Romanticism
*(c)* Imperialism      *(d)* Materialism

**412.** In which poem do the following lines appear:
"Stone walls do not a prison make,
Nor iron bars a cage."
*(a)* "To Lucasta"
*(b)* 'To Althea, from Prison'
*(c)* Ballad Upon a Wedding
*(d)* None of these

**413.** Which one among the following was not a cavalier poet
*(a)* Herrick         *(b)* Thomas Carew
*(c)* John Suckling    *(d)* Robert Bridges

**414.** Which age in English literature is known as the Augustan Age
*(a)* That of Dryden
*(b)* That of Dr. Johnson
*(c)* That of Shakespeare
*(d)* That of Pope

**415.** Who wrote to Pope in 1706 :
"The best of the modern poets in all languages are those that have nearest copied the ancients."
*(a)* Addison       *(b)* Steele
*(c)* Walsh         *(d)* Dryden

**416.** The Age of Queen Anne in England was an era of
*(a)* political stability
*(b)* political upheavals
*(c)* great social unrest
*(d)* great natural calamities

**417.** When was Swift born?
*(a)* 1660         *(b)* 1661
*(c)* 1680         *(d)* 1667

**418.** Which is Swift's most powerful general satire
*(a)* Gulliver's Travels
*(b)* The Tale of a Tub
*(c)* The Battle of Books
*(d)* Nothing can be said in this connection

**419.** Who characterized D.G. Rossetti's poetry as belonging to "the fleshly school of poetry"
*(a)* Eliot         *(b)* M. Arnold
*(c)* Robert Buchanan    *(d)* Yeats

**420.** In which poem does the following line occur :
"The wild wine slips with the weight of its leaves."—Swinburne
*(a)* The Blessed Damozel
*(b)* Atalanta in Calydon
*(c)* The Hounds of Spring
*(d)* None of these

**421.** Which of the following should be regarded as the presiding deity of the Victorian period
*(a)* Mrs. Grundy     *(b)* Mammon
*(c)* Cupid         *(d)* Venus

**422.** Who is the heroine of 'Vanity Fair'
*(a)* Sophia       *(b)* Estella
*(c)* Dora         *(d)* Becky Sharp

**423.** The period of Edward VII's rule in England lasted from 1901 to .........
*(a)* 1912        *(b)* 1910
*(c)* 1909        *(d)* 1913

**424.** When was Old Age Pensions Act passed in England
*(a)* 1909        *(b)* 1907
*(c)* 1906        *(d)* 1908

**425.** In which decade in the nineteenth century did the Chartist Movement take a concrete shape in England?
*(a)* Thirties      *(b)* Twenties
*(c)* Fifties       *(d)* Sixties

**426.** Which one among the following was not the reason for the failure of the Chartist Movement?
*(a)* Peel's reforms and the growth of prosperity
*(b)* Lack of a powerful leader among the working classes
*(c)* Fake signatures of people presented to parliament
*(d)* Natural calamities

**427.** Which age is generally called the Age of Prose and Reason?
*(a)* Eighteenth century
*(b)* Seventeenth century
*(c)* Nineteenth century
*(d)* Sixteenth century

**428.** Who can be said to be the greatest writer of the Comedy of Humours?

   *(a)* Dryden         *(b)* Ben Jonson
   *(c)* Congreve       *(d)* Etherege

**429.** Which one among the following is not a play by Ben Johnson?
   *(a)* Volpone
   *(b)* Alchemist
   *(c)* Every man out of His Honour
   *(d)* The Way of the World

**430.** Who is the writer of the book "Prince"
   *(a)* Ovid          *(b)* Boccaccio
   *(c)* Machiavelli     *(d)* Montaigne

**431.** Who is the writer of the essay "Simulation and Dissimulation"?
   *(a)* Montaigne      *(b)* Lamb
   *(c)* De Quincey      *(d)* Bacon

**432.** Name the figure of speech for which Lyly is chiefly remembered
   *(a)* Malapropism     *(b)* Euphuism
   *(c)* Melodramaticism    *(d)* None of these

**433.** Utopia was written by
   *(a)* Walter Raleigh
   *(b)* Sir Thomas Moore
   *(c)* Daniel Defoe
   *(d)* None of these

**434.** The other name for Euphues is
   *(a)* The Anatomy of Melancholy
   *(b)* The Anatomy of Joy
   *(c)* The Anatomy of Wit
   *(d)* None of these

**435.** Ferrex and Porrex is the other name for
   *(a)* The Spanish Tragedy
   *(b)* Dr. Faustus
   *(c)* Goboduc
   *(d)* None of these

**436.** In the 'Spanish Tragedy', there is the ghost of
   *(a)* Andrea        *(b)* Horatio
   *(c)* Balthazar      *(d)* Lorenzo

**437.** Which one among the following belongs to the group known as University Wits
   *(a)* Shakespeare     *(b)* Congreve
   *(c)* Dryden        *(d)* Marlowe

**438.** Astrophel and Stella is a
   *(a)* play          *(b)* novel
   *(c)* sonnet sequence    *(d)* short story

**439.** In the Duchess of Malfi, Ferdinand was the Duke of

   *(a)* Milan        *(b)* Calabria
   *(c)* Rome        *(d)* None of these

**440.** The Alchemist was published in
   *(a)* 1610         *(b)* 1611
   *(c)* 1612         *(d)* 1609

**441.** In the Duchess of Malfi, who spoke the following words "O horror, that not the fear of him which binds the devils can prescribe man obedicence."
   *(a)* Ferdinand      *(b)* Cardinal
   *(c)* Bosola        *(d)* Antonio

**442.** In 'Sons and Lovers', Paul Moral is the son of
   *(a)* John Morel     *(b)* Joseph Morel
   *(c)* Walter Morel    *(d)* James Morel

**443.** Which of the following is not one of the five movements in 'The Wasteland'
   *(a)* The Burial of the Dead
   *(b)* The Game of Chess
   *(c)* The Fire Sermon
   *(d)* The Joy of Riding

**444.** When was St. Thomas canonized : in
   *(a)* 1170         *(b)* 1171
   *(c)* 1173         *(d)* 1175

**445.** Who appointed St. Thomas Becket a Chancellor
   *(a)* Henry III      *(b)* Henry I
   *(c)* Henry II       *(d)* None of these

**446.** T.S. Eliot died in
   *(a)* 1960         *(b)* 1962
   *(c)* 1961         *(d)* 1965

**447.** When was Erewhon first published
   *(a)* 1871         *(b)* 1872
   *(c)* 1873         *(d)* 1874

**448.** What is the Greek meaning of 'Utopia'
   *(a)* An ideal place
   *(b)* A healthy place
   *(c)* A lovely place
   *(d)* Not a place (=ou=not; topos=a place)

**449.** What are the last words of Vanity Fair
   *(a)* Shantih! Shantih! Shantih
   *(b)* Vanitas Vanitatum!
   *(c)* Amen!
   *(d)* Let it be

**450.** 'Virtue Rewarded' is the other name for
   *(a)* Pamela       *(b)* Joseph Andrews
   *(c)* Clarissa       *(d)* Tom Jones

**451.** The word "Volksgeist" means
(a) The spirit of the age
(b) (As per) tradition, custom and consensus
(c) The essence of something
(d) None of these

**452.** When did the hundred years' war which started in 1337 come to an end?
(a) 1450      (b) 1451
(c) 1452      (d) 1453

**453.** The Age of chivalry was basically an age of
(a) war
(b) love
(c) love, war and religion
(d) religion

**454.** Cervantes practically rang the death-knell of
(a) war      (b) love
(c) religion      (d) chivalry

**455.** The "Black Death" in England as came in 1348 was known by this name because
(a) Black, knotty boils appeared on the bodies of the victims
(b) The country was attached by black vultures feeding on dead bodies
(c) The whole country became black with dead bodies
(d) It was a mournful event compelling people to wear black dress.

**456.** When did Peasants' Revolt take place in England?
(a) In 1380      (b) In 1384
(c) In 1381      (d) In 1390

**457.** Who was the king in England at the time of Peasants' Revolt?
(a) Richard II      (b) Richard III
(c) Henry I      (d) King John

**458.** Which one of the following was a contemporary of Chaucer
(a) Spenser      (b) Herrick
(c) Robert Graves      (d) John Gower

**459.** The famous work of Boccaccio is
(a) Decameron
(b) Divine Comedy
(c) Essays
(d) A collection of sonnets

**460.** When did Petrarch die?
(a) 1382      (b) 1389
(c) 1370      (d) 1374

**461.** Who has written the following line :
"Chaucer symbolises, as no other writer does, The Middle Ages."
(a) Legouis      (b) Hugh Walker
(c) Compton-Rickett      (d) Hudson

**462.** What is meant by "Grub Street"?
(a) The literary scene of hacks' crowds during Pope's period.
(b) Unhygienic streets of London
(c) Streets full of worms
(d) Plague-infested streets

**463.** Who wrote: "Idylls of the King"?
(a) Tennyson      (b) Browning
(c) Spenser      (d) Keats

**464.** Who started the Lollards' Movement?
(a) John Gower      (b) Langland
(c) Wyclif      (d) Wat Tylar

**465.** Who wrote the following lines :
"He loved gold in special, For, gold in physic is a cordial."
(a) Langland      (b) Wyclif
(c) John Ball      (d) Chaucer

**466.** Sir Andrew Freeport is a member of
(a) The Royal Society of Science
(b) The Spectator Club
(c) The Royal Academy of Art
(d) The Royal Society of Physicians

**467.** What could be another name for Renaissance
(a) The New Learning
(b) The Reformation
(c) The Prostantism
(d) Humanism

**468.** Who wrote: 'Hudibras'
(a) Butler      (b) Addison
(c) Steele      (d) Goldsmith

**469.** When was the poet John Gay born?
(a) 1675      (b) 1681
(c) 1685      (d) 1687

**470.** "London" by Dr. Johnson is
(a) An epic      (b) A verse satire
(c) A prose satire      (d) A critical work

**471.** Cowper was born in
(a) 1730      (b) 1733
(c) 1731      (d) 1729

**472.** Who wrote Moll Flanders?

(a) Richardson    (b) Fielding
(c) Smollett    (d) Defoe

**473.** The Gothic novel was primarily a novel of
(a) Pity
(b) Terror
(c) Love
(d) Description of nature

**474.** When did Areopagitica appear?
(a) In 1641    (b) In 1642
(c) In 1643    (d) In 1644

**475.** The main plank of Areopagitica's argument was for the freedom of
(a) the press
(b) worship
(c) movement
(d) forming a political party

**476.** Philip Wakem is a character in
(a) The Middlemarch
(b) Great Expectations
(c) The Mill on the Floss
(d) Waiting for Godot

**477.** When was Walter Pater born?
(a) In 1836    (b) In 1837
(c) In 1839    (d) In 1841

**478.** Which one of the following writers is not dealt with in Pater's 'Appreciations'
(a) Southey    (b) Lamb
(c) Coleridge    (d) Rossetti

**479.** 'Unto This Last' is a work by
(a) Carlyle    (b) Pater
(c) Oscar Wilde    (d) John Ruskin

**480.** Thomas Gradgrind is a character that occurs in
(a) Hard Times    (b) Candida
(c) Wasteland    (d) Jude the Obscure

**481.** Which one among the following cannot strictly be called the writer of novels of purpose
(a) Dickens    (b) Newman
(c) Jane Austen    (d) Kingsley

**482.** Who among the following cannot be termed one of the Four Wheels of English Novel in the Eighteenth century?
(a) Jane Austen    (b) Smollett
(c) Sterne    (d) Fielding

**483.** Who is the writer of "The Blessed Damozel"?

(a) Christina Rossetti    (b) Emile Bronte
(c) D.G. Rossetti    (d) W.B. Yeats

**484.** Which is the correct chronological order?
(a) Utopia—Dr. Faustus—Areopagitica—Maud
(b) Henry V—The Faery Queene—Lyrical Ballads—The Compleat Angler
(c) Christabel—Canterbury Tales—Queen Mab—Corsair
(d) Kubla Khan—Othello—Paradise Lost—Michael

**485.** The word "compromise" is used with...age
(a) Elizabethan    (b) Modern
(c) Victorian    (d) Chaucerian

**486.** Which one of the following poets may to some extent be considered a continental poet
(a) Tennyson    (b) Spenser
(c) Eliot    (d) Byron

**487.** Which one among the following favoured most the imperialistic tendencies
(a) Shelley    (b) Spenser
(c) Eliot    (d) Kipling

**488.** Who among the following was not a critic?
(a) M. Arnold    (b) Ruskin
(c) Dryden    (d) Tennyson

**489.** "Liberty, Equality, Fraternity" was the slogan of
(a) French Revolution
(b) Bolshevik Revolution
(c) American Civil War
(d) Indian Freedom Movement

**490.** Francis Thompson the poet, died in
(a) 1910    (b) 1909
(c) 1907    (d) 1906

**491.** The most important aspect of Jane Austen's novels is
(a) Superb characterization
(b) Perfect Plot construction
(c) High moral sense
(d) Lively dialogues

**492.** The circle of Jane Austen's novels is
(a) The whole universe
(b) The whole word
(c) The whole of England
(d) A limited number of families

**493.** Which one among the following was not a contemporary or predecessor of Shakespeare?
  *(a)* Marlowe      *(b)* Kyd
  *(c)* Fry      *(d)* Greene

**494.** Who among the following was not a prose writer
  *(a)* Ascham      *(b)* Coleridge
  *(c)* Hooker      *(d)* Raleigh

**495.** Who among the following was not a character writer
  *(a)* Wordsworth
  *(b)* Joseph Hall
  *(c)* John Earle
  *(d)* Sir Thomas Overbury

**496.** Who among the following was not an essayist of the seventeenth century.
  *(a)* Halifax
  *(b)* Sir Thomas Browne
  *(c)* Hazlitt
  *(d)* Sir William Temple

**497.** About whom has it been said :
  "He knew small Latin and less Greek"
  *(a)* Ben Jonson      *(b)* Shakespeare
  *(c)* Milton      *(d)* Aristotle

**498.** Who said about Shakespeare:
  "He was not of age but of ages"
  *(a)* Jonson      *(b)* Johnson
  *(c)* Dryden      *(d)* Arnold

**499.** Pinpoint the correct chronological sequence
  *(a)* Petrarch—Spenser—Wordsworth—Marlowe
  *(b)* Wyclif—Lyly—Shelley—Tennyson
  *(c)* Pope—Chaucer—Donne—Yeats
  *(d)* M. Arnold—Dryden—Sidney—Yeats

**500.** Who wrote: 'Modern Painters.'
  *(a)* Rossetti      *(b)* Reynolds
  *(c)* Hazlitt      *(d)* Ruskin

**501.** When was Somerset Maugham born
  *(a)* 1871      *(b)* 1872
  *(c)* 1873      *(d)* 1874

**502.** In which book do the following lines occur :
  "Around the ancient track marched, rank on rank,
  The army of unalterable law."
  *(a)* Sons and Lovers
  *(b)* Michael

  *(c)* 'Love in the Valley' by George Meredith
  *(d)* Hyperion

**503.** Who is the writer of the following lines :
  "Laugh and be merry, remember, better the world with a song.
  Better the world with a blow
  in the teeth of a wrong."
  *(a)* Wordsworth      *(b)* Browning
  *(c)* John Masefield      *(d)* Yeats

**504.** When did Landon die?
  *(a)* 1870      *(b)* 1874
  *(c)* 1872      *(d)* 1873

**505.** Which one of the following is not the work of Lamb
  *(a)* Of Style      *(b)* All Fools' Day
  *(c)* Dream Children      *(d)* Grace Before Meat

**506.** Whose is the following line:
  "A child's a plaything for an hour."
  *(a)* Charles Lamb      *(b)* Mary Lamb
  *(c)* Shelley      *(d)* Tagore

**507.** Who wrote the following line :
  "The moon is nothing
  But a circumambulatory aphrodisiac."
  *(a)* Yeats      *(b)* Shelley
  *(c)* Keats      *(d)* Fry

**508.** Who is stated to have said :
  "veni, vidi, vici"
  *(a)* Julius Caesar      *(b)* Alexander
  *(c)* Napoleon      *(d)* Homer

**509.** The War of Troy was fought between
  *(a)* The Greeks and the French
  *(b)* The Greeks and the Trojans
  *(c)* The Trojans and the Austrians
  *(d)* The Trojans and the Turks

**510.** One of the heroes in the War of Troy bore the name of a city
  *(a)* Paris      *(b)* Prague
  *(c)* Madrid      *(d)* Rome

**511.** Who wrote : "The Advancement of Learning"
  *(a)* Pope      *(b)* Tennyson
  *(c)* Bacon      *(d)* Eliot

**512.** Who said : "My essays ........ come home, to men's business, and bosoms."
  *(a)* Lamb      *(b)* Bacon
  *(c)* Hazlitt      *(d)* Stevenson

**513.** In which year did the 'Glorious Revolution' take place in England?
    *(a)* 1685          *(b)* 1680
    *(c)* 1681          *(d)* 1688

**514.** Who wrote: "We are hollow men."
    *(a)* Eliot          *(b)* Yeats
    *(c)* Tagore          *(d)* Ezekiel

**515.** Who used the term "The perpetual struggle for room and food."
    *(a)* Amartya Sen          *(b)* Laski
    *(c)* Malthus          *(d)* Marx

**516.** In which book do the following lines appear :
"O thou art fairer than the evening air, Clad in the beauty of a thousand stars."
    *(a)* Dr. Faustus
    *(b)* Tamburlaine
    *(c)* The Spanish Tragedy
    *(d)* Faerie Queene

**517.** Who wrote the following line :
"Our swords shall play the orators for us."
    *(a)* Shakespeare          *(b)* Marlowe
    *(c)* Greene          *(d)* Eliot

**518.** By which character is the following line in Shakespeare's Julius Caesar spoken?
"I'm well-armed in honesty."
    *(a)* Caesar          *(b)* Cassius
    *(c)* Brutus          *(d)* Cicero

**519.** Who said: "I teach you the superman. Man is something that is to be surpassed."
    *(a)* Mallarme          *(b)* Zola
    *(c)* Ibsen          *(d)* Nietzsche

**520.** Who is stated to have called Turkey "a seriously sick man."
    *(a)* Edward II          *(b)* Nicholas I of Russia
    *(c)* Napoleon          *(d)* Churchill

**521.** Who gave the definition of a gentleman as "one who never inflicts pain."
    *(a)* Nash          *(b)* Wordsworth
    *(c)* Newman          *(d)* Yeats

**522.** To whom is the statement "Laws were made to be broken" originally ascribed
    *(a)* Goldsmith, Oliver
    *(b)* Christopher North (John Wilson)
    *(c)* Bacon
    *(d)* Hazlitt

**523.** Who wrote the following lines :

**524.** Who said: "He comes too near that comes to be denied."
    *(a)* Milton          *(b)* Overbury
    *(c)* Addison          *(d)* Stevenson

"My subject is war, and the pity of war. The poetry is in the pity."
    *(a)* George Washington     *(b)* Napoleon
    *(c)* Tolstoy          *(d)* Wilfred Owen

**525.** "Who wrote : "The dropping of rain hollows out of a stone."
    *(a)* Milton          *(b)* Shakespeare
    *(c)* Virgil          *(d)* Ovid

**526.** In which book do the following words appear :
"The mass of men lead dead lives of quiet desperation."
    *(a)* Glimpses of World History
    *(b)* Outline of World History
    *(c)* Walden
    *(d)* Emerson's Essays

**527.** In which book did Jawaharlal Nehru quote the following words of Goethe:
"If the Romans were great enough to invent things like that, we at least should be great enough to believe them."
    *(a)* The Discovery of India
    *(b)* Glimpses of World History
    *(c)* An Autobiography
    *(d)* None of these

**528.** Who said about Jawaharlal Nehru:
"...Thus there emerges the image of Jawaharlal Nehru as a humanist, full of the deepest tenderness for men everywhere, a polytheist who accepted all the gods of the world, a universalist."
    *(a)* R.K. Narayan          *(b)* Mulk Raj Anand
    *(c)* Khushwant Singh     *(d)* Indira Gandhi

**529.** Who said: "Nothing can harm a good man, either in life or after death."
    *(a)* Newman          *(b)* Chaucer
    *(c)* Shakespeare          *(d)* Socrates

**530.** Who said, "From forty to fifty a man is at heart either a stoic or a satyr."
    *(a)* Sir Thomas Moore
    *(b)* Sir Arthur Pinero
    *(c)* Horace Walpole
    *(d)* Yeats

531. 'The Way of All Flesh' was written by
(a) Swift
(b) Congreve
(c) Butler
(d) Addison

532. In which poem does the following line occur :
"Our birth is but a sleep and a forgetting."
(a) Tintern Abbey
(b) Hymn on Intellectual Beauty
(c) Ode on Intimations of Immortality
(d) Adam's Curse

533. In which play does the character "Maura" occur
(a) Riders to the Sea
(b) Lady's Not for Burning
(c) Murder in the Cathedral
(d) The Playboy of the Western World

534. When was 'The Wind Among The Reeds' written
(a) 1897
(b) 1899
(c) 1896
(d) 1900

535. Who was the chief co-founder of the (Irish) Abbey Theatre with W.B. Yeats
(a) Lady Gregory
(b) Shaw
(c) Galsworthy
(d) Maud Gonne

36. When did Housman die?
(a) 1933
(b) 1935
(c) 1936
(d) 1937

537. P.G. Wodehouse is generally known as a
(a) sad man
(b) 'Funny man' of contemporary literature
(c) man of romance
(d) None of these

538. Who said the following words :
"To be alone is the fate of all great minds."
(a) Plato
(b) Socrates
(c) The Buddha
(d) Arthur Schopenhauer

539. "There is no cure for birth and death save to enjoy the interval."
Who said the words mentioned above?
(a) Socrates
(b) George Santayana
(c) M.K. Gandhi
(d) Vivekananda

540. Who said, "I am the grass; I cover all."
(a) Whitman
(b) Frost
(c) Sandburg
(d) Emily Dickinson

541. Who is the writer of the line :
"Look back, and smile at perils past."
(a) Shakespeare
(b) Scott
(c) Wordsworth
(d) Yeats

542. Who wrote : "I must—I will—I can—I ought—I do. "
(a) Congreve
(b) Carlyle
(c) R.B. Sheridan
(d) Etherege

543. Who is the writer of "The Good Companions"
(a) A.G. Gardiner
(b) Chatterton
(c) Hazlitt
(d) J.B. Priestley

544. Who among the following poets can be said to be a catalogue writer
(a) Lowell
(b) Auden
(c) Eliot
(d) Whitman

545. Which poet among the following can be said to be a poet of multitudes
(a) Auden
(b) Yeats
(c) Whitman
(d) Sandburg

546. Who is the writer of the poem 'Vagabond'?
(a) MacNeice
(b) Masefield
(c) Sir Henry Newbolt
(d) Rupert Brooke

547. Who said, "French is the only modern language fit for literature"
(a) Coleridge
(b) Yeats
(c) Conrad
(d) Synge

548. Which poem of Kipling was considered an offence to democracy
(a) 'Recessional'
(b) 'Rowers'
(c) 'Our Lady of the Snows'
(d) 'A Servant when He Reigneth

549. Which one among the following was not one of the Decadents
(a) Oscar Wilde
(b) Aubrey Beardsley
(c) Tennyson
(d) Rupert Brooke

550. "If I should die, think only this of me." Who wrote the above line?
(a) Housman
(b) Mare
(c) Yeats
(d) Brooke

551. Which of the following statements is true :
(a) Browning's work is more original in content than that of Tennyson
(b) Wordsworth was the older brother of Coleridge

    *(c)* Shelley was a pessimistic poet

    *(d)* James Joyce received the Nobel Prize in 1933

**552.** Which of the following statements is true :

    *(a)* Fanny Burney was a poetess of the first rank.

    *(b)* Wordsworth and Coleridge were always at daggers' drawn with each other

    *(c)* Keats died at the age of fifty

    *(d)* Mrs. Virginia Woolf committed suicide

**553.** Which of the following statements is true :

    *(a)* Goldsmith hated mankind

    *(b)* Horace Walpole is an historian of the second order

    *(c)* Crashaw was a Victorian novelist

    *(d)* Donne was the grandson of Spenser

**554.** Which of the following statements is true :

    *(a)* Mrs. Montagu is one of the queens of the Blue Stockings

    *(b)* French Revolution had no effect on Shelley

    *(c)* Southey fought in the battle of Blenheim

    *(d)* Lamb had his hut in a forest

**555.** Dryden's comedy 'The Wild Gallant' belongs to the year

    *(a)* 1661        *(b)* 1663

    *(c)* 1665        *(d)* 1667

**556.** Sir Thomas Browne was overwhelmingly a

    *(a)* poet of the first order

    *(b)* a prose writer

    *(c)* a dramatist

    *(d)* a novelist

**557.** "Gallathea" in written by

    *(a)* Spenser       *(b)* Herbert

    *(c)* Lyly         *(d)* Shelley

**558.** In which category should Lyly's "Love's Metamorphosis" be counted:

    *(a)* Tragedy      *(b)* Historical Play

    *(c)* Pastoral      *(d)* None of these

**559.** When was James Thomson born

    *(a)* 1701        *(b)* 1700

    *(c)* 1702        *(d)* 1699

**560.** In which year was Jane Austen born

    *(a)* 1775        *(b)* 1772

    *(c)* 1780        *(d)* 1778

**561.** Blackwood's magazine was founded in

    *(a)* 1815        *(b)* 1817

    *(c)* 1816        *(d)* 1818

**562.** Which one among the following was a periodical

    *(a)* The Spectator

    *(b)* The Doll's House

    *(c)* The Portrait of a Lady

    *(d)* Shepherd's Calendar

**563.** The dramas of the nineteenth century England appeal to

    *(a)* the eye      *(b)* the imagination

    *(c)* the reason    *(d)* the conscience

**564.** Who wrote: "The Harp of India"

    *(a)* Govind Chunder Dutt

    *(b)* Michael Madhusudan Dutt

    *(c)* Henry L.V. Derozio

    *(d)* V.K. Gokak

**565.** "King Porus—A Legend of Old" is written by

    *(a)* Henry Derozio

    *(b)* Toru Dutt

    *(c)* Sarojini Naidu

    *(d)* Michael Madhusudan

**566.** Who is the writer of the poem "The Dance of the Eunuchs"

    *(a)* Nissim Ezekiel    *(b)* Kamala Das

    *(c)* Daruwallah     *(d)* A.K. Ramanujan

**567.** Which Indian poet wrote the poem "The Trojan War"

    *(a)* Vikram Seth

    *(b)* Keki N. Daruwalla

    *(c)* Sri Aurbindo

    *(d)* Tagore

**568.** Who wrote: "Jonathan Wild"

    *(a)* Richardson     *(b)* Smollett

    *(c)* Defoe        *(d)* Fielding

**569.** Which one among the following is not a Gothic novelist

    *(a)* Mrs. Anne Radicliffe

    *(b)* Virginia Woolf

    *(c)* Horace Walpole

    *(d)* Matthew Gregory Lewis

**570.** Horace Walpole was the .......... of Mr. Walpole, the Prime Minister of England.

    *(a)* son        *(b)* brother

    *(c)* cousin      *(d)* father

**571.** Which one among the following cannot be regarded as a stream-of-consciousness novelist?

    *(a)* Dorothy M. Richardson

*(b)* Thackeray
*(c)* Virginia Woolf
*(d)* James Joyce

**572.** What is it to which Stephen Dedalus finally gets inclined in "A Portrait of the Artist as A Young Man"?
*(a)* Religion      *(b)* Art
*(c)* Nature      *(d)* God

**573.** George Eliot's real name was
*(a)* Mary Evans      *(b)* Maggie
*(c)* Sophia      *(d)* Miss Crompton

**574.** Which one of the following novels created a lot of controversy even in America
*(a)* A Tale of Two Cities
*(b)* Ulysses
*(c)* The Mill on the Floss
*(d)* Pride and Prejudice

**575.** Which characters does Forster consider better in his Aspects of the Novel
*(a)* Flat      *(b)* Oblong
*(c)* Rich      *(d)* Round

**576.** Stephen Guest is a character in
*(a)* Adam Bede
*(b)* The Middlemarch
*(c)* The Mill on The Floss
*(d)* Silas Marner

**577.** "Of Revenge" is one of the essays of
*(a)* Lamb      *(b)* Hazlitt
*(c)* Gardiner      *(d)* Bacon

**578.** "Reading maketh a full man; conference a ready man; and writing an exact man."
In which of Bacon's essays does the sentence mentioned above appear?
*(a)* Of Studies
*(b)* Of King
*(c)* Of Simulation and Dissimulation
*(d)* Of Revenge

**579.** In which category should Samuel Pepys be placed
*(a)* A novelist      *(b)* a poet
*(c)* a diarist      *(d)* a dramatist

**580.** Addison wrote the autobiography of a coin. What was it?
*(a)* a pound      *(b)* a shilling
*(c)* a pence      *(d)* a half-crown

**581.** Which one among the following was the periodical to which Addison did not contribute his works?
*(a)* The Tafler
*(b)* The Edinburg Review
*(c)* The Spectator
*(d)* The Guardian

**582.** What secured Addison political patronage
*(a)* a poem      *(b)* a drama
*(c)* an essay      *(d)* a novel

**583.** 'Meditation on a Broomstick' by Swift is primarily a
*(a)* study in nature
*(b)* an anatomy of love
*(c)* a bitter criticism of human nature
*(d)* a dive into the spiritual world

**584.** Goldsmith died in
*(a)* 1772      *(b)* 1770
*(c)* 1774      *(d)* 1771

**585.** "Beau Tibbs" by Goldsmith is a satire on
*(a)* fops and beaus      *(b)* politicians
*(c)* astrologers      *(d)* social reformers

**586.** When did De Quincey die
*(a)* in 1860      *(b)* in 1862
*(c)* in 1861      *(d)* in 1859

**587.** About whom did Wordsworth write the following line?
"She was a phantom of delight."
*(a)* about Dorothy      *(b)* his beloved
*(c)* his wife      *(d)* Mrs. Coleridge

**588.** Who is one of the persons described in De Quincey's "Wordsworth's Household"
*(a)* Dorothy      *(b)* Mary Shelley
*(c)* Jane Austen      *(d)* Emile Bronte

**589.** Who accompanied Wordsworth when he was alone in the lap of nature?
*(a)* Mrs. Hutchinson      *(b)* Dorothy
*(c)* His children      *(d)* Coleridge

**590.** Who wrote: "The Confessions of An English Opium-Eater"?
*(a)* Coleridge      *(b)* Shelley
*(c)* De Quincey      *(d)* James Joyce

**591.** Charles Lamb was born in
*(a)* 1775      *(b)* 1776
*(c)* 1774      *(d)* 1778

**592.** Who among the following is called the Prince of Essayists?
- (a) Bacon
- (b) Hazlitt
- (c) De Quincey
- (d) Lamb

**593.** In which of his essays does Lamb use the oxymoron "busy-idle" diversions
- (a) All Fools's Day
- (b) Dream Children
- (c) St. Valentine's Day
- (d) Bachelors' Complaint Against the Behaviour of Married People.

**594.** What, according to Lamb, as in his essay " The Convalescent," comprise the mind of a sick man?
- (a) humanism
- (b) rationalism
- (c) complete self-absorption
- (d) philanthropy

**595.** Who focused attention on the metaphysical poets in the 20th century?
- (a) Yeats
- (b) Joyce
- (c) Virginia Woolf
- (d) T.S. Eliot

**596.** Mention the date of Eliot's Hollow Men
- (a) 1922
- (b) 1925
- (c) 1927
- (d) 1921

**597.** Who wrote the poem "Rhapsody on a Windy Day"?
- (a) Yeats
- (b) Spenser
- (c) Eliot
- (d) Housman

**598.** Who wrote the line :
"The weariness, the fever, and the fret"
- (a) Shelley
- (b) Keats
- (c) Southey
- (d) Swinburne

**599.** In which poem does the following poem by Keats occur?
"For ever wilt thou love
and she be fair."
- (a) Ode to a Nightingale
- (b) Hyperion
- (c) Ode to a Grecian Urn
- (d) Ode on Indolence

**600.** Who was Pericles?
- (a) A great French poet
- (b) A German philosopher
- (c) An Italian sonnet-writer
- (d) A great Athenian statesman

**601.** Who wrote : "The Parliament of Foules"
- (a) Chaucer
- (b) Gower
- (c) Langland
- (d) Dunbar

**602.** When did Chaucer die?
- (a) 1401
- (b) 1402
- (c) 1400
- (d) 1399

**603.** Of the following periods, which does not belong to Chaucer?
- (a) The Period of French
- (b) The Period of German
- (c) The Period of Italian
- (d) The English period or The Period of Maturity

**604.** Who wrote : "Epithalamion"?
- (a) Chaucer
- (b) Milton
- (c) Spenser
- (d) Lovelace

**605.** In which of Shakespeare's plays does the following line appear?
"Sigh no more, ladies, sigh no more."
- (a) Midsummer Night's Dream
- (b) Merchant of Venice
- (c) As You Like It
- (d) Much Ado About Nothing

**606.** In which of Dryden's poems does the following line occur :
"Love is that madness which all lovers have."
- (a) Aureng-Zebe
- (b) Absalom and Achitophel
- (c) The Hind and the Panther
- (d) The Conquest of Granada

**607.** Who said, "Pope's poetry exhibits always an equilibrium of many separate forces."
- (a) Dryden
- (b) Johnson
- (c) Tillotson
- (d) Hugh Walter

**608.** When did Spenser die?
- (a) 1592
- (b) 1599
- (c) 1595
- (d) 1600

**609.** When was Milton born?
- (a) 1606
- (b) 1602
- (c) 1608
- (d) 1605

**610.** When did Victoria ascend the throne?
- (a) In 1835
- (b) In 1837
- (c) In 1838
- (d) In 1839

**611.** Queen Victoria's period in literature is generally considered to start from

(a) 1839      (b) 1840
(c) 1845      (d) 1850

**612.** Who wrote :
"How fast has brother followed brother,
From sunshine to the sunless land!"
(a) Wordsworth      (b) Coleridge
(c) Shelley      (d) Yeats

**613.** Who is the writer of:
"Cast a cold eye
on life, on death,
Horseman, pass by!"
(a) Wordsworth      (b) Keats
(c) Shelley      (d) Yeats

**614.** Browning's Pauline was published in
(a) 1832      (b) 1833
(c) 1834      (d) 1835

**615.** 'Sartor Resartus' was written by
(a) Oscar Wilde      (b) Ruskin
(c) Carlyle      (d) Pafer

**616.** When did the French Revolution start?
(a) 1788      (b) 1785
(c) 1787      (d) 1789

**617.** When was slave trade abolished in England?
(a) 1805      (b) 1807
(c) 1806      (d) 1810

**618.** Which of the following writers did not belong to the 18th century?
(a) Cowper      (b) Goldsmith
(c) Burke      (d) Pafer

**619.** Which one of the following poets was not a Victorian poet?
(a) Keats      (b) Swinburne
(c) Browning      (d) Morris

**620.** Name of writer who "tried almost every kind of novel known to the 19th century."
(a) Charlotte Bronte      (b) Emile Bronte
(c) G. Eliot      (d) Bulwer Lytton

**621.** By writing "Truce of the Bear" which country did Kipling offend?
(a) Russia      (b) Germany
(c) America      (d) Canada

**622.** Which of Kipling's poems commemorate England's entrance into the First World War?
(a) Recessional
(b) For All We Have and Are
(c) The Ballad of Red Earl
(d) Ballad of East and West

**623.** When did Kipling receive the Nobel Prize?
(a) In 1905      (b) In 1902
(c) In 1907      (d) In 1904

**624.** Who was the Editor of the Cornhill Magazine?
(a) Thackeray      (b) Coleridge
(c) Hazlitt      (d) Goldsmith

**625.** Which of the following is not the work of Bunyan?
(a) The Holy War
(b) Grace Abounding....
(c) The Life and Death of Mr. Badman
(d) Samson Agonistes

**626.** Shakespeare's use of prose is usually limited to
(a) asides      (b) plays within plays
(c) comic scenes      (d) tragic scenes

**627.** Who said, "If Pope is not the poet, where is poetry to be found?"
(a) Dryden      (b) Dr. Johnson
(c) Addison      (d) Steele

**628.** "Fans" is a humorous essay by
(a) Addison      (b) Sheridan
(c) Lamb      (d) De Quincey

**629.** To commemorate whose death did M. Arnold write "Thyrsis"?
(a) Wordsworth
(b) Dr. Johnson
(c) Tennyson
(d) Arthur Hugh Clough

**630.** In which year was "The Princess" published
(a) 1850      (b) 1847
(c) 1849      (d) 1848

**631.** In which book of "The Task" by Cowper does the following line appear?
"God made the country, and men made the town".
(a) Bk I      (b) Bk II
(c) Bk III      (d) Bk IV

**632.** In which book of "The Task" does the following line appear?
"England, with all thy faults, I love thee still."
(a) Bk I      (b) Bk II
(c) Bk III      (d) Bk IV

**633.** In which drama of Shakespeare does the following line appear?

"Tu-whit, tu-who—a merry note."
(a) Midsummer Night's Dream
(b) Measure for Measure
(c) Love's Labours Lost
(d) As You Like It

**634.** Where is the scene of "The Devil's Disciple" located?
(a) London     (b) Manchester
(c) Wessex     (d) New Hampshire

**635.** Who wrote the following line :
"Much have I travelled in the realms of gold."
(a) Shelley     (b) Wordsworth
(c) Morris     (d) Keats

**636.** Burns' father was a
(a) poor peasant     (b) rich business man
(c) collier     (d) bank official

**637.** Who took Gray abroad?
(a) Blake     (b) Gladstone
(c) Horace Walpole     (d) Wilberforce

**638.** Wilberforce was mainly working for .........in the eighteenth century
(a) prison reforms
(b) the liberation of the slaves
(c) women's emancipation
(d) universal franchise

**639.** Who wrote the lines :
"There is not flesh in man's obdurate heart, It does not feel for man."
(a) Blake     (b) Gray
(c) Cowper     (d) Goldsmith

**640.** Which one of the following was not a part of the general nature of the Anglo-Saxons?
(a) love of personal freedom
(b) love of religion
(c) fondness for lewd way of living
(d) respect for women

**641.** The main aspect of the Anglo-Saxon language was
(a) Vigour     (b) Sweetness
(c) Obscurity     (d) Incoherence

**642.** The first important expression of melody is made in the works of
(a) Langland     (b) Dunbar
(c) Spenser     (d) Chaucer

**643.** Which one among the following could not be described as the 'matter' of early verse romances

(a) Matter of France     (b) Spain
(c) Rome     (d) Britain

**644.** In which year was Armada defeated?
(a) 1585     (b) 1587
(c) 1588     (d) 1590

**645.** When did Bacon die?
(a) 1622     (b) 1626
(c) 1630     (d) 1621

**646.** When was first the Divine Right of Kings proclaimed?
(a) 1605     (b) 1601
(c) 1604     (d) 1608

**647.** Who wrote the Ode , "Come Leave the Loathed Stage."?
(a) Milton     (b) Massinger
(c) Fletcher     (d) Ben Jonson

**648.** How many dramatists were with Ben Jonson in fighting against the romantic tendency?
(a) He was alone     (b) 2
(c) 3     (d) So many

**649.** Which metre has Chaucer used in his Troilus and Criseyde
(a) Iambic pentametre
(b) Rime Royal
(c) Terza Rima
(d) None of these

**650.** Who is the writer of 'Piers Plowman'?
(a) Chaucer     (b) Dunbar
(c) Langland     (d) Wyclif

**651.** Who is the writer of the poem :
The Pied Piper of Hamelin?
(a) Tennyson     (b) M. Arnold
(c) Wordsworth     (d) Browning

**652.** The sculptures on the gateway of the Sanchi Stupa built by Emperor Ashoka in the 3rd century B.C., illustrate, *inter alia,*
(a) Jataka stories
(b) The stories of Aesop
(c) Stories from the Panchtantra
(d) Stories from the Punch

**653.** In which poem of Shelley does the following line occur :
"O antique verse and high romance."
(a) Ode to a Skylark
(b) Epipsychidion

*(c)* Hymn to Intellectual Beauty

*(d)* Hellas

**654.** Who is the writer of the following lines :
"Learn hence for ancient rules a just esteem
To copy Nature is to copy, them."
*(a)* Dryden         *(b)* Ben Jonson
*(c)* M. Arnold       *(d)* Pope

**655.** Who wrote about Vivekananda,
"If you want to know India, study Vivekananda.
In him everything is positive, nothing negative."
*(a)* Gandhi         *(b)* Jawaharlal Nehru
*(c)* Tagore         *(d)* Sarojini Naidu

**656.** When did Swami Vivekananda die?
*(a)* July 2, 1902
*(b)* June 3, 1902
*(c)* July 14, 1902
*(d)* July 04, 1902

**657.** In which year did Vivekananda participate in the Parliament of Religions in Chicago, USA?
*(a)* 1891         *(b)* 1893
*(c)* 1895         *(d)* 1890

**658.** Who wrote : "Science and Life"?
*(a)* Newton       *(b)* Einstein
*(c)* V.C. Ramana    *(d)* J.B.S. Haldane

**659.** Who wrote the following line :
"History is largely a record of self-deception."
*(a)* A.G. Gardiner     *(b)* Lynd
*(c)* J.B. Priestley      *(d)* Lucas

**660.** Who spoke the following words in his defence in the court :
"I believe that only God is really wise, and ...... that man's wisdom is worth little or nothing."
*(a)* Gandhi        *(b)* St. Joan
*(c)* Socrates       *(d)* Oscar Wilde

**661.** In which work does the following sentence appear :
"Philosophy teaches us to feel uncertain about the things that seem to us self-evident."
*(a)* 'Skeptial Essays' by Russell
*(b)* 'An Autobiography' by Jawaharlal Nehru
*(c)* 'My Experiments with Truth' by M.K. Gandhi
*(d)* 'Brave New World Revisited' by Aldous Huxley

**662.** What kind of book is "Three Men In A Boat"?
*(a)* A funny or humorous book
*(b)* A melodramatic book
*(c)* A narrative book
*(d)* An extremely serious work

**663.** Which of the following is not concerned with fun or humour?
*(a)* Irony         *(b)* Pathetic Fallacy
*(c)* Understatement    *(d)* Exaggeration

**664.** In which book do the following words appear :
"...man is a brief episode in the life of a small plant in a little corner of the universe."
*(a)* Emerson's 'Essays'
*(b)* Huxley's 'Music At Night'
*(c)* Russell's 'Unpopular Essay'
*(d)* Gandhi's 'My Experiments with Truth.'

**665.** In which of Shakespeare's play does a character speak the following words:
"If your leisure serv'd,
I would speak with you."
*(a)* The Merchant of Venice
*(b)* Much Ado About Nothing
*(c)* Julius Caesar
*(d)* Cymbeline

**666.** Which kind of life can be best described as led by Dr. Jekyll in R.L. Stevenson's "The Strange case of Dr. Jekyll and Mr. Hyde."
*(a)* a double life     *(b)* a single life
*(c)* a happy life      *(d)* a sad life

**667.** Who was the founder of the system of philosophy known as "Positivism"
*(a)* Goethe        *(b)* Victor Hugo
*(c)* Proust         *(d)* Auguste Comte

**668.** What is meant by "sing-song tone"
*(a)* a happy tone
*(b)* a rash or flourishing tone
*(c)* a boring childish tone
*(d)* None of these

**669.** What is meant by 'jink and muck'?
*(a)* a new dress
*(b)* a colourful thing
*(c)* a dancing toy
*(d)* old thing of little or no value

**670.** Delphi was a place in ancient Greece which was known for the oracle of

    *(a)* Apollo         *(b)* Urania
    *(c)* Venus         *(d)* God Mercury

**671.** Who said the following words :
    "I must set God's command above everything."
    *(a)* Plato         *(b)* Socrates
    *(c)* Christ         *(d)* Gandhi

**672.** What is meant by the expression "Homeric Fight"?
    *(a)* a great fight         *(b)* a foolish fight
    *(c)* a cowardly fight         *(d)* a stylish fight

**673.** Henry Dunant was associated with :
    *(a)* Clearing of mines
    *(b)* Red cross
    *(c)* Anti-smuggling laws
    *(d)* Demonstrations against the use and maintenance of nuclear weapons

**674.** The name of Shelley's wife who committed suicide was
    *(a)* Mary         *(b)* Sophia
    *(c)* Hutchinson         *(d)* Harriet

**675.** The philosopher who influenced Pope was
    *(a)* Bolingbroke         *(b)* Godwin
    *(c)* Nietzsche         *(d)* Kant

**676.** Who is the writer of the book "The Impact of Science on Society"?
    *(a)* Huxley         *(b)* Priestley
    *(c)* B. Russell         *(d)* Gardiner

**677.** Who wrote the following line :
    "What, there's nothing in the moon noteworthy?" (in 'One Word More')
    *(a)* Tennyson         *(b)* Browning
    *(c)* Keats         *(d)* Wordsworth

**678.** Who was Michelangelo?
    *(a)* A physician         *(b)* A painter
    *(c)* A musician         *(d)* A statesman

**679.** Mention which of the following Tagore was not—
    *(a)* school teacher         *(b)* novelist
    *(c)* dramatist         *(d)* painter

**680.** Who is the writer of the following lines as quoted by M. Arnold at the start of his "Thyrsis".
    "Thus yesterday, today, tomorrow come,
    They hustle one another and they pass."
    *(a)* Ovid         *(b)* Lucretius
    *(c)* Pericles         *(d)* Chaucer

**681.** When did Arthur Hugh Clough die?
    *(a)* 1861         *(b)* 1864
    *(c)* 1863         *(d)* 1865

**682.** In which poem of M. Arnold does the following line appear?
    "Where ignorant armies
    clash by night."
    *(a)* Sohrab and Rustam  *(b)* Thyrsis
    *(c)* Dover Beach         *(d)* The Scholar Gipsy

**683.** Who is the writer of the play "The Miracle Merchant"
    *(a)* Tagore         *(b)* Synge
    *(c)* Barrie         *(d)* Saki

**684.** 'The Miracle Merchant" was based on the story
    *(a)* 'The Hen'
    *(b)* Monkey's Paw
    *(c)* Dusk
    *(d)* The Open Window

**685.** The essay "An Apology for Idlers" is written by
    *(a)* Russell         *(b)* Huxley
    *(c)* R.L. Stevenson         *(d)* Goldsmith

**686.** Who is the writer of the following line in his introduction to a book on social history :
    "And Reality, if rightly interpreted is grander than Fiction."
    *(a)* Macaulay         *(b)* Trevelyan
    *(c)* Legouis         *(d)* Crompton

**687.** Who used the term "Dry as dust" for the antiquarian or historical researcher?
    *(a)* Trevelyan         *(b)* Macaulay
    *(c)* Carlyle         *(d)* Legouis

**688.** Who among Chaucer's characters spoke the following lines :
    "Wold the see were kept for anything
    Betwixt Middleburgh and Orewell
    *(a)* Knight         *(b)* Squire
    *(c)* Nun         *(d)* Merchant

**689.** Under what category, should Langland's 'The Piers Plowman' be placed
    *(a)* Romance
    *(b)* Pastoral
    *(c)* Religious allegory
    *(d)* Supernatural poetry

**690.** In which work do the following lines appear :
    "Labourers that have no land to live on but their hands

Deigned not dine a day on worts a night old."
*(a)* Piers Plowman
*(b)* Prologue to the Canterbury Tales
*(c)* Faerie Queene
*(d)* Song to the Men of England

**691.** Wat Tyler was slain at......... in the presence of the mob be led
*(a)* London      *(b)* Manchester
*(c)* Smithield      *(d)* None of these

**692.** About which character does Chaucer say the following words :
"It snowed in his house of meat and drinke ofalle dainties that men could think."
*(a)* Merchant      *(b)* Franklin
*(c)* Knight      *(d)* Parson

**693.** By whom was Christ's Hospital founded?
*(a)* Edward II      *(b)* Henry II
*(c)* Edward VI      *(d)* Henry V

**694.** Kett's rising in Norfolk in 1549 was a
*(a)* Peasants' rising
*(b)* Factory workers' rebellion
*(c)* Barons' rebellion against the king
*(d)* Priests' uprising

**695.** Who is the writer of "Angler"
*(a)* Blake      *(b)* Cowper
*(c)* Izaak Walton      *(d)* Goldsmith

**696.** Name the writer of the book "Illusion and Reality"
*(a)* Christopher Caudwell
*(b)* Ruskin
*(c)* Carlyle
*(d)* Oscar Wilde

**697.** When did George II die?
*(a)* 1780      *(b)* 1760
*(c)* 1762      *(d)* 1765

**698.** George IV reigned from
*(a)* 1820-30      *(b)* 1820-25
*(c)* 1820-33      *(d)* 1820-35

**699.** Who wrote: 'Wealth of Nations'
*(a)* Malthus      *(b)* Marx
*(c)* Engels      *(d)* Adam Smith

**700.** Dr. Chalmers was associated with
*(a)* Evangelical revival
*(b)* Peasants' revolt
*(c)* Adult Franchise movement
*(d)* Restoration of monarchy

**701.** In which play of Shakespeare there exists "The Forest of Arden"
*(a)* Winter's Tale
*(b)* Merry Wives of Windsor
*(c)* Tempest
*(d)* As You Like It

**702.** What is the other name for Euphues
*(a)* The Anatomy of Melancholy
*(b)* The Anatomy of Wit
*(c)* The Anatomy of Wisdom
*(d)* The Anatomy of Joy

**703.** Heathcliff is the most important character in the novel
*(a)* Jane Eyre      *(b)* Hard Times
*(c)* Wuthering Heights      *(d)* Vanity Fair

**704.** 'Wuthering Heights' is the name of a farm owned by
*(a)* Earnshaws      *(b)* Lintons
*(c)* Bennets      *(d)* Georges

**705.** How many knights enter the cathedral to kill St. Thomas in 'Murder in the Cathedral.'
*(a)* Three      *(b)* Four
*(c)* Five      *(d)* Six

**706.** Which country could most probably stand for Samuel Butler's Erewhon which otherwise means nowhere?
*(a)* Australia      *(b)* West Indies
*(c)* Bahamas      *(d)* New Zealand

**707.** In which novel of Hardy does the character 'Arabella' exist?
*(a)* Jude the Obscure
*(b)* The Return of the Native
*(c)* Tess
*(d)* Far From the Madding Crowd

**708.** Most of Hardy's novels are
*(a)* Comedies      *(b)* Histories
*(c)* Tragedies      *(d)* Romances

**709.** What hastened Mr. Tulliver's death in "The Mill on the Floss".
*(a)* His terminal illness
*(b)* His uncordial relations with Tom
*(c)* His bankruptcy
*(d)* His fall from the horse

**710.** 'Rawdon Crawley' is a character in
*(a)* The Mayor of Casterbridge
*(b)* Vanity Fair

*(c)* Erewhon

*(d)* Don Quixote

**711.** In which poem do the following lines occur :
"Before the beginning of years
There came to the making of man
Time, with a gift of tears."
*(a)* Hellas
*(b)* Ode to Melancholy
*(c)* Dunciad
*(d)* Atlanta and Calydon

**712.** How many lines does each stanza of the "Scholar Gipsy" consist of
*(a)* Eight      *(b)* Six
*(c)* Ten      *(d)* Nine

**713.** Milton wrote 'Paradise Lost' mainly to
*(a)* justify ways of God to man
*(b)* justify ways of man to God
*(c)* get himself established as a great poet
*(d)* subtly reject the life in Charles II's court

**714.** The Rubaiyat of Omar Khayyam (English translation) is written in
*(a)* Six line stanzas
*(b)* Quatrains
*(c)* Couplets
*(d)* Three line stanzas

**715.** 'Maud' is a poem by
*(a)* Tennyson      *(b)* Shelley
*(c)* Keats      *(d)* Swinburne

**716.** In which poem does the following lyric in blank verse appear :
"Come down, O maid."
*(a)* Maud
*(b)* The Princess
*(c)* In Memoriam
*(d)* Sohrab and Rustam

**717.** What is the rhyme scheme of "In Memoriam"
*(a)* a b b a      *(b)* a b a b
*(c)* a a b b      *(d)* a b b b

**718.** Who satirised Wordsworth's poetic diction in the following lines :
"Who both by precept and example, shows
That prose is verse, and verse is merely prose."
*(a)* Tennyson      *(b)* Arnold
*(c)* Byron      *(d)* Eliot

**719.** Who is the writer of the following :

"Let me not to the marriage of true minds
Admit impediments..."
*(a)* Milton      *(b)* Spenser
*(c)* Sidney      *(d)* Shakespeare

**720.** Who wrote :
"Oh east is east and west is west,
And never the twain shall meet."
*(a)* Tennyson      *(b)* Robert Bridges
*(c)* Kipling      *(d)* Eliot

**721.** Who wrote : "English Bards and Scotch Reviewers"
*(a)* Burns      *(b)* Byron
*(c)* Scott      *(d)* Yeats

**722.** Who is the writer of the tragedy "Prometheus Bound."
*(a)* Shelley      *(b)* Aeschylus
*(c)* Sophocles      *(d)* Euripides

**723.** How many poems did Wordsworth contribute to Lyrical Ballads :
*(a)* 16      *(b)* 17
*(c)* 18      *(d)* 19

**724.** Samuel Gulliver in Gulliver's Travels is a
*(a)* merchant      *(b)* sailor
*(c)* surgeon      *(d)* carpenter

**725.** How many imaginary countries does Gulliver visit
*(a)* Three      *(b)* Four
*(c)* Five      *(d)* Six

**726.** Who is the writer of "Leviathan"
*(a)* Rousseau      *(b)* Locke
*(c)* Adam Smith      *(d)* Hobbes

**727.** Robinson Crusoe was published
*(a)* 1718      *(b)* 1717
*(c)* 1719      *(d)* 1720

**728.** In the Dunciad, Pope has satirised
*(a)* fallen literary standards
*(b)* the contemporary political scenario
*(c)* the ancient literary standards
*(d)* the miserable economic scene

**729.** "The Rape of the Lock" is a ........ poem
*(a)* mock-heroic
*(b)* tragedy
*(c)* comedy
*(d)* dramatic monologue

**730.** The following lines occur in
"........ in Logic a great critic,

Profoundly skill'd in Analytic;
He could, distinguish and divide
A hair twixt south and south-west side."
*(a)* Macflecknoe
*(b)* Deserted Village
*(c)* Hudibras
*(d)* The Rape of the Lock

**731.** In which country was TS Eliot born :
*(a)* England          *(b)* USA
*(c)* Germany          *(d)* Scotland

**732.** The 'Forsyte Saga' was written by
*(a)* Shaw          *(b)* H.G. Wells
*(c)* Galsworthy          *(d)* Eliot

**733.** Arnold Bennet died in
*(a)* 1930          *(b)* 1931
*(c)* 1933          *(d)* 1932

**734.** Who is the writer of the comedy 'The Wild Gallant'
*(a)* Dryden          *(b)* Pope
*(c)* Shakespeare          *(d)* Lyly

**735.** When was Crashaw born
*(a)* 1610          *(b)* 1615
*(c)* 1617          *(d)* 1612

**736.** Who wrote the following line :
"Death, thou wast once an uncouth hideous thing."
*(a)* Donne          *(b)* Herbert
*(c)* Crashaw          *(d)* Lovelace

**737.** Robert Herrick died in
*(a)* 1670          *(b)* 1672
*(c)* 1674          *(d)* 1679

**738.** Thomas Carew died in
*(a)* 1636          *(b)* 1637
*(c)* 1638          *(d)* 1639

**739.** Hobbes can be regarded as a precursor and pioneer of modern
*(a)* poetry          *(b)* prose
*(c)* drama          *(d)* fiction

**740.** Which of the following is not a comic character
*(a)* Justice Shallow          *(b)* Othello
*(c)* Juliet's nurse          *(d)* Falstaff

**741.** To whom can "courtly wit" be ascribed :
*(a)* Lyly          *(b)* Ford
*(c)* Heyword          *(d)* Dekker

**742.** Who is the writer of the comedy "A New Way To Pay Old Debts."
*(a)* Webster          *(b)* Massinger
*(c)* Lyly          *(d)* Jonson

**743.** In one of whose works does the character 'Sir Epicure Mammon' exist
*(a)* Jonson          *(b)* Massinger
*(c)* Ford          *(d)* Fletcher

**744.** Who is now said to have collaborated with Fletcher in writing the following plays :
The False one, The Spanish Curate,
The Beggar's Bush, etc.
*(a)* Jonson          *(b)* Field
*(c)* Massinger          *(d)* Rowley

**745.** 'The Woman-Hater' is a mock-heroic comedy by
*(a)* Fletcher          *(b)* Beaumont
*(c)* Ford          *(d)* Massinger

**746.** 'Four Prentices of London' is written by
*(a)* Ford          *(b)* Massinger
*(c)* Heywood          *(d)* Fletcher

**747.** In Epicoene, Jonson's chief aim is
*(a)* to moralise
*(b)* to please the public
*(c)* to satirize old customs
*(d)* to catharsise the element of fear

**748.** In 'The Poetaster' Jonson presents one of the following as a bad poet
*(a)* Aristophanes          *(b)* Fletcher
*(c)* Martson          *(d)* Dryden

**749.** Who is the writer of the following lines :
"I'll strip the ragged follies of the time,
Naked as at their birth."
*(a)* Jonson          *(b)* Fletcher
*(c)* Dryden          *(d)* Shelley

**750.** Constantinople fell to the Turks in
*(a)* 1450          *(b)* 1453
*(c)* 1456          *(d)* 1459

**751.** In whose Ashram did Shakuntala live?
*(a)* Kanva          *(b)* Vashisht
*(c)* Indra          *(d)* Durvasa

**752.** The name of the king who came to the ashram where Shakuntala lived was
*(a)* Porus          *(b)* Arjuna
*(c)* Dushyanta          *(d)* Nala

**753.** Meghdoot was written by
*(a)* Bharitrihari          *(b)* Valmiki
*(c)* Patanjali          *(d)* Kalidas

**754.** Who is the writer of the following sentence:
"I think one of the reasons why I stopped writing novels is that the social aspect of the world changed so much."
*(a)* Tagore  *(b)* Forster
*(c)* Joyce  *(d)* Henry James

**755.** Who wrote the following:
"Agriculture is not one industry among many, but is a way of life."
*(a)* Macaulay  *(b)* Jawaharlal Nehru
*(c)* Trevelyan  *(d)* Birla

**756.** From which year is the modern period of English literature generally accepted to have started.
*(a)* 1897  *(b)* 1899
*(c)* 1901  *(d)* 1900

**757.** Who wrote the following sentence :
"It was in 1915 the old world ended."
*(a)* Forster  *(b)* Huxley
*(c)* Lawrence  *(d)* Russell

**758.** When did G.K. Chesterton die?
*(a)* 1932  *(b)* 1934
*(c)* 1936  *(d)* 1938

**759.** Who wrote 'The Second World War' (in six volumes)
*(a)* Stalin  *(b)* Trevelyan
*(c)* Lenin  *(d)* Winston Churchill

**760.** In which year was I.A. Richard's "The Meaning of Meaning" published
*(a)* 1930  *(b)* 1921
*(c)* 1923  *(d)* 1927

**761.** When did J.M. Barrie die?
*(a)* 1935  *(b)* 1939
*(c)* 1938  *(d)* 1937

**762.** When did Sean O'Casey die?
*(a)* 1961  *(b)* 1964
*(c)* 1971  *(d)* 1960

**763.** When did John Osborne die?
*(a)* 1981  *(b)* 1991
*(c)* 1994  *(d)* 1996

**764.** Who among the following may be described as a naturalist?
*(a)* Shaw  *(b)* Aldous Huxley
*(c)* Noel Coward  *(d)* None of these

**765.** Who among the following is a model more of Juvenalian rather than Horatian satire?

*(a)* Swift  *(b)* Addison
*(c)* Steele  *(d)* Goldsmith

**766.** Comedy of Manners flourished in the .......... period
*(a)* Elizabethan  *(b)* Restoration
*(c)* Victorian  *(d)* Romantic

**767.** Which of the following is not a fictional satirist?
*(a)* Mark Twain  *(b)* Rabelais
*(c)* Lamb  *(d)* Cervantes

**768.** "Sestina" is
*(a)* the other name for a sonnet
*(b)* a complex French lyrical form
*(c)* the old English word 'seista'
*(d)* None of these

**769.** What is meant by "Envoy" in context with 'sestina'
*(a)* A message
*(b)* The first three lines
*(c)* The last three lines
*(d)* The first quatrain

**770.** What is the correct chronological sequence in the following :
*(a)* Alastor—Lycidas—Epithalamion—Lucy Gray
*(b)* Epithalamion—Alastor—Lucy Gray—Lycidas
*(c)* Lucy Gray—Epithalamion—Lycidas—Alastor
*(d)* Epithalamion—Lycidas—Lucy Gray—Alastor

**771.** Point out the correct chronological sequence
*(a)* Maud—Shakespeare—To Autumn—Christabel
*(b)* Christabel—To Autumn—Maud—Shakespeare
*(c)* To Autumn—Maud—Christabel—Shakespeare
*(d)* Shakespeare—Maud—Christabel—To Autumn

**772.** When did Coleridge die?
*(a)* 1836  *(b)* 1837
*(c)* 1834  *(d)* 1841

**773.** In which of the following poems of Chaucer do the following lines occur?
"O hateful harm! condicion of poverte!

With thrust, with cold, with hunger so confounded."
(a) The Prologe of the Mannes Tale of Lawe
(b) Prologue to the Canterbury Tales
(c) The Pardoner's Tale
(d) The Nonne Preeste's Tale

774. Spenser wooed Elizabeth Boyle (whom he later married) in his
(a) Faerie Queene        (b) Amoretti
(c) Epithalamion        (d) None of these

775. In his command of metaphor, Shakespeare
(a) has his peer in Milton
(b) has so many peers
(c) is alone
(d) cannot excel Yeats

776. In which book of Paradise Lost does Milton say—"God is light"
(a) Bk I        (b) Bk II
(c) Bk III        (d) Bk VII

777. In which book of Paradise Lost does the following line occur :
"A Paradise within thee, happier far."
(a) Bk I        (b) Bk II
(c) Bk VII        (d) Bk XII

778. In which book of Milton does the following line occur :
"All is best, though we oft doubt."
(a) Paradise Lost        (b) Samson Agonistes
(c) Comus        (d) L'Allegro

779. Goldsmith's 'The Traveller' was published in
(a) 1761        (b) 1767
(c) 1763        (d) 1764

780. Who said the following words about Goldsmith:
"One of the first men we now have as an author."
(a) Jonson        (b) Johnson
(c) Addison        (d) Stevenson

781. Dr. Primrose is a character in
(a) Vanity Fair
(b) David Copperfield
(c) The Vicar of Wakefield
(d) The Mill on the Floss

782. Who is the writer of "Ode To Duty"
(a) Shelley        (b) Plato
(c) Wordsworth        (d) Byron

783. Who wrote: "The Retreat"

(a) Wordsworth        (b) George Herbert
(c) Herrick        (d) Vaughan

784. 'The Cloister and the Hearth" is a masterpiece by
(a) Trollope        (b) Charles Reade
(c) Bulwer Lytton        (d) Kingsley

785. Charlotte Bronte died in
(a) 1855        (b) 1857
(c) 1851        (d) 1853

786. Burton's Anatomy of Melancholy appeared in
(a) 1620        (b) 1621
(c) 1623        (d) 1622

787. The first regular newspaper "The Weekly News" appeared in
(a) 1621        (b) 1623
(c) 1622        (d) 1627

788. Bacon died in
(a) 1625        (b) 1626
(c) 1627        (d) 1628

789. About whom can it be most appropriately said, "a man of grief who makes the world glad"
(a) Wordsworth        (b) Tennyson
(c) Shakespeare        (d) Coleridge

790. What is the name of the hero in Shaw's 'The Devil's Disciple'
(a) Burgoyne        (b) The Clergyman
(c) Dick        (d) None of these

791. Who is the writer of "Waiting"
(a) Yeats        (b) Katharine Tynan
(c) Synge        (d) Barrie

792. Who is the writer of Novun Organum
(a) Bacon        (b) Lamb
(c) Montaigne        (d) Stevenson

793. Who said: "the world owes some of its greatest debts to man from whose memory the world recoils."
(a) Socrates        (b) Stubb
(c) Pope        (d) Shakespeare

794. Who is the writer of the lines :
"And as for me, though that my wit be lytë,
On bookës for to rede I am delytë."
(a) Chaucer        (b) Langland
(c) Gower        (d) Dunbar

795. In which play of Shakespeare do the following lines appear :

"On, on, you noblest English,
Follow your spirit."
(a) Henry IV      (b) Julius Caesar
(c) Hamlet      (d) Henry V

**796.** The complete cycle of early Miracle play of England was presented every year beginning on
(a) Corpus Christi day   (b) Christmas day
(c) Good Friday      (d) Easter day

**797.** Which of the following is not one of the known cycles of the Miracle play in England?
(a) Chester cycle      (b) Manchester cycle
(c) York cycle      (d) Wakefield

**798.** King Charles I ascended the throne in
(a) 1622      (b) 1625
(c) 1627      (d) 1621

**799.** Literary tastes of King James I were
(a) enlightened      (b) average
(c) mean      (d) uncertain

**800.** Who ruled over England from 1649-60
(a) James I      (b) Charles I
(c) Olive Cromwell      (d) James II

**801.** Which of the following was not the one who carried forward the tradition of Donne
(a) Vaughan      (b) Marvell
(c) Crashaw      (d) Swinburne

**802.** Which one among the following was not a Cavalier
(a) Herrick      (b) Lovelace
(c) Donne      (d) Suckling

**803.** Who wrote 'Cooper's Hill'
(a) Suckling      (b) John Denham
(c) Marvell      (d) Cowley

**804.** Name the writer of "Pindarique Odes"
(a) Cowley      (b) Wordsworth
(c) Shelley      (d) Keats

**805.** Who believed in the hedonist philosophy of 'eat, drink and be merry'
(a) Metaphysical poets   (b) Puritans
(c) Cavaliers      (d) Romantics

**806.** Name the writer of "Life of Cowley"
(a) Dr. Johnson      (b) Boswell
(c) Dryden      (d) Herbert

**807.** Marvell's love poem "To His Coy Mistress" is written in the ........... tradition.

(a) metaphysical      (b) romantic
(c) Elizabethan      (d) Chaucerian

**808.** Who among the following formed prominently part of a Cambridge community of poets known as "the sons of Ben Jonson"
(a) Herrick      (b) Herbert
(c) Vaughan      (d) Dryden

**809.** Which one among the following should be considered a heroic play rather than a comedy
(a) Dryden's 'All for Love'
(b) Wycherley's 'The Country Wife'
(c) Farquhar's 'The Beaux Stratagem'
(d) Congreve's 'The Way of the World'

**810.** Which poet among the following may be said to be belonging to the Caroline period
(a) Dryden      (b) Pope
(c) Donne      (d) Tennyson

**811.** Which one among the following is prominently a satire
(a) Hudibras
(b) Otway's Venice Preserv'd
(c) Pilgrim's Progress
(d) The Country Wife

**812.** Who among the following cannot be said to treat poetry with fashionable irresponsibility?
(a) Earl of Rochester   (b) Dryden
(c) Sir Charles Sedley   (d) Earl of Dorset

**813.** Name the writer of "Humphry Clinker"
(a) Sterne      (b) Smollet
(c) Richardson      (d) Trollope

**814.** William Collins was born in
(a) 1722      (b) 1724
(c) 1721      (d) 1723

**815.** Boswell died in
(a) 1795      (b) 1791
(c) 1794      (d) 1793

**816.** Thomas Paine wrote "Rights of Man"
(a) in reply to Burke's Reflections on the French Revolution
(b) to express his personal views
(c) to elaborate the views of Rousseau
(d) as a reply to Godwin's 'Political Justice'

**817.** According to the French poet Baudelaire, romanticism was situated in
(a) mode of feelings   (b) choice of subjects
(c) exact truth      (d) None of these

**818.** Who said: "the essence of romantic art is that in it the spirit counts far more than the form"
*(a)* Hugh Walker      *(b)* Grierson
*(c)* I.A. Richards      *(d)* Abererombie

**819.** Which one of the following Lamb loved
*(a)* new books      *(b)* new faces
*(c)* new years      *(d)* old books

**820.** In which of Lamb's essay do the following sentences occur :
"Is the world all from up?
Is childhood dead?"
*(a)* Old Benchers of the Inner Temple
*(b)* New Yrars Eve
*(c)* Imperfect Sympathies
*(d)* All Fools' Day

**821.** Of which play of Shakespeare Desdemona is the heroine
*(a)* Othello
*(b)* Macbeth
*(c)* King Lear
*(d)* Antony and Cleopatra

**822.** Napoleon was defeated finally in the Battle of Waterloo in
*(a)* 1805      *(b)* 1815
*(c)* 1830      *(d)* 1810

**823.** Swift's Yahoos are creatures of
*(a)* reason
*(b)* impulse
*(c)* high ideals
*(d)* acute analytical minds

**824.** Who wrote the following lines :
"Bliss was it in that dawn to be alive,
But to be young was very heaven."
*(a)* Wordsworth      *(b)* Shelley
*(c)* Byron      *(d)* Coleridge

**825.** In which canto of Childe Harold's Pilgrimage does the following line occur :
"There is a pleasure in the pathless woods"
*(a)* I      *(b)* II
*(c)* III      *(d)* IV

**826.** In which poem does the following line occur:
"Thou wast not born for death, immortal bird"
*(a)* Ode To a Skylark
*(b)* To the Cuckoo
*(c)* Ode To a Nightingale
*(d)* None of these

**827.** In which year was "The Origin of Species" published?
*(a)* 1859      *(b)* 1861
*(c)* 1862      *(d)* 1857

**828.** Who was the most representative poet of the Victorian age
*(a)* Browning      *(b)* Tennyson
*(c)* Arnold      *(d)* Robert Bridges

**829.** In which work do two sisters Laura and Lizzy exist
*(a)* Goblin Market
*(b)* David Copperfield
*(c)* Thyrsis
*(d)* The Prince's Progress

**830.** Which of the following works is not by Mrs. Gaskell
*(a)* Cranford      *(b)* Ruth
*(c)* Hypatia      *(d)* North and South

**831.** Who wrote : "Westward Ho!"
*(a)* Kingsley      *(b)* Mrs. Gaskell
*(c)* Thackeray      *(d)* Hemingway

**832.** Which one among the following was Dickens' first work
*(a)* The Pickwick Papers
*(b)* Sketches by Boz
*(c)* Oliver Twist
*(d)* Nicholas Nickleby

**833.** Which is the correct chronological sequence
*(a)* The Happy Prince—The Newcomer—Michael—Adam Bede
*(b)* Adam Bede—The Newcomer—Michael—The Happy Prince
*(c)* Michael—The Newcomer—Adam Bede—The Happy Prince
*(d)* The Newcomer—Adam Bede—The Happy Prince—Michael

**834.** Who is the writer of "Vox Clamantis"
*(a)* Chaucer      *(b)* Langland
*(c)* Wyclif      *(d)* Gower

**835.** Gower was a contemporary of
*(a)* Chaucer      *(b)* Spenser
*(c)* Donne      *(d)* Dryden

**836.** Theophrastus was a ............ writer
*(a)* Greek      *(b)* Roman
*(c)* Latin      *(d)* German

**837.** La Bruy'ere was a ............ writer

(a) Greek     (b) Latin
(c) French     (d) Roman

**838.** Who wrote 'The Sound and the Fury"
(a) Saul Bellow     (b) Hemingway
(c) Flaubert     (d) Faulkner

**839.** Who wrote the character of 'Charles II'
(a) Halifax     (b) Overbury
(c) Hall     (d) None of these

**840.** In writing the characters of Virtues and Vices, Hall was influenced by
(a) Aristophanes     (b) Theophrastus
(c) Euripides     (d) Sophocles

**841.** A play which is usually written to be read rather than acted or performed is called a
(a) closet drama     (b) melodrama
(c) comic play     (d) an interlude

**842.** A pause in a line of verse necessary for the natural rhythm of the language is known as
(a) an acrostic     (b) an allusion
(c) an assonance     (d) a caesura

**843.** Copernicus brought about a revolution in the field of
(a) astronomy     (b) astrology
(c) literature     (d) science

**844.** Who among the following was not a university wit
(a) Marlowe     (b) Lodge
(c) Shakespeare     (d) Greene

**845.** In literature the term "Purism" *inter alia* means
(a) exclusion of dance from drama
(b) exclusion of music from drama
(c) maintenance of absolute standards of correctness in writing
(d) rejection of all kinds of immorality

**846.** In which play of Shakespeare, does the following line appear :
"Doomsday is near; die all, merrily"
(a) Henry V     (b) Cymbeline
(c) Tempest     (d) Henry IV, Part I

**847.** Who speaks the following words in Eliot's Murder in the Cathedral :
"We are not here to triumph by fighting....
...We have only to conquer
Now, by suffering."
(a) Thomas Becket
(b) Ist Knight
(c) IInd Knight
(d) 3rd Knight

**848.** Who is the writer of "Frogs"
(a) Aeschylus     (b) Aristophanes
(c) Euripides     (d) Plato

**849.** Which of the following is not the internal element of tragedy as enunciated by Aristotle
(a) Plot     (b) Character
(c) Thought     (d) Diction

**850.** Which is the only kind of poetry that Plato allows in his Republic
(a) that in the form of hymn to the gods and praises of famous men
(b) epic
(c) lyrical
(d) dramatic

---

## ANSWERS

| 1 | 2 | 3 | 4 | 5 | 6 | 7 | 8 | 9 | 10 |
|---|---|---|---|---|---|---|---|---|---|
| (c) | (a) | (d) | (c) | (b) | (c) | (d) | (c) | (b) | (d) |
| **11** | **12** | **13** | **14** | **15** | **16** | **17** | **18** | **19** | **20** |
| (a) | (c) | (b) | (d) | (b) | (c) | (a) | (c) | (a) | (d) |
| **21** | **22** | **23** | **24** | **25** | **26** | **27** | **28** | **29** | **30** |
| (b) | (c) | (a) | (c) | (a) | (a) | (b) | (a) | (b) | (a) |
| **31** | **32** | **33** | **34** | **35** | **36** | **37** | **38** | **39** | **40** |
| (b) | (a) | (b) | (c) | (b) | (a) | (c) | (c) | (c) | (c) |

| 41 | 42 | 43 | 44 | 45 | 46 | 47 | 48 | 49 | 50 |
|----|----|----|----|----|----|----|----|----|----|
| (d) | (d) | (d) | (a) | (b) | (c) | (c) | (b) | (a) | (c) |
| 51 | 52 | 53 | 54 | 55 | 56 | 57 | 58 | 59 | 60 |
| (a) | (d) | (c) | (c) | (c) | (d) | (b) | (a) | (d) | (b) |
| 61 | 62 | 63 | 64 | 65 | 66 | 67 | 68 | 69 | 70 |
| (a) | (b) | (c) | (c) | (d) | (a) | (b) | (c) | (b) | (a) |
| 71 | 72 | 73 | 74 | 75 | 76 | 77 | 78 | 79 | 80 |
| (b) | (c) | (a) | (d) | (c) | (c) | (a) | (c) | (b) | (b) |
| 81 | 82 | 83 | 84 | 85 | 86 | 87 | 88 | 89 | 90 |
| (c) | (b) | (a) | (b) | (c) | (c) | (b) | (d) | (c) | (b) |
| 91 | 92 | 93 | 94 | 95 | 96 | 97 | 98 | 99 | 100 |
| (c) | (c) | (d) | (d) | (b) | (c) | (d) | (c) | (b) | (a) |
| 101 | 102 | 103 | 104 | 105 | 106 | 107 | 108 | 109 | 110 |
| (d) | (c) | (b) | (a) | (d) | (c) | (c) | (c) | (d) | (c) |
| 111 | 112 | 113 | 114 | 115 | 116 | 117 | 118 | 119 | 120 |
| (a) | (d) | (d) | (c) | (c) | (a) | (c) | (d) | (a) | (b) |
| 121 | 122 | 123 | 124 | 125 | 126 | 127 | 128 | 129 | 130 |
| (c) | (a) | (d) | (b) | (c) | (d) | (b) | (d) | (b) | (b) |
| 131 | 132 | 133 | 134 | 135 | 136 | 137 | 138 | 139 | 140 |
| (c) | (c) | (c) | (d) | (d) | (b) | (d) | (c) | (d) | (b) |
| 141 | 142 | 143 | 144 | 145 | 146 | 147 | 148 | 149 | 150 |
| (c) | (c) | (a) | (c) | (d) | (b) | (a) | (c) | (d) | (c) |
| 151 | 152 | 153 | 154 | 155 | 156 | 157 | 158 | 159 | 160 |
| (d) | (b) | (c) | (c) | (a) | (b) | (b) | (c) | (b) | (a) |
| 161 | 162 | 163 | 164 | 165 | 166 | 167 | 168 | 169 | 170 |
| (b) | (c) | (a) | (b) | (b) | (a) | (c) | (c) | (d) | (a) |
| 171 | 172 | 173 | 174 | 175 | 176 | 177 | 178 | 179 | 180 |
| (c) | (d) | (c) | (d) | (a) | (b) | (a) | (b) | (c) | (a) |
| 181 | 182 | 183 | 184 | 185 | 186 | 187 | 188 | 189 | 190 |
| (c) | (b) | (d) | (c) | (a) | (c) | (d) | (b) | (a) | (c) |
| 191 | 192 | 193 | 194 | 195 | 196 | 197 | 198 | 199 | 200 |
| (b) | (a) | (d) | (d) | (d) | (b) | (a) | (a) | (b) | (c) |
| 201 | 202 | 203 | 204 | 205 | 206 | 207 | 208 | 209 | 210 |
| (d) | (c) | (a) | (b) | (c) | (a) | (c) | (b) | (b) | (a) |
| 211 | 212 | 213 | 214 | 215 | 216 | 217 | 218 | 219 | 220 |
| (c) | (c) | (d) | (a) | (b) | (c) | (b) | (d) | (d) | (b) |
| 221 | 222 | 223 | 224 | 225 | 226 | 227 | 228 | 229 | 230 |
| (b) | (c) | (d) | (b) | (c) | (d) | (c) | (d) | (c) | (a) |
| 231 | 232 | 233 | 234 | 235 | 236 | 237 | 238 | 239 | 240 |
| (b) | (b) | (d) | (c) | (b) | (a) | (d) | (c) | (a) | (c) |
| 241 | 242 | 243 | 244 | 245 | 246 | 247 | 248 | 249 | 250 |
| (a) | (b) | (c) | (b) | (a) | (d) | (b) | (d) | (c) | (b) |

| | | | | | | | | | |
|---|---|---|---|---|---|---|---|---|---|
| 251 | 252 | 253 | 254 | 255 | 256 | 257 | 258 | 259 | 260 |
| (b) | (c) | (c) | (d) | (c) | (a) | (d) | (c) | (b) | (d) |
| 261 | 262 | 263 | 264 | 265 | 266 | 267 | 268 | 269 | 270 |
| (a) | (d) | (c) | (b) | (c) | (d) | (c) | (a) | (d) | (b) |
| 271 | 272 | 273 | 274 | 275 | 276 | 277 | 278 | 279 | 280 |
| (a) | (d) | (c) | (d) | (d) | (a) | (b) | (c) | (b) | (c) |
| 281 | 282 | 283 | 284 | 285 | 286 | 287 | 288 | 289 | 290 |
| (b) | (a) | (d) | (b) | (b) | (a) | (b) | (b) | (c) | (b) |
| 291 | 292 | 293 | 294 | 295 | 296 | 297 | 298 | 299 | 300 |
| (d) | (c) | (a) | (d) | (b) | (d) | (a) | (a) | (c) | (b) |
| 301 | 302 | 303 | 304 | 305 | 306 | 307 | 308 | 309 | 310 |
| (d) | (c) | (a) | (b) | (c) | (a) | (c) | (b) | (a) | (b) |
| 311 | 312 | 313 | 314 | 315 | 316 | 317 | 318 | 319 | 320 |
| (b) | (b) | (c) | (b) | (c) | (a) | (b) | (c) | (b) | (d) |
| 321 | 322 | 323 | 324 | 325 | 326 | 327 | 328 | 329 | 330 |
| (c) | (a) | (c) | (a) | (c) | (b) | (a) | (d) | (c) | (b) |
| 331 | 332 | 333 | 334 | 335 | 336 | 337 | 338 | 339 | 340 |
| (b) | (c) | (a) | (c) | (a) | (b) | (a) | (d) | (c) | (b) |
| 341 | 342 | 343 | 344 | 345 | 346 | 347 | 348 | 349 | 350 |
| (c) | (a) | (b) | (d) | (d) | (c) | (b) | (d) | (b) | (d) |
| 351 | 352 | 353 | 354 | 355 | 356 | 357 | 358 | 359 | 360 |
| (c) | (a) | (c) | (b) | (c) | (b) | (c) | (c) | (d) | (b) |
| 361 | 362 | 363 | 364 | 365 | 366 | 367 | 368 | 369 | 370 |
| (c) | (d) | (b) | (c) | (a) | (c) | (b) | (d) | (c) | (b) |
| 371 | 372 | 373 | 374 | 375 | 376 | 377 | 378 | 379 | 380 |
| (c) | (c) | (b) | (c) | (d) | (b) | (c) | (d) | (b) | (c) |
| 381 | 382 | 383 | 384 | 385 | 386 | 387 | 388 | 389 | 390 |
| (d) | (a) | (c) | (d) | (c) | (a) | (c) | (a) | (c) | (d) |
| 391 | 392 | 393 | 394 | 395 | 396 | 397 | 398 | 399 | 400 |
| (a) | (c) | (d) | (c) | (a) | (b) | (b) | (a) | (d) | (c) |
| 401 | 402 | 403 | 404 | 405 | 406 | 407 | 408 | 409 | 410 |
| (c) | (b) | (c) | (a) | (d) | (c) | (a) | (c) | (d) | (b) |
| 411 | 412 | 413 | 414 | 415 | 416 | 417 | 418 | 419 | 420 |
| (a) | (b) | (d) | (d) | (c) | (a) | (d) | (a) | (c) | (c) |
| 421 | 422 | 423 | 424 | 425 | 426 | 427 | 428 | 429 | 430 |
| (a) | (d) | (b) | (d) | (a) | (d) | (a) | (b) | (d) | (c) |
| 431 | 432 | 433 | 434 | 435 | 436 | 437 | 438 | 439 | 440 |
| (d) | (b) | (b) | (c) | (c) | (a) | (d) | (c) | (b) | (c) |
| 441 | 442 | 443 | 444 | 445 | 446 | 447 | 448 | 449 | 450 |
| (a) | (c) | (d) | (c) | (c) | (d) | (b) | (d) | (b) | (a) |
| 451 | 452 | 453 | 454 | 455 | 456 | 457 | 458 | 459 | 460 |
| (b) | (d) | (c) | (d) | (a) | (c) | (a) | (d) | (a) | (d) |

| | | | | | | | | | |
|---|---|---|---|---|---|---|---|---|---|
| **461** | **462** | **463** | **464** | **465** | **466** | **467** | **468** | **469** | **470** |
| (c) | (a) | (a) | (c) | (d) | (b) | (a) | (a) | (c) | (b) |
| **471** | **472** | **473** | **474** | **475** | **476** | **477** | **478** | **479** | **480** |
| (c) | (d) | (b) | (d) | (a) | (c) | (c) | (a) | (d) | (a) |
| **481** | **482** | **483** | **484** | **485** | **486** | **487** | **488** | **489** | **490** |
| (c) | (a) | (c) | (a) | (c) | (d) | (d) | (d) | (a) | (c) |
| **491** | **492** | **493** | **494** | **495** | **496** | **497** | **498** | **499** | **500** |
| (b) | (d) | (c ) | (b) | (a) | (c) | (b) | (a) | (b) | (d) |
| **501** | **502** | **503** | **504** | **505** | **506** | **507** | **508** | **509** | **510** |
| (d) | (c) | (c) | (b) | (a) | (b) | (d) | (a) | (b) | (a) |
| **511** | **512** | **513** | **514** | **515** | **516** | **517** | **518** | **519** | **520** |
| (c) | (b) | (d) | (a) | (c) | (a) | (b) | (c) | (d) | (b) |
| **521** | **522** | **523** | **524** | **525** | **526** | **527** | **528** | **529** | **530** |
| (c) | (b) | (d) | (b) | (d) | (c) | (a) | (b) | (d) | (b) |
| **531** | **532** | **533** | **534** | **535** | **536** | **537** | **538** | **539** | **540** |
| (c) | (c) | (a) | (b) | (a) | (c) | (b) | (d) | (b) | (c) |
| **541** | **542** | **543** | **544** | **545** | **546** | **547** | **548** | **549** | **550** |
| (b) | (c) | (d) | (b) | (c) | (b) | (c) | (d) | (c) | (d) |
| **551** | **552** | **553** | **554** | **555** | **556** | **557** | **558** | **559** | **560** |
| (a) | (d) | (b) | (a) | (b) | (b) | (c) | (c) | (b) | (a) |
| **561** | **562** | **563** | **564** | **565** | **566** | **567** | **568** | **569** | **570** |
| (b) | (a) | (b) | (c) | (d) | (b) | (c) | (d) | (b) | (a) |
| **571** | **572** | **573** | **574** | **575** | **576** | **577** | **578** | **579** | **580** |
| (b) | (b) | (a) | (b) | (d) | (c) | (d) | (a) | (c) | (b) |
| **581** | **582** | **583** | **584** | **585** | **586** | **587** | **588** | **589** | **590** |
| (b) | (a) | (c ) | (c) | (a) | (d) | (c) | (a) | (b) | (c) |
| **591** | **592** | **593** | **594** | **595** | **596** | **597** | **598** | **599** | **600** |
| (a) | (d) | (b) | (c) | (d) | (b) | (c) | (b) | (c) | (d) |
| **601** | **602** | **603** | **604** | **605** | **606** | **607** | **608** | **609** | **610** |
| (a) | (c) | (b) | (c) | (d) | (d) | (c) | (b) | (c) | (b) |
| **611** | **612** | **613** | **614** | **615** | **616** | **617** | **618** | **619** | **620** |
| (d) | (a) | (d) | (b) | (c) | (d) | (b) | (d) | (a) | (d) |
| **621** | **622** | **623** | **624** | **625** | **626** | **627** | **628** | **629** | **630** |
| (a) | (b) | (c) | (a) | (d) | (c) | (b) | (a) | (d) | (b) |
| **631** | **632** | **633** | **634** | **635** | **636** | **637** | **638** | **639** | **640** |
| (a) | (b) | (c) | (d) | (d) | (a) | (c) | (b) | (c) | (c) |
| **641** | **642** | **643** | **644** | **645** | **646** | **647** | **648** | **649** | **650** |
| (a) | (d) | (b) | (c) | (b) | (c) | (d) | (a) | (b) | (c) |
| **651** | **652** | **653** | **654** | **655** | **656** | **657** | **658** | **659** | **660** |
| (d) | (a) | (b) | (d) | (c) | (d) | (b) | (d) | (c) | (c) |
| **661** | **662** | **663** | **664** | **665** | **666** | **667** | **668** | **669** | **670** |
| (d) | (a) | (b) | (c) | (b) | (a) | (d) | (c) | (d) | (a) |

| | | | | | | | | | |
|---|---|---|---|---|---|---|---|---|---|
| **671** | **672** | **673** | **674** | **675** | **676** | **677** | **678** | **679** | **680** |
| (b) | (a) | (b) | (d) | (a) | (c) | (b) | (b) | (a) | (b) |
| **681** | **682** | **683** | **684** | **685** | **686** | **687** | **688** | **689** | **690** |
| (a) | (c) | (d) | (a) | (c) | (b) | (c) | (d) | (c) | (a) |
| **691** | **692** | **693** | **694** | **695** | **696** | **697** | **698** | **699** | **700** |
| (c) | (b) | (c) | (a) | (c) | (a) | (b) | (a) | (d) | (a) |
| **701** | **702** | **703** | **704** | **705** | **706** | **707** | **708** | **709** | **710** |
| (d) | (b) | (c) | (a) | (b) | (d) | (a) | (c) | (c) | (b) |
| **711** | **712** | **713** | **714** | **715** | **716** | **717** | **718** | **719** | **720** |
| (d) | (c) | (a) | (b) | (a) | (b) | (a) | (c) | (d) | (c) |
| **721** | **722** | **723** | **724** | **725** | **726** | **727** | **728** | **729** | **730** |
| (b) | (b) | (d) | (c) | (b) | (d) | (c) | (a) | (a) | (c) |
| **731** | **732** | **733** | **734** | **735** | **736** | **737** | **738** | **739** | **740** |
| (b) | (c) | (b) | (a) | (d) | (b) | (c) | (d) | (b) | (b) |
| **741** | **742** | **743** | **744** | **745** | **746** | **747** | **748** | **749** | **750** |
| (a) | (b) | (a) | (c) | (b) | (c) | (b) | (c) | (a) | (b) |
| **751** | **752** | **753** | **754** | **755** | **756** | **757** | **758** | **759** | **760** |
| (a) | (c) | (d) | (b) | (c) | (c) | (c) | (c) | (d) | (c) |
| **761** | **762** | **763** | **764** | **765** | **766** | **767** | **768** | **769** | **770** |
| (d) | (b) | (c) | (d) | (a) | (b) | (c) | (b) | (c) | (d) |
| **771** | **772** | **773** | **774** | **775** | **776** | **777** | **778** | **779** | **780** |
| (b) | (c) | (a) | (b) | (c) | (c) | (d) | (b) | (d) | (b) |
| **781** | **782** | **783** | **784** | **785** | **786** | **787** | **788** | **789** | **790** |
| (c) | (c) | (d) | (b) | (a) | (b) | (c) | (b) | (d) | (c) |
| **791** | **792** | **793** | **794** | **795** | **796** | **797** | **798** | **799** | **800** |
| (b) | (a) | (b) | (a) | (d) | (a) | (b) | (b) | (c) | (c) |
| **801** | **802** | **803** | **804** | **805** | **806** | **807** | **808** | **809** | **810** |
| (d) | (c) | (b) | (a) | (c) | (a) | (a) | (a) | (a) | (c) |
| **811** | **812** | **813** | **814** | **815** | **816** | **817** | **818** | **819** | **820** |
| (a) | (b) | (b) | (c) | (a) | (a) | (a) | (b) | (d) | (a) |
| **821** | **822** | **823** | **824** | **825** | **826** | **827** | **828** | **829** | **830** |
| (a) | (b) | (b) | (a) | (d) | (c) | (a) | (b) | (a) | (c) |
| **831** | **832** | **833** | **834** | **835** | **836** | **837** | **838** | **839** | **840** |
| (a) | (b) | (c) | (d) | (a) | (a) | (c) | (d) | (a) | (b) |
| **841** | **842** | **843** | **844** | **845** | **846** | **847** | **848** | **849** | **850** |
| (a) | (d) | (a) | (c) | (c) | (d) | (a) | (b) | (d) | (a) |

———————

# ENGLISH LANGUAGE

# 1. Comprehension Passages

## ENGLISH LANGUAGE COMPREHENSION

The objective of language comprehension test is to ascertain the ability of the candidates to understand the passage properly. Therefore candidates are required to take notice of the following points:

1. Read the full passage very attentively and intelligently.
2. Try to comprehend the gist of it.
3. Make a mental note of all the important details and points given in the passage.
4. Read the passage for the second time in case you have not been able to understand it satisfactorily.
5. Divide the time proportionately for all the passages.
6. Answer the questions on the basis of facts, as given in the paragraph.
7. Don't waste much time in answering the questions of any one passage.
8. Check all the answers once again, very carefully, to see whether any question is left unanswered by mistake.

## MODEL QUESTIONS (FOR PRACTICE)

**Directions:** *Each of the following passages is followed by five questions. Read the passage carefully and then answer the questions that follow each. For each question, four probable answers A, B, C and D are given. Only one out of these is correct. Choose the correct answer.*

### PASSAGE-1

The use of words like 'welcome', 'thank you', 'please', etc., at the right moment reflects a polite nature. The civic sense also lies within the scope of good manners. We should not shout or talk loudly in public places like hospitals and libraries and create disturbance. We should not cheat people or make fun of them. Cleanliness is also necessary. We must not throw the waste on roads and make use of dustbins. We should not harm the public property as it belongs to all of us. While in a queue, discipline should be maintained. We must give fair chance to others.

1. Expressions like 'welcome' 'thank you' and 'please' reflect
   A. happiness          B. discipline
   C. civic sense        D. polite nature

2. While in a library, we should
   A. respect others     B. avoid arguments
   C. talk in low tone   D. be courteous

3. A public property belongs to
   A. nobody
   B. all of us
   C. government
   D. one who maintains it

**4.** Discipline is
   A. the rule of proper conduct or action
   B. the rule of road sense
   C. making use of dustbins
   D. forming a queue

**5.** The most appropriate title for this passage would be
   A. Polite Nature
   B. Courtesy
   C. Good Manners
   D. Civic Sense

## PASSAGE-2

There is an old proverb 'Early to bed and early to rise makes a man healthy and wise.' I am in the habit of getting up early in the morning and have formed the habit of taking long morning walks in the past two years. It is a light exercise and best for physical fitness. The morning air which is fresh and pure is beneficial for the lungs. The early rays of the rising sun are good for healthy skin. 'Health is wealth' and doctors also recommend morning walk to their patients for gaining sound health and freshness of energy.

**1.** What is good for lungs?
   A. Sunrays     B. Fresh air
   C. Sound sleep     D. Light exercise

**2.** What is a light exercise?
   A. Early to bed
   B. Early to rise
   C. Morning walk
   D. Gaining sound health

**3.** What is good for skin?
   A. Fresh air
   B. Morning air
   C. Morning walk
   D. Rising sun's rays

**4.** What is best for physical fitness?
   A. Light exercise
   B. Long morning walk
   C. Early to rise
   D. Fresh and pure air

**5.** Long morning walk
   A. bring sound sleep
   B. ensures physical fitness

C. ensures healthy skin
D. keeps healthy, wealthy and wise

## PASSAGE-3

Mahatma Gandhi lived a splendid long life and has set great moral standards before us. He showed to the world the true way to peace. He wished to see India prosper but he became a martyr for the noble cause of Hindu-Muslim unity at the time of partition when a religious fanatic, Nathuram Godse, shot him dead on January 30, 1948. His last words were 'Hey Ram'. He lived and died for his country and countryman.

**1.** Mahatma Gandhi showed the world the true way to
   A. prosperity     B. love
   C. truth     D. peace

**2.** Mahatma Gandhi became a martyr for the noble cause of
   A. truth
   B. non-violence
   C. freedom of India
   D. Hindu-Muslim unity

**3.** Mahatma Gandhi was shot dead
   A. before India achieved independence
   B. by a mad man
   C. by an intolerant religious person
   D. by a non-religious person

**4.** Mahatma Gandhi set great moral standards. It means
   A. he was a great religious teacher
   B. he was a great moralist
   C. he made India morally stronger
   D. moral was everything to him

**5.** Gandhiji lived and died for his country and countryman. It means
   A. he was born in India and died in India
   B. he was a patriot
   C. he was a great moralist
   D. he sacrified his life for India and her people

## PASSAGE-4

On one hot day a crow felt very thirsty. He flew from one place to another in search of water. After long hours of labour he found a pitcher. Eagerly, he perched on the mouth of the pitcher. He found that the water was at the bottom of the vessel. He tried his best to dip his beak but did not succeed. He did not know what to do. Suddenly some pebbles lying nearby gave him an idea. One by one he dropped the pebbles with his beak into the pitcher. The level of water slowly came up to the mouth of the pitcher. The crow then drank the water and quenched his thirst.

1. The crow found a pitcher
   A. as it flew
   B. after many hours of labour
   C. full of water
   D. which was empty

2. What is the moral of the passage?
   A. No pains, no gains
   B. God helps those who help themselves
   C. Necessity is the mother of invention
   D. Try and try again, you will succeed at last

3. The crow flew from place to place
   A. in search of pitcher
   B. in search of pebbles
   C. in search of water
   D. in search of a vessel

4. The pitcher, the crow found
   A. was full of water
   B. was dry
   C. had little water in the bottom
   D. had water up to its mouth

5. As the crow dropped pebbles into the pitcher, what happend?
   A. The pitcher broke down
   B. The water leaked one of the pitcher
   C. The level of water into the pitcher rose up slowly
   D. Water level immediately rose to the mouth of the pitcher

## PASSAGE-5

Once upon a time a crane and a fox lived in a forest. They were good friend. One day the fox invited the crane to a feast. He made a tasty food and served it before the crane on a plate. The crane could not eat anything because of the long beak. But the fox licked all his food. The crane felt insulted. He decided to teach the fox a lesson.

Next day he invited the fox. He prepared the same tasty food and placed it in front of the fox inside a narrow glass. The crane ate easily while the fox looked on. Now, it was the fox's turn to remain hungry.

1. What is the moral of the passage?
   A. Beware of the wicked
   B. One good turn deserves another
   C. Be contented with what you have
   D. Tit for tat

2. The crane could not eat tasty food because the
   A. food was served in a shallow plate
   B. food was very hot
   C. food was served in a long jar
   D. crane was not hungry

3. The fox had to remain hungry because
   A. the food served was not enough in quantity
   B. the food was served inside a narrow glass
   C. the food served was not tasty
   D. the food was all liquid

4. Why did the crane feel insulted?
   A. Because he was invited to feast but he could not eat anything
   B. Because the food was served in a shallow plate and he could not eat
   C. Because the food was too hot
   D. Because the fox gulped all the food quickly

5. The crane successfully taught a lesson to the fox when he invited the fox to a feast and served the food
   A. in a narrow glass
   B. in a large plate
   C. in a broken plate
   D. in a long jar

## PASSAGE-6

The family set down at the table and began to talk about the summer holidays. They had to decide a place to visit during the vacation. Should they go to their village or to a hill station? The parents preferred the village while the children wished to go the hill station. After few moments of discussion the elders decided to visit both the places. First they shall go to the village for a week and then stay at the hill station for the remaining days. For the first time the family shall be together during the holidays. The children were happy with the holiday plan.

1. The purpose for which the family set down at the table was
   A. to decide a place to visit during the vacation
   B. to educate the children how to carry articles during a visit to a hill station
   C. to decide the date when they should start their journey
   D. to tell the children that they will visit a hill station during this vacation

2. The final plan was to visit
   A. their village
   B. a hill station
   C. their village as well as a hill station
   D. their home town

3. The final decision was made by
   A. the boys          B. the girls
   C. the women         D. the elders

4. They decided first to go to their village and stay there for
   A. a day             B. a week
   C. ten days          D. a fortnight

5. Why were children happy?
   A. Because a hill station was included in their holiday plan
   B. Because a visit to their village was excluded from their holiday plan
   C. Because their choice prevailed
   D. Because they were going all alone to the hill station

1. Govind intended to go
   A. for a business trip
   B. to a hill station
   C. on a long journey to a sacred place
   D. to his home town for a long period

2. Why did Govind leave his box of jewellery with Mirind?
   A. Because it was not safe to take the box with him on a long journey
   B. Because Mirind was his fast friend
   C. Because the box was very heavy
   D. Because his house was unsafe

3. Why did Govind take Mirind to a lonely place?
   A. To tell him that the box contained valuable jewellery
   B. So that no third person could see box
   C. To show him what was within the box
   D. To tell him that the box will remain with him

4. Where did Govind hand over the box of jewellery to Mirind?
   A. At Mirind's house
   B. At his own house
   C. In a lonely place
   D. In a lonely place under a tree

5. It was not safe to leave the box in a lone house. Here the word 'lone house' means
   A. a house in a deserted place
   B. a house where none lives
   C. a house without door and lock
   D. a house near the forest

## PASSAGE-7

Once Govind intended to go on pilgrimage with his family. He asked Mirind to accompany. But for his trade's reason, he did not go with him. So Govind thought it safe to leave the box of his jewellery with him, as it was dangerous to leave it in a lone house or take it on the journey. So he went to him with the box. He took him to a lonely place under a tree and handed it over to him. He told Mirind, "Keep it safe with you. I shall return from the journey after six month then I shall take it back from you." Mirind said, "Don't worry, I shall keep it as safe as own."

## PASSAGE-8

Zahir-ud-din Babar was the first Mughal emperor of India. A descendent of Timur on father's side and Changez Khan on his mother's side, Babar was a brave warrior. After defeating Ibrahim Lodhi in the First Battle of Panipat in 1526 he entered Delhi and soon gained control over Agra. After many more battles with Rajputs he extended his empire over Punjab, Uttar Pradesh and north Bihar. He died at a young age of 48 years in 1530 at his capital Agra without getting much time to consolidate his victories.

**1.** Zahir-ud-din Babar was the first
   A. Muslim ruler of India
   B. Mughal ruler of India
   C. Afghan ruler of India
   D. Turk ruler of India

**2.** Babar was born in the years
   A. 1480      B. 1482
   C. 1492      D. 1962

**3.** Babar first occupied
   A. Punjab      B. Agra
   C. Delhi      D. Panipat

**4.** Babar was a brave warrior. Here brave warrior means
   A. courageous soldier
   B. a kind hearted soldier
   C. a clever fighter
   D. a victorious general

**5.** Babar extended his empire over Punjab and Uttar Pradesh after many more battles with the
   A. Afghans      B. Rajputs
   C. Mughals      D. Lodhies

## PASSAGE-9

Our National Flag is tricolour. It has three equal horizontal strips. The strip at the top is saffron, in the middle is white and at the bottom is green. The ratio of width to length of the flag is 2 : 3. In the centre of the white strip is a wheel in navy blue. The wheel represents the *chakra*. Its design is similar to the wheel which appears on the abacus of the Sarnath Lion Capital of Ashoka. Its diameter approximates to the width of the white strip. The wheel has 24 spokes. It was adopted by Constituent Assembly on July 22, 1947. We love our national flag. We respect it. We are ready to sacrifice our life to protect its honour. It represents the nation. So it is a symbol of national honour.

**1.** In our national flag the wheel is located in the centre of
   A. saffron strip      B. white strip
   C. green strip      D. blue strip

**2.** In our national flag which of the strips is at the bottom in our national flag
   A. blue      C. saffron
   B. white      D. green

**3.** Why do we love our national flag?
   A. Because it is tricolour
   B. Because it has three strips
   C. Because it has a wheel at the centre
   D. Because it is a symbol of national honour

**4.** Our national flag was approved by
   A. President
   B. Lok Sabha
   C. Parliament
   D. Constituent Assembly

**5.** The diameter approximates to the width of the white strip. Here the word 'approximates' means
   A. is more or less equal
   B. is exactly equal
   C. is not equal
   D. is related

## PASSAGE-10

Distance in large cities are long. All the people do not have their own means of transport. They have to depend upon the state or private buses. The number of bus users is very large. Every bus stop is, therefore, crowded. The number of buses is not adequate. Thus people suffer the torture of long wait at the bus stop. Some bus stops are quite orderly. People form queues and get into the buses turn by turn. However, often this order is forgotten and confusion spreads when the bus comes and the law of jungle prevails.

**1.** Why are the bus stops crowded?
   A. Because they are small is size
   B. Because the number of passengers is very large
   C. Because they are situated at some busy centre
   D. Because people do not form queues

**2.** Long wait at the bus stop is the result of
   A. over-crowding in the buses
   B. late running of buses
   C. shortage of buses
   D. slow speed of buses

**3.** Some bus stops are quite orderly where
   A. there is no crowd
   B. the number of buses is adequate

C. people do not have to wait for long
D. people form queues and enter the buses one by one

**4.** Most of the people who travel by buses are
A. non-working
B. do not have their own vehicles
C. have to go a long distance
D. live in large cities

**5.** What happens when people do not have their own transport?
A. They have to wait for a bus at a bus stop
B. They have to depend upon the state or private buses
C. They have to travel long distances
D. They form queues and get into buses one by one

## PASSAGE-11

A certain king once fell ill and doctors said that only a sudden fright would restore his health but the king was not a man for anyone to play tricks on, except his fool. One day, when the fool was with him in his boat he cleverly pushed the king into water but he was rescued and put to bed. The fright, the bath and bed cured the diseased king, but he was so angry with the fool that he turned him out of the country.

**1.** What did the doctor say about the king?
A. Only a sudden fright would restore the king's health
B. Only fool would cure the king
C. Only a boat trick could cure the king
D. The king had suffered a sudden fright

**2.** He cleverly pushed the king into water but *he* was rescued and put to bed. In this sentence *he* refers to
A. the king　　　　B. the fool
C. the doctor　　　D. the river

**3.** When the fool pushed the king into water they were
A. in the palace　　B. in the bed
C. in the garden　　D. in a boat

**4.** Who played the trick on the king?
A. The doctor　　　B. The boatman
C. The fool　　　　D. The fright

**5.** The fool who cured the king was
A. rewarded
B. thrown into water
C. turned out of the country
D. put into jail

## ANSWERS

| Passage 1. | 1 | 2 | 3 | 4 | 5 | Passage 7. | 1 | 2 | 3 | 4 | 5 |
|---|---|---|---|---|---|---|---|---|---|---|---|
| | D | C | B | A | C | | C | A | B | D | B |
| Passage 2. | 1 | 2 | 3 | 4 | 5 | Passage 8. | 1 | 2 | 3 | 4 | 5 |
| | B | C | D | B | B | | B | B | C | A | B |
| Passage 3. | 1 | 2 | 3 | 4 | 5 | Passage 9. | 1 | 2 | 3 | 4 | 5 |
| | D | D | C | B | D | | B | D | D | D | A |
| Passage 4. | 1 | 2 | 3 | 4 | 5 | Passage 10. | 1 | 2 | 3 | 4 | 5 |
| | B | C | C | C | C | | B | C | D | B | B |
| Passage 5. | 1 | 2 | 3 | 4 | 5 | Passage 11. | 1 | 2 | 3 | 4 | 5 |
| | D | A | B | B | A | | A | A | D | C | C |
| Passage 6. | 1 | 2 | 3 | 4 | 5 | | | | | | |
| | A | C | D | B | A | | | | | | |

# 2. English Grammar



| Part of speech | Definition or Function | Examples |
|---|---|---|
| Noun | Name of a person, place, animal, quality or thing | Ram, boy, dog pen, sun, Delhi, truth, honesty |
| Pronoun | Used in place of a noun | I, you, he she, they |
| Articles & Determiners | Points out indefinite and definite nouns | a, an, the, few, some |
| Adjective | Describes a noun or pronoun | big, honest, wooden valuable, quiet, deep, soft, narrow |
| Adverb | Describes a verb, an adjective or another adverb | silently, widely, softly, quietly, very, carefully |
| Verb | Tells about action or state of something or someone | is, am, was, have, do, like, walk, work, make, throw, tell |
| Conjuction | Joins words, clauses or sentences | and, but, when, yet, while, else |
| Preposition | Links a noun or pronoun to another word | at, to, after, on for, under, over, with |
| Interjection | Expresses sudden feelings or emotions | Ah!, Alas!, oh!, ouch!, hi!, well!, Hurrah! |

## NOUNS

A word which denotes a person, a thing, an animal or a place is said to be a noun.

There are two noun numbers in English — the *Singular* and the *Plural*.

**Singular Numbers :** A noun that denotes one person or one thing, is said to be in the Singular number. For example — book, pencil, bird, dog, hen etc. are in singular number.

**Plural Number :** A noun that denotes more than one person or one thing is said to be in plural number. For example — boys, pens, lions, girls, men etc. are in plural number.

### REMEMBER

| *Singular* | *Plural* |
|---|---|
| Cat | Cats |
| Book | Books |
| Pen | Pens |
| Room | Rooms |
| Tree | Trees |
| Bus | Buses |
| Bush | Bushes |
| Box | Boxes |
| Glass | Glasses |
| Dish | Dishes |
| Judge | Judges |
| Tax | Taxes |
| Watch | Watches |
| Calf | Calves |
| Thief | Thieves |
| Knife | Knives |

| *Singular* | *Plural* |
|---|---|
| Scarf | Scarves |
| Wife | Wives |
| Leaf | Leaves |
| Wolf | Wolves |
| Half | Halves |
| Monarch | Monarchs |
| Roof | Roofs |
| Hoof | Hoofs |
| Gulf | Gulfs |
| Staff | Staffs |
| Radio | Radios |
| Bamboo | Bamboos |
| Folio | Folios |
| Hero | Heroes |
| Volcano | Volcanoes |
| Mango | Mangoes |
| Potato | Potatoes |
| Photo | Photos |
| Piano | Pianos |
| Baby | Babies |
| Fly | Flies |
| Country | Countries |
| Lady | Ladies |
| Boy | Boys |
| Monkey | Monkeys |
| Ox | Oxen |
| Child | Children |
| Man | Men |
| Woman | Women |
| Tooth | Teeth |
| Axis | Axes |
| Basis | Bases |
| Foot | Feet |
| Goose | Geese |
| Englishman | Englishmen |
| Radius | Radii |
| Vertex | Vertices |
| Stimulus | Stimuli |

**1.** Note the plurals of the following nouns:

| *Singular* | *Plural* | *Singular* | *Plural* |
|---|---|---|---|
| copy | copies | cry | cries |
| baby | babies | duty | duties |
| body | bodies | country | countries |
| family | families | diary | diaries |
| fly | flies | fairy | fairies |
| city | cities | spy | spies |
| army | armies | storey | storeys |
| bay | bays | monkey | monkeys |

**2.** The following nouns do not undergo any change in plural form, in general.

| *Singular* | *Plural* | *Singular* | *Plural* |
|---|---|---|---|
| deer | deer | sheep | sheep |
| thousand | thousand | pair | pair |
| hundred | hundred | score | score |
| dozen | dozen | gross | gross |

**Note:** We can write—

(*a*) thousands of men; (*b*) two pairs of shoes; (*c*) dozens of mangoes; (*d*) scores of people etc. But—

(*a*) two thousand rupees; (*b*) three hundred men; (*c*) five dozen eggs, etc.

**3.** The following nouns are usually used in plural forms. They take a plural verb after them—

| | | |
|---|---|---|
| eatables | fetters | surroundings |
| riches | alms | spectacles |
| trousers | pants | scissors |
| premises | thanks | annals |
| congratulations | goods | shorts |
| tongs | pains | arms |
| breeches | (for troubles) | |

**4.** The following are the nouns which are plural in appearance but are usually used in singular number. They are followed by a singular verb—

| | | |
|---|---|---|
| news | politics | physics |
| mathematics | economics | ethics |
| politics | classics | gallows |
| statistics | athletics | innings |
| mechanics | summons | mumps |

**5.** Collective nouns often used as plurals—

| | | |
|---|---|---|
| public | police | cattle |
| audience | clergy | folk |
| people | poultry | nation |
| elite | gentry | glitterati |

**6.** The nouns that are usually used in singular forms—

| | | |
|---|---|---|
| advice | hair | rice |
| fuel | alphabet | machinery |
| offspring | issue | furniture |
| mischief | stationery | luggage |
| bedding | information | abuse |

**7.** Material nouns are always used in singular number—

gold          copper         milk

water         silk          wool

**Note:** They may be used in plural with a different meaning.

copper coins (coppers), chains or fetters (irons), cans made of tin (tins).

## GENDERS

The difference in sex is denoted by Gender in grammar. The various genders are as follows :

1. **Masculine Gender :** A noun that denotes a male is said to be of the masculine gender, as man, uncle, ox, boy etc.
2. **Feminine Gender :** A noun that denotes a female is said to be of feminine gender, as woman, aunt, princess, cow etc.
3. **Common Gender :** Nouns which denote both males and females are said to be of the common gender, as friend, cousin, person, parent, baby etc.
4. **Neuter Gender :** A noun that denotes the name of object without life is said to be of neuter gender, as file, table, pencil.

### REMEMBER

| Masculine | Feminine |
|---|---|
| Boy | Girl |
| Son | Daughter |
| Brother | Sister |
| Murderer | Murderess |
| Sorcerer | Sorceress |
| Son-in-law | Daughter-in-law |
| Father-in-law | Mother-in-law |
| Man-servant | Maid-servant |
| Land-lord | Land-lady |
| Bachelor | Maid |
| Gentleman | Lady |
| Monk | Nun |
| Earl | Countess |
| Lad | Lass |
| Sir | Madam |
| Duke | Dutchess |
| Emperor | Empress |
| Milk-man | Milk-maid |
| Pea-cock | Pea-hen |

| Masculine | Feminine |
|---|---|
| Step-father | Step-mother |
| Hero | Heroine |
| Viceroy | Vicerine |
| Mr. | Mrs. |
| Governor | Governess |
| Master | Mistress |
| Wizard | Witch |
| Heir | Heiress |
| Host | Hostess |
| Lion | Lioness |
| Mayor | Mayoress |
| Actor | Actress |
| Buck | Doe |
| Colt | Filly |
| Dog | Bitch |
| Horse | Mare |
| Count | Countess |
| Hunter | Huntress |
| Prince | Princess |
| Abbot | Abbess |
| God | Goddess |
| Author | Authoress |
| Ox | Cow |
| Widower | Widow |
| Grand-father | Grand-mother |
| He-goat | She-goat |
| Milk-man | Milk-woman |
| Bridegroom | Bride |
| Tiger | Tigress |
| Priest | Priestess |
| Poet | Poetess |
| Shepherd | Shepherdess |
| Nephew | Niece |
| Stag | Hind |

## PRONOUNS

The repetition of a noun in a sentence or a set of sentences is really boring. So, instead of repeating the noun, we can use a word (for that noun) called the pronoun.

"A pronoun is a word that we use instead of a noun".

**Example:**

This is *Sachin. He* plays cricket.

**Note:** *He* is the pronoun used in place of *Sachin.*

## Kinds of Pronouns

1. **Personal pronouns :** A pronoun which is used instead of the name of a person is known as a 'Personal Pronoun'. A list of the 'Personal pronouns' is listed below :

   I, my, mine, me, we      (First Person)

   You, your, yours      (Second Person)

   He, his, him, she, her, hers, it,

   its, they, their, theirs, them  (Third Person)

2. **Demonstrative, Indefinite and Distributive Pronouns :**

   **(a) Demonstrative Pronouns :** Pronouns used to point out the objects to which they refer are called Demonstrative Pronouns.

   **Examples :**
   (i)  *This* is a present from my uncle.
   (ii)  *These* are merely excuses.
   (iii) Bembay mangoes are better than *those* of Bangaluru.

   **(b) Indefinite Pronouns :** All pronouns which refer to persons or things in a general way and do not refer to any particular person or thing are called Indefinite Pronouns.

   **Examples :**
   (i)  *Somebody* has stolen my watch.
   (ii)  *Few* escaped unhurt.
   (iii) Did you ask *anybody* to come?

   **(c) Distributive Pronouns :** Each, either, neither are called distributive pronouns because they refer to persons or things one at a time. For this reason they are always singular and followed by the verb in singular.

   **Examples :**
   (i)  *Each* of the men received a reward.
   (ii)  *These* men received *each* a reward.
   (iii) *Either* of you can go.

3. **Relative Pronouns :** A relative pronoun refers or relates to some noun going before, which is called its Antecedent.

   **Examples :**
   (i)  I met Hari *who* used to live here.
   (ii)  I have found the pen *which* I had lost.
   (iii) Here is the book *that* you lent me.

4. **Interrogative Pronouns :** These pronouns, are used for asking questions.

   **Examples :**
   (i)  *Whose* book is this?
   (ii)  *What* will all the neighbours say?
   (iii) *Which* do you prefer, tea or coffee?

   **Note :** Interrogative pronouns can also be used in asking indirect questions. Consider the following examples :
   (i)  I asked *who* was speaking.
   (ii)  Tell me *what* you have done.
   (iii) Say *which* you would like best.

## Behaviour of the Pronouns

1. If three pronouns are used together in the same sentence they are arranged in the following order :

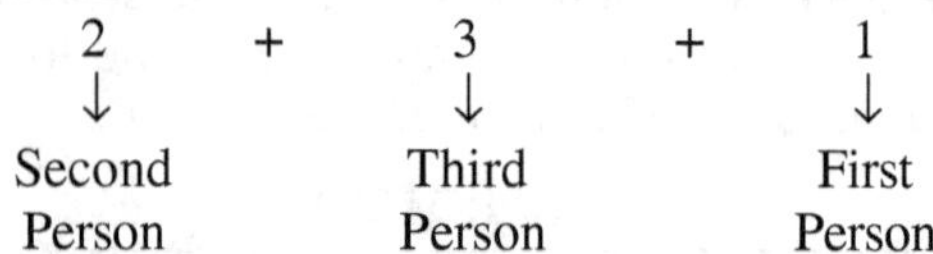


   **Examples :**
   I, you and he must help *that* poor man.
   (Incorrect)
   You, he and I must help *that* poor man.
   (Correct)

2. When two or more singular nouns are joined by and, the pronoun used for them should be plural.

   **Examples :**
   Mohan and Sohan are friends. *They* play football. *They* live at Lajpat Nagar.

3. But if these nouns joined by and refer to the same person or thing, the pronoun used should be singular.

   **Examples :**
   (i)  Delhi, the beautiful city and the capital of India, is famous for *its* historical monuments.
   (ii)  The manager and owner of the firm expressed *his* views on the demands of the workers.

4. When two nouns are used with as well as, the pronoun agrees with the first subject.

   **Examples :**

   (a) Mohan as well as his friends is doing *his* work.

   (b) The students as well as their teachers are doing *their* work.

5. When two singular nouns joined by 'and' are preceded by *each* or *every,* the pronoun used must be singular and should agree in gender with the second noun.

   **Examples :**

   (a) Every man and every woman will do *her* best for the nation.

   (b) Each boy and each girl went to *her* house.

6. When two nouns are joined by using 'with', the pronoun agrees with the noun coming before 'with'.

   **Examples :**

   (a) The boy with *his* parents has gone to see a movie.

   (b) The children with *their* parents have gone to picnic.

7. When two different nouns are joined by either.......... or; neither .......... nor, the pronoun is used according to the number and gender of the second noun.

   **Examples :**

   (a) Either your sister or you have done *your* work.

   (b) Neither the students nor the teacher was in *his* class.

8. The pronoun coming after 'than' must be in the same case as that coming before 'than'.

   **Examples :**

   (a) She plays better than *me.*      (Incorrect)
       She plays better than *I.*      (Correct)

   (b) His elder brother is more intelligent than *him.*      (Incorrect)
       His elder brother is more intelligent than *he.*      (Correct)

9. 'Many a' always takes a singular pronoun and singular verb.

   **Example :**

   Many a soldier has met *his* death in the battle field.

10. 'Who', 'Whose', 'Whom' are used only for persons.

    **Examples :**

    (a) *Who* is knocking at the door?
    (b) *Whose* pen is this?
    (c) *What* do you want?

11. 'Which' is used for things.

    **Example :**

    *Which* game do you like?

## MULTIPLE CHOICE QUESTIONS

**Directions:** *In the following questions choose the correct options to fill the blanks.*

1. The place was so dirty that ..... wished to run away from there.
   A. everybody        B. anybody
   C. few              D. some

2. ..... was there to help me.
   A. Somebody        B. Anything
   C. Anybody         D. Nobody

3. Is there ....... to eat?
   A. some            B. something
   C. any             D. few

4. ..... of the students were making a great noise.
   A. Anyone          B. Somebody
   C. Many            D. Nobody

5. ..... of the students can solve this sum.
   A. Someone         B. Anybody
   C. Somebody        D. None

6. ...... of us should try our best to make India a heaven.
   A. Any             B. Somebody
   C. Anybody         D. All

7. ...... of us do not know the real meaning of our lives.
   A. Any             B. Something
   C. Several         D. Many

8. My .......... black.
   A. hairs are       B. hair is
   C. hairs shall     D. hair will

**9.** She saw two .......... on the last Sunday.
A. thiefs
B. theifs
C. thieves
D. theives

**10.** My sister is a .......... .
A. bacheloress
B. bachelor
C. unmaried
D. spinster

**11.** One is supposed to do .......... .
A. our duty
B. their duty
C. one's duty
D. his duty

**12.** Take anything .......... you want.
A. that
B. which
C. than
D. then

**13.** I cannot tolerate .......... .
A. separated you
B. your separation
C. separation from you
D. you separated

**14.** He is .......... faithful partner.
A. Yours
B. You
C. Your
D. Your's

**15.** Ajay is more smart than .......... .
A. her
B. hers
C. herself
D. she

**16.** Vivek works harder than .......... .
A. me
B. I
C. her
D. his

**17.** They should help .......... .
A. the poor people
B. the poor
C. the poor persons
D. the poor peoples

**18.** .......... are mad.
A. All his sons
B. His all sons
C. Sons all his
D. All sons his

**19.** The poor fellow .......... to fate.
A. resigned
B. resigned himself
C. resigned itself
D. resigned themselves

**20.** Nobody will help you but .......... .
A. I
B. me
C. ours
D. his

**21.** It is a good chance, You must avail .......... this opportunity.
A. of
B. yourself of
C. for
D. from

**22.** The person who is elected .......... my relative.
A. is
B. he is
C. his
D. him

**23.** He made .......... .
A. yours mention
B. mention of you
C. mention for you
D. mention about you

**24.** .......... I know, he is quite faithful.
A. As far as
B. So far as
C. So far this
D. So far so

**25.** It is a duty of a person to take .......... for his family.
A. pain
B. pains
C. pain-killers
D. pained

**26.** She does not love .......... husband.
A. his
B. her
C. its
D. their

**27.** Let .......... work together.
A. him and me
B. he and I
C. he and him
D. I and me

**28.** Copper, Silver and Gold .......... .
A. each will do
B. either will do
C. any one will do
D. any will do

**29.** Jessica and Roma are very irregular .......... habits.
A. in her
B. in their
C. in its
D. in every

**30.** One likes to enjoy .......... who was a great poet.
A. The sonnets of Shakespeare
B. Shakespeare's sonnets
C. Sonnets
D. Shakespeare

**31.** That is the boy .......... everybody loves.
A. whom
B. who
C. that
D. whose

**32.** That is the girl .......... won the first prize.
A. whom
B. who
C. whose
D. which

**33.** That is the man .......... purse was lost.
A. who
B. whom
C. whose
D. their

## ANSWERS

| 1 | 2 | 3 | 4 | 5 | 6 | 7 | 8 | 9 | 10 |
|---|---|---|---|---|---|---|---|---|----|
| A | D | B | C | D | D | D | B | C | D |
| **11** | **12** | **13** | **14** | **15** | **16** | **17** | **18** | **19** | **20** |
| C | A | C | C | D | B | B | A | B | B |
| **21** | **22** | **23** | **24** | **25** | **26** | **27** | **28** | **29** | **30** |
| B | A | B | A | B | B | A | C | B | A |
| **31** | **32** | **33** | | | | | | | |
| A | B | C | | | | | | | |

## ARTICLES

The family of the articles has only three members. They are : A, An and The. However, they fall under two groups :

*(a)* Definite Article *(b)* Indefinite Article

'The' is known as definite article whereas 'a' and 'an' are known as indefinite articles.

## Use of the Definite Article 'The'

### 'The' is used before

1. The superlative degree :
   He is the ablest man of the town.
   (ablest is a superlative degree)

2. The name of states, countries etc. having a descriptive name :
   (i) The J & K is a small state. (J & K is a descriptive name)
   (ii) He lives in the U.S.A. (U.S.A. is a descriptive name)
   (But the Delhi and the America are wrong because neither Delhi nor America is a descriptive name)

3. The names of the scriptures :
   The Gita is a holy book. (Gita is a scripture)

4. Name of newspapers :
   The Tribune is published from Chandigarh.

5. Name of rivers, canals, seas, oceans, bays, gulfs, groups of islands etc. :
   (i) The Ganga is a holy river.
   (ii) The Indian Ocean is the deepest ocean.
   (iii) The Persian Gulf is a narrow gulf.

6. The name of famous buildings :
   The Taj is one of the best buildings in India.

7. The names of nationals, sects and communities:
   (i) The English defeated the Germans in the World War.
   (ii) The rich should help the poor.
   (iii) The Hindus believe in the caste system.

8. Proper nouns used as common nouns :
   (i) Kalidas is the Shakespeare of India.
   (ii) Delhi is the London of India.

9. Famous historical events :
   The Industrial Revolution changed the face of England.

10. The directions and the celestial bodies:
    The sun rises in the east.

11. Titles :
    Akbar, the Great was loved by his subjects.

## Do not use 'the'

1. Before languages :
   The English is an international language. (Incorrect)
   English is an international language. (Correct)

2. Before the names of games :
   The hockey is a popular game. (Incorrect)
   Hockey is a popular game. (Correct)

## Use of the Indefinite Articles 'A' and 'An'

### 'A' is used before :

1. All singular common nouns beginning with a consonant :
   (i) A boy sings a song.

(ii) A black and a white cow were grazing in the field.

2. If a word begins with a vowel but gives the sound of a consonant, 'a' should be used before it :
   (i) He was helped in his work by a European.
   (ii) He is a one-eyed man.
   (iii) It is a useful work.

## 'An' is used as follows :

1. All singular common nouns beginning with a vowel (*i.e.*, a, e, i, o, u) :
   (i) He is an artist.
   (ii) He is an old man.
   (iii) I intend to buy an umbrella.

2. If a word starts with a consonant but gives the sound of a vowel, "an" should be used before it :
   (i) Brutus is an honourable man.
   (ii) He is an honour to his profession.
   (iii) He is an L.L.B.

(iv) He is an M.A.
(v) You will reach there in an hour.

## Demonstratives, that, these and those

1. The demonstrative adjectives and pronouns are for objects nearby the speaker:
   this (singular) those (plural)
   and for objects far away from the speaker.
   That (singular) those (plural)

2. Demonstratives are the only adjectives that agree in number with their nouns.
   That hat is nice.
   Those hats are nice.

3. When there is the idea of selection, the pronoun "one" (or "ones") often follows the demonstrative.
   I want a book. I'll get this (one).
   If the demonstrative is followed by an adjective, "one"(or "ones") must be used.
   I want a book. I'll get this big one.

## MULTIPLE CHOICE QUESTIONS

**Directions:** *In the following questions choose the correct options to fill the blanks.*

**1.** ......... will have to be paid for this material.
   A. Half rupee       B. Half a rupee
   C. A half rupee     D. An half rupee

**2.** .......... is taking keen interest in India.
   A. The USA          B. USA
   C. An USA           D. A USA

**3.** Only .......... can save our country.
   A. the Hitler       B. a Hitler
   C. Hitler           D. an Hitler

**4.** I can run for .......... .
   A. hundred miles    B. the hundred miles
   C. a hundred miles  D. an hundred miles.

**5.** .......... man-eater has been killed.
   A. The              B. A
   C. An               D. Either A or B

**6.** What .......... fine idea!
   A. the              B. an
   C. a                D. No article

**7.** .......... earth is moving around the sun.
   A. An               B. A

   C. The              D. No article

**8.** This is .......... first example while I got.
   A. the              B. a
   C. an               D. No article

**9.** This is .......... house which was built during earthquake.
   A. a                B. an
   C. the              D. No article

**10.** .......... America is a rich country.
   A. The              B. An
   C. A                D. No article

**11.** .......... U.S.A. is a developed country.
   A. A                B. An
   C. The              D. No article

**12.** .......... Bible is a holy book.
   A. A                B. The
   C. An               D. No article

**13.** .......... rich  should help the poor.
   A. The              B. A
   C. An               D. No article

**14.** .......... Gold is a costly metal.
   A. The              B. A
   C. An               D. No article

**15.** Kalidas is .......... Shakespeare of India.
A. a  B. an
C. the  D. No article

**16.** I cannot do .......... difficult work.
A. a such  B. the such
C. such the  D. such a

**17.** How foolish .......... plan it is!
A. a  B. an
C. the  D. No article

**18.** An ink is .......... useful article.
A. an  B. a
C. the  D. No article

**19.** There are .......... husband and wife.
A. a  B. an
C. the  D. No article

**20.** He is learning .......... French
A. the  B. a
C. an  D. No article

## ANSWERS

| 1 | 2 | 3 | 4 | 5 | 6 | 7 | 8 | 9 | 10 |
|---|---|---|---|---|---|---|---|---|----|
| B | A | B | C | D | C | C | A | C | D |

| 11 | 12 | 13 | 14 | 15 | 16 | 17 | 18 | 19 | 20 |
|----|----|----|----|----|----|----|----|----|----|
| C | B | A | D | C | D | A | B | D | D |

## ADJECTIVES & ADVERBS

An Adjective is a word which adds something to the meaning of a noun or a pronoun.

Mridula is an *intelligent* girl.

He has a *black* goat.

He is a *brilliant* student.

She is a *clever* girl.

It is a *beautiful* picture.

In the sentences given above, the words in italics are adjectives.

An Adverb is a word which qualifies the meaning of a Verb, an Adjective or another Adverb.

(*i*) He talks *slowly*.

(*ii*) He is a *very* good student.

(*iii*) He talks *very* slowly.

In sentence (*i*), *slowly* qualifies the verb *talks*.

In sentence (*ii*), *very* qualifies the adjective *good*.

In sentence (*iii*), *very* qualifies the adverb *slowly*.

Adjectives have three degrees of comparison :

1. **Positive Degree :** It expresses the common form of an adjective.

   **Example :**

   Ram is a *tall* boy.

   In the above sentence *tall* is an adjective and expresses the common form.

2. **Comparative Degree :** It expresses the more of the same form.

**Example :**

Ram is *taller* than Mahesh.

In the above sentence *taller* is an adjective that expresses the more of the common form of the adjective *tall*.

**"When and How to Use" Comparative Degree?**

(a) Comparative Degree is used when two persons or two groups of persons or things are compared.

   **Examples :**

   (a) He is *wiser* than his younger brother.

   (b) This glass is *cleaner* than the other.

(b) When two different qualities in the same person are compared, more is used instead of 'er' to form the comparative. The formula used in this case should be :

   **More + Positive Degree**

   She is *fairer* than polite.　　(Incorrect)

   She is *more fair* than polite.　　(Correct)

(c) When selection of one out of two persons or things is meant, the degree of comparison is followed by of and *the* is used before it.

   **Example :**

   Zia is abler of *the* two sisters.

(d) If two comparatives are used in the same sentence to impress upon an idea, both should be preceded by the definite article.

**Examples :**
(i) The higher you go, the cooler it is.
(ii) The more we get, the more we desire.

(e) When one person or thing is compared with another of the same kind, other is used after the comparative degree. In such sentences other is normally preceded by any or all.

**Examples :**
(i) Kalidas is greater than any dramatist. (Incorrect)

    Kalidas is greater than any other dramatist. (Correct)

(ii) Lead is heavier than all metals. (Incorrect)

    Lead is heavier than all other metals. (Correct)

(f) Senior, junior, superior, inferior, prior, anterior (earlier than) and posterior (later than) are always followed by 'to'.

**Examples :**
(i) Ram is senior *to* Mohan by three years.
(ii) That pen is inferior *to* that.
(iii) He is junior *to* me in rank.
(iv) This event was posterior *to* that.

**Note:** Never use *than* after the above mentioned adjectives.

## Important Information

(a) 'Preferable' is also used as an adjective of the comparative degree. As such, it is always followed by *to* and not *a*.

Death is preferable than dishonour. (Incorrect)
Death is preferable *to* dishonour. (Correct)

(b) To intensify the Degree of comparison, we use *far* or *much* before the comparative.

**Examples :**
(i) This book is *far* better than that.
(ii) His performance was *much* better than Mohan's.

**Warning :** Always avoid the use of double comparatives.

**Don't say :** Ram is more cleverer than his younger brother.

**Say:** Ram is cleverer than his younger brother.

3. **Superlative Degree :** It expresses the most of the common form of an adjective.

**Example :**
He is the ablest man of the town.

## How and when to use the Superlative Degree?

(a) The Superlative Degree is used when more than two persons or things are compared.

(b) The Superlative Degree is generally preceded by 'the' and followed by 'of' in most of the cases or otherwise.

(c) When an adjective of the superlative degree is preceded by a Possessive Adjective or a Noun in the Possessive case, 'the' should not be used before it.

**Example :**
Which is Kalidas' best play?
It will be a blunder to use 'the' before the Superlative Degree in such cases.

**Don't say :** Which is Kalidas' the best play.

(d) To intensify the degree of comparison, *by far* is used before the superlative degree.

**Example :**
India is *by far* the most beautiful country of the world.

**Note:** Always avoid the use of double superlatives.

**Don't say :** He is the most strongest boy in the class.

**Say :** He is the strongest boy in the class.

## Use of some Important Adjectives

1. (a) 'Some' is used as follows :
(i) With countable nouns where it means— a little, a small quantity.
(ii) In a question which shows some request.

**Examples :**
(i) There is some water in the bottle.
(ii) Some of the students were absent yesterday.
(iii) Will you have some milk?
(iv) Will you buy some fruit for me?

(b) 'Any' is used as follows :
(i) In negative sentences.
(ii) In interrogative sentences.

(iii) After 'Hardly', 'Scarcely' and 'Barely'.

(iv) After 'If'.

**Examples :**

(i)   There is not any sugar in the pot.

(ii)  We haven't any rice in the house.

(iii) I have hardly any money.

(iv) There are scarcely any plants in this field.

(v)  If there is any danger, blow the whistle.

2. (a) **Older :** Older (and oldest) are used for persons animals and things. But 'Older' and 'Oldest' refer to the persons who do not belong to the same family.

**Examples :**

(i)   Radha is older than Shyama.

(ii)  John is the oldest member of the staff. 'Older' and 'Oldest' refer to the persons who do not belong to the same family.

(b) **Elder** (and **eldest**) are used in respect of the members of the same family like sons, daughters, brothers, sisters.

**Examples :**

(i)   My elder sister is a lecturer.

(ii)  Meenakshi is the eldest of the three sisters.

**Note :**

(i)   'Elder' is not followed by 'than'.

(ii)  'Elder' and 'Eldest' cannot be used for things.

3. (a) **'Few'** is negative and is the opposite of 'Many'. It means 'not many'.

(b) **'A few'** is positive and means 'some at least'. It is the opposite of 'None'.

(c) **'The few'** means 'minority' and suggests 'whether there is'.

**Examples :**

(i)   We have few holidays in school.

(ii)  Only a few boys will fail in the examination.

(iii) The few poems that he wrote are very popular.

4. (a) **Further** means 'something additional'.

(b) **Farther** means 'a greater distance'.

**Examples :**

(i)   Further discussion will be held in the office of the principal.

(ii)  Amritsar is farther from Delhi than Ambala.

5. (a) **Little** is negative. It means, 'not much', or 'hardly any'.

(b) **A little** is positive. It means 'some quantity'.

(c) **The little** denotes quantity. It means, 'not much but all that is, or whatever quantity there is'.

**Examples :**

(i)   There is little hope of his success.

(ii)  He knows a little of everything.

(iii) I have spent the little money I had.

(iv) The little knowledge of shoe-making proved very useful to me.

6. (a) **'Much'** expresses 'quantity'.

(b) **'Many'** expresses 'number'.

(c) **'Many a'**—'Singular noun' and 'Singular verb' are used with 'many a'.

**Examples :**

(i)   There is not *much* water in the jug.

(ii)  *Many* boys are absent today.

(iii) *Many* a battle has been fought on the soil of India.

7. (a) **'Less'** denotes 'in a small degree'.

(b) **'Fewer'** denotes 'number'.

**Examples :**

(i)   He devotes less time to his studies.

(ii)  There are no fewer than ten chairs in this room.

8. (a) **'Each'** is used for a single number of 'two persons' or 'things'.

(b) **'Every'** is used for a single number of 'many persons' or 'things'.

**Examples :**

(i)   Each boy must take part in games.

(ii)  There are only two poets. Each poet recited his poem.

(iii) Every man dies in this world.

(iv) Every man is expected to do his duty.

9. (a) **'Either'** means one of the two or both.

(b) **'Neither'** is negative of the either.

**Examples :**

(i)   You may buy either of these two chairs.

(ii)  Neither of them could speak on the stage.

10.(a) **'Later'** expresses 'late in time'.

(b) **'Latter'** means 'second in position or order'.

**Examples :**

(i)   My father reached later than I expected.

(ii)  The latter position was better than the former.

## Use of some Important Adverbs

1. (a) Also, too, enough:

(i)   He taught English. Also, he edited the school magazine

(ii)  He is a writer and also he is a painter.

(iii) He is too obstinate to listen to any reason.

(iv)  This is too difficult a piece for the junior students.

(v)   Sarla was kind enough to help the poor.

(vi)  He is brave enough to help the truth.

**Note:** 'Too' is used in a negative sense, but enough is used in a positive sense.

(b) Fairly and rather: Both suggest the meaning 'moderately'. But, mainly 'fairly' is used with the words that denote a positive meaning and rather is used with the words that denote a negative meaning:

(i)   Rita did fairly well in that competition, but her performance was rather poor in sports.

(ii)  Mona is fairly rich, but she is rather stingy.

**Note:** 'Rather' can also be used in a positive sense.

(i)   This is a rather interesting job.

(ii)  That boy is rather smart.

(c) Hardly, barely, scarcely: These words mostly convey the negative suggestions and are almost similar.

(i)   I have hardly any strength now.

(ii)  There was barely any supply to the township,

(iii) There were scarcely a hundred guests present.

**Note:** With slight variance in the meaning, the words given above convey the idea of 'very little', 'not enough', 'lack of quantity and number'.

(d) Yet, Still: These adverbs can often be used to connect the sentence units:

(i)   He has been defeated many times in the contest; still he wants to be a competitor.

(ii)  Mona was sick; yet she went on doing her work.

(e) Alone:

(i)   He alone (none else) is capable of handling that fire,

(ii)  He hunted all alone in the forest. (not in any company)

**Special Note:**

(a) Apart from their conventional positions the adverbs might be used in different positions with different meanings and angles.

(i)   He had only four books.

(ii)  John only contacted his friend in need.

(iii) He greeted me only.

(iv)  Only he greeted me there.

(b) Inversion: Some adverbs can be inverted *i.e.* placed in the beginning of the sentence and then be followed by an interrogative form. The most common of these adverb are: so, seldom, never, nowhere, under no circumstances, hardly, scarcely etc.

(i)   So big was the bus that it could not enter the narrow lane.

(ii)  Hardly had he reached the station when he received the message.

## MULTIPLE CHOICE QUESTIONS

**Directions:** *In the following questions choose the correct options to fill the blanks.*

**1.** The girl whom you met is the .......... sister of Ravi.

A.  eldest

B.  elder

C.  older

D.  oldest

**2.** The historical place is .......... .

A.  seeing worth

B.   worthy of seeing
C.   worth seeing
D.   worthy seeing

**3.** These flowers smell .......... .
A.   sweet                B.   sweetly
C.   more sweetly     D.   sweetest

**4.** .......... aspirant cannot pass the entrance examination.
A.   Each               B.   Every
C.   All                 D.   No

**5.** Harivansh Rai .......... second Shakespeare.
A.   is a               B.   is
C.   is the            D.   is an

**6.** .......... student in the class got prizes.
A.   Each and every     B.   Every and each
C.   Every            D.   Never

**7.** It is .......... picture than the one we saw last Monday.
A.   interesting       B.   much interesting
C.   more interesting   D.   most interesting

**8.** She is clever .......... .
A.   that her mother is
B.   as her mother is
C.   to her mother is
D.   than her mother is

**9.** They will get .......... .
A.   Red, green and black paper
B.   Red, green black paper
C.   Red and green and black paper
D.   Red green black paper

**10.** Health is .......... wealth.
A.   preferable to
B.   more preferable than
C.   more preferable to
D.   most preferable then

**11.** .......... water that was in the jug evaporated.
A.   Little            B.   The little
C.   Small           D.   A small

**12.** He has not sung .......... songs.
A.   much             B.   most
C.   more             D.   many

**13.** Srishti has searched .......... office.
A.   whole the       B.   the whole
C.   a whole         D.   some whole

**14.** Premchand was ....... best and ....... famous writer.
A.   a, the most       B.   the, a most
C.   the, more         D.   the, the most

**15.** William Shakespeare is famous as .......... .
A.   a poet and a dramatist
B.   a poet and dramatist
C.   the poet and the dramatist
D.   a poet and the dramatist

**16.** What does .......... leader suggest?
A.   other            B.   another
C.   others           D.   anothers

**17.** He .......... money.
A.   has few          B.   have few
C.   has little       D.   have little

**18.** The .......... boys are rewarded.
A.   first two        B.   two first
C.   firsts two      D.   two's first

**19.** He is .......... brave.
A.   stronger than
B.   stronger then
C.   more strong then
D.   more strong than

**20.** No sooner said .......... .
A.   so done          B.   and done
C.   then done      D.   but done

**21.** She returned .......... than I had thought.
A.   quickly          B.   more quicker
C.   more quickly     D.   quicker

**22.** He is .......... foolish person.
A.   rather the       B.   a rather
C.   rather a        D.   rather

**23.** This pen .......... rupees.
A.   costs twenty
B.   twenty costs only
C.   costs only twenty
D.   only costs twenty

**24.** It is .......... pride.
A.   nothing else but
B.   nothing else than
C.   else nothing than
D.   but

**25.** This tea is .......... to drink.
A.   too hot          B.   very hot
C.   enough hot     D.   much hot

## ANSWERS

| 1 | 2 | 3 | 4 | 5 | 6 | 7 | 8 | 9 | 10 |
|---|---|---|---|---|---|---|---|---|---|
| A | C | A | B | A | C | C | C | A | A |

| 11 | 12 | 13 | 14 | 15 | 16 | 17 | 18 | 19 | 20 |
|----|----|----|----|----|----|----|----|----|----|
| B | D | B | D | B | B | C | A | D | C |

| 21 | 22 | 23 | 24 | 25 |
|----|----|----|----|----|
| C | C | C | A | A |

## DETERMINERS

Determiners are actually Adjectives. They are always followed by nouns.

Determiners are of the following kinds:

**1. Demonstrative Determiners**
   this, that, these, those

**2. Possessive Determiners**
   my, our, your, his, her, its, their

**3. Quantitative Determiners**
   some, any, much, enough, sufficient, whole, a little, the little, little, all, both

**4. Numerical Determiners**
   a few, some, few, the few, any, several, many, no, etc.

   One, two, three ...                    (Cardinals)

   First, second, third ...               (Ordinals)

**5. Distributive Determiners**
   either, neither

**6. Articles**
   **Indefinite:** a, an

   **Definite:** the

## MULTIPLE CHOICE QUESTIONS

**Directions:** *In the following questions choose the correct options to fill the blanks.*

1. Give me ......... rice.
   A. some
   B. few
   C. a few
   D. any

2. ......... sheep grazing on the slope of the hill had gone away.
   A. Any
   B. The few
   C. This
   D. Much

3. Have you got ......... magazines to read?
   A. all
   B. much
   C. some
   D. little

4. I have ....... money that I want to spend on shares.
   A. any
   B. much
   C. less
   D. some

5. There is ......... owl on the branch of the tree.
   A. a
   B. the
   C. an
   D. some

6. My brother is ......... MBA.
   A. a
   B. an
   C. the
   D. any

7. Have you got ......... cheese?
   A. some
   B. many
   C. a few
   D. few

8. No, I have not got ......... cheese.
   A. many
   B. few
   C. any
   D. some

9. There is only ......... milk left in the bottle.
   A. enough
   B. few
   C. much
   D. a little

10. There is ......... hope of his recovery.
    A. any
    B. little
    C. many
    D. few

11. ......... dogs were barking at the strangers.
    A. Some
    B. Any
    C. Much
    D. Less

**12.** The girl bought her father ......... juice.
  A. few                    B. some
  C. any                    D. many

**13.** You should take ......... honey everyday.
  A. any                    B. many
  C. a little               D. a few

**14.** ......... boy was punished by the teacher.
  A. Either                 B. All
  C. Any                    D. Many

**15.** ......... girl was asked to join the army.
  A. None                   B. Neither
  C. All                    D. Any

**16.** ......... water in the jug has been drunk by Mohan.

  A. The little             B. The few
  C. A few                  D. Few

**17.** I shall play ......... piano at the party.
  A. some                   B. any
  C. the                    D. few

**18.** ......... labourers were found dead in the mine.
  A. Any                    B. Fewer
  C. Many                   D. Less

**19.** Could I borrow ......... umbrella?
  A. our                    B. your
  C. yours                  D. my

**20.** My brother is standing in the ......... row.
  A. any                    B. many
  C. some                   D. first

## ANSWERS

| 1 | 2 | 3 | 4 | 5 | 6 | 7 | 8 | 9 | 10 |
|---|---|---|---|---|---|---|---|---|---|
| A | B | C | D | C | B | A | C | D | B |

| 11 | 12 | 13 | 14 | 15 | 16 | 17 | 18 | 19 | 20 |
|----|----|----|----|----|----|----|----|----|----|
| A | B | C | A | B | A | C | C | B | D |

## THE VERB

A Verb is a word that tells something about the action or state of or happenning to a person or thing.

A Verb tells the following:

**1.** What a person or thing does.
  Sachin goes to school daily.
  The bell *rang* loudly.
  Many birds fly in the sky.
  She *sang* a song.

**2.** What a person or thing is.
  India *is* the biggest democracy in the world.
  Ram Mehar *is* very rich.
  They *are* happy.

**3.** What is done to a person or thing.
  You *are liked* by all.
  Two thieves *were arrested.*
  Four students *were punished* by the teacher.

**4.** What happens to a person or thing.
  His maternal uncle *died* last week.
  Two ships *sank* yesterday.
  Leaves *turn* yellow in autumn.

**5.** What a person or thing has, had, and so on.
  I *have* a new car.
  He *had* a scooter last year.

He *has* several cows and goats.

It goes without saying that a verb is the most important part of a sentence. No sentence is complete without a Verb.

## Important Information

1. If two or more singular nouns are joined by 'and' the verb used will be plural.

  **Example:**
  (i)  He and I were going to the market.
  (ii) Ram and Mohan are friends.

2. If two singular nouns joined by 'and' points out to the same thing or person, the verb used must be singular.

  **Example:**
  (i)  Rice and curry is the favourite food of the Punjabis.
  (ii) The Collector and District Magistrate is away.

3. In case two subjects are joined by 'as well as' the verb agrees with the first subject.

  **Example :**
  (i)  Kanta as well as her children is playing.
  (ii) Children as well as their mother are playing.

In the case of first sentence the verb (is) agrees with Kanta and in the case of second sentence the verb (are) agrees with the children.

4. 'Neither', 'Either', 'Every', 'Each', 'Everyone', and 'Many a' are followed by a singular verb.
   **Example :**
   (i)   Either of the plans is to be adopted.
   (ii)  Neither of the two brothers is sure to pass.
   (iii) Every student is expected to be obedient.
   (iv)  Everyone of them desires this.
   (v)   Many a person is drowned in the sea.

5. If two subjects are joined by 'Either ....... or' / 'Neither .......... nor', the verb agrees with the subject near to it.

   **Example :**
   (i)   Either my brother or I am to do this work.
   (ii)  Neither he nor they are prepared to do this work.

6. 'A great many' is always followed by a 'plural noun' and a 'plural verb'. For example :
   A great many students have been declared successful.

7. Similarly if two subjects are joined by 'with', 'together with', 'no less than', in addition to 'and not', etc. the verb agrees with the first subject.
   **Example :**
   (i)   The boy with his parents has arrived.
   (ii)  He, no less than I, is to blame.

8. Nouns, plural in form, but singular in meaning, take a singular verb.
   **Example :**
   This news was broadcast from television yesterday.

## MULTIPLE CHOICE QUESTIONS

**Directions:** *In the following questions choose the correct options to fill the blanks.*

1. The bus with all its passengers .......... lost.
   A. were          B. was
   C. are           D. would

2. You as well as I .......... responsible for this work.
   A. am            B. are
   C. was           D. is

3. Raghava like all his companions .......... a spoiled child.
   A. are           B. were
   C. is            D. will be

4. Pen and ink .......... required for me.
   A. are           B. were
   C. is            D. has required

5. Every girl and every boy .......... attended the seminar.
   A. have          B. has
   C. is            D. are

6. Not only she but all her sisters ...... been married.
   A. has           B. have
   C. is            D. are

7. There .......... nothing but miseries in life.
   A. is            B. are
   C. were          D. will be

8. Neither prose nor poem .......... given.
   A. were          B. was
   C. has           D. have

9. Either he or I .......... wrong.
   A. is            B. are
   C. am            D. were

10. Either Sulekha or Rekha .......... coming here.
    A. are          B. is
    C. were         D. have

11. .......... the child or his parents to blame?
    A. Is           B. Are
    C. Were         D. Has

12. You and I .......... neighbours.
    A. am           B. are
    C. was          D. has

13. The house with all its belongings ..... sold away.
    A. were         B. are
    C. was          D. must

14. Either water or juice .......... required.
    A. is           B. are
    C. were         D. has

15. There were not as many tables as .......... required.
    A. was          B. were
    C. is           D. are

16. They each .......... a book.
    A. have              B. are
    C. has               D. is
17. He and I .......... class friends.
    A. is                B. am
    C. was               D. are
18. She as well as I .......... guilty.
    A. is                B. are
    C. am                D. must be
19. Purushottam ....... not read more on this chapter.
    A. needs             B. has been need
    C. need              D. had been need
20. He came .......... to his aunt.
    A. run               B. running
    C. to run            D. in run
21. She dislikes .......... meat.
    A. eat to            B. to eat
    C. eating            D. to eating
22. He likes ........... .
    A. sing to           B. singing
    C. to sing           D. to singing
23. We are ready .......... the match.
    A. play to           B. to playing
    C. playing           D. to play
24. .......... is injurious to health.
    A. Smoking           B. To smoke
    C. To smoking        D. Smoke to
25. He loves .......... raw vegetables.
    A. eaten             B. eating
    C. to eating         D. eat to
26. He seemed .......... finished his homework.
    A. have to           B. to have
    C. having            D. to having

## ANSWERS

| 1 | 2 | 3 | 4 | 5 | 6 | 7 | 8 | 9 | 10 |
|---|---|---|---|---|---|---|---|---|----|
| B | B | C | C | B | B | A | B | C | B |

| 11 | 12 | 13 | 14 | 15 | 16 | 17 | 18 | 19 | 20 |
|----|----|----|----|----|----|----|----|----|----|
| A | B | C | A | B | A | D | A | C | B |

| 21 | 22 | 23 | 24 | 25 | 26 |
|----|----|----|----|----|----|
| C | B | D | A | B | B |

## CONJUNCTIONS

A conjunction is a word which connects words, clauses or sentences.

Look at the following sentences.

(i) He bought apples *and* mangoes.

(ii) God made the country *and* man made the town.

(iii) The door was open *but* there was no one in the house.

(iv) He knows that I am here *and* that I want to see him.

In the sentence (i), *and* connects two words—*apples* and *mangoes*.

In the sentence (ii), *and* connects two sentences—*God made the country* and *man made the town.*

In the sentence (iii), *but* connects two sentences—*The door was open* and *there was no one in the house.*

In the sentence (iv), *and* connects two clauses—*that I am here* and *that I want to see him.*

The main coordinating conjunctions are:

and, but, for, or, nor, also, either ..... or, neither ..... nor.

There are some conjunctions which are used in pairs. They are:

either .... or, .... neither .... nor, both .... and, though .... yet, whether .... or, not only .... but also.

**Example:** *Either* take it *or* leave it.

It is *neither* useful *nor* ornamental.

They *both* like *and* respect me.

*Though* he is suffering from high fever, *yet* he does not cry.

He does not care *whether* you go *or* stay.

He is *not only* doltish, *but also* obstinate.

The conjunctions which are used in pairs in this way, are called correlative conjunctions, or merely correlatives.

## Use of Important Conjunctions

1. **As soon as :** As soon as denotes simultaneous time.
   **Example :** As soon as he saw his enemy, he took to his heels.

2. **No sooner .......... than :**
   (a) 'No sooner' is always followed by 'than'.
   (b) Please remember that 'No sooner' is always followed by do/does/did. As such only first form of the verb should be used after the subject.
   **Example :**
   No sooner did he see his enemy than he took to his heels.

3. **Hardly :** Hardly is followed by when.
   **Examples :**
   (i) Hardly had I left the house when it started raining.
   (ii) We had hardly come into the room when his father began chastising him.
   **Note :**
   A. Hardly is never followed by than.
   B. 'Scarcely' can also be used in the sense and manner of 'Hardly'.

4. **Lest :** Lest is used in the sense of so that .......... not. It is always followed by should. Lest is negative in sense. Hence 'not' should never be used with it.
   **Example :**
   Work hard lest you should fail.
   **Note :** 'Lest' is always followed by 'should' and not 'may'.

5. **Unless :** Unless expresses condition. It is also used in the negative sense. Use of 'not' is not allowed with unless because unless is already in the negative sense.
   **Example :**
   Unless you labour hard you will not pass.

6. **Until :** 'Until' expresses time. It means 'till not'.
   **Example :**
   Wait here until I return.
   **Note :** Until is in the negative sense. So 'not' should not be used with it. Example :
   Wait here until I do not return.    (Incorrect)
   Wait here until I return.             (Correct)

7. **As well as :** When two subjects are joined by 'as well as', the verb always agrees with the first subject.
   **Examples :**
   (i) The teacher as well as students is playing.
   (ii) Students as well as the teacher are playing.
   **Note :** 'Both' and 'as well as' cannot be used together in the same sentence.
   **Examples :**
   Both Sita as well as Kanta are beautiful.
                                        (Incorrect)
   Sita as well as Kanta is beautiful.  (Correct)
   Both Sita and Kanta are beautiful. (Correct)

8. **As if :** 'As if' is used in the sense of pretension. While using 'as if' in a sentence, we should see that even the third person singular subject gets 'were'.
   **Example :**
   He talks as if he were mad.

9. **Till :** Till expresses time. Till is always used in the affirmative.
   **Example :**
   We did not come back till sunset.

10. **Rather than :** 'Rather than' is used in the sense of 'preference'. 'Rather' is always followed by 'than'.
    **Example :**
    I would rather die than submit.

11. **As long as/so long as :** Both express time during which an action or event takes place.
    **Example :**
    As long as there is life, there is hope.

12. **However :** It is both a subordinate and co-ordinate clause.
    **Examples :**
    (a) Mala worked hard, she however, failed.
    (b) However hard he may work, he cannot pass.

13. **Such as :** 'Such as' gives us the sense of 'like'. Such is always followed by 'as'.
    **Example :**
    Life is such a puzzle as cannot be solved.

# MULTIPLE CHOICE QUESTIONS

**Directions:** *In the following questions choose the correct options to fill the blanks.*

1. Neither he .......... his friend is good.
   - A. or
   - B. and
   - C. but
   - D. nor

2. The officer asked the peon .......... why he was late.
   - A. that
   - B. if
   - C. but
   - D. No word needed

3. Both Ajay .......... Vijay are intelligent.
   - A. or
   - B. nor
   - C. and
   - D. No word needed

4. No Sooner did the thief see the public .......... he ran away.
   - A. then
   - B. and
   - C. but
   - D. than

5. Abhinav .......... his brothers was going to Mumbai.
   - A. but
   - B. yet
   - C. No word needed
   - D. together with

6. He behaves .......... he were the captain of the team.
   - A. as if
   - B. as
   - C. No word needed
   - D. that

7. Either Rupali .......... Sonali is going to attend the meeting.
   - A. and
   - B. but
   - C. nor
   - D. or

8. Neither Nirmal .......... Ashwinee is going to listen the speech.
   - A. and
   - B. but
   - C. nor
   - D. or

9. Ravi .......... Prakash are going to Kolkata.
   - A. or
   - B. nor
   - C. but
   - D. and

10. Rice .......... curry is my usual breakfast.
    - A. and
    - B. but
    - C. then
    - D. than

11. Hardly had he left .......... his brother came.
    - A. then
    - B. than
    - C. when
    - D. that

12. I would rather have a copy .......... a book.
    - A. then
    - B. than
    - C. when
    - D. that

13. He is no other .......... my friend.
    - A. then
    - B. than
    - C. when
    - D. but

14. He saw a snake ..........he awoke.
    - A. then
    - B. when
    - C. than
    - D. No word needed

15. Ten years have passed .......... my grandmother died.
    - A. since
    - B. when
    - C. then
    - D. than

16. She is .......... good .......... bad.
    - A. either, not
    - B. neither, or
    - C. neither, nor
    - D. neither, than

17. The cellphone is both cheap .......... best.
    - A. than
    - B. and
    - C. then
    - D. or

18. No sooner did the rogue see the police .......... he disappeared.
    - A. then
    - B. than
    - C. so
    - D. because

19. Srishti will go .......... Sanju goes.
    - A. if
    - B. than
    - C. then
    - D. although

20. She is wise .......... timid.
    - A. and
    - B. yet
    - C. but
    - D. however

21. Make hay ........ the sun shines.
    - A. though
    - B. while
    - C. after
    - D. before

22. He is so weak .......... he cannot walk.
    - A. but
    - B. that
    - C. then
    - D. so

23. Although he is rich, ........ he is unhappy.
    - A. but
    - B. yet
    - C. so
    - D. still

24. Wait here ....... I come back.
    - A. till
    - B. until
    - C. before
    - D. after

**25.** He is my friend ............ I shall help him.
   A. so
   B. hence
   C. that is why
   D. therefore

**26.** He must go away .................... he will be beaten.
   A. otherwise      B. and
   C. or      D. else

**27.** God loves good men .......... good men love God.

     A. and      B. or
     C. that      D. those

**28.** He was late ............. he was not punished.
   A. but      B. yet
   C. still      D. therefore

**29.** Walk slowly .............., you may fall.
   A. and      B. or
   C. so      D. otherwise

**30.** Work hard, ............ you will fail.
   A. and      B. or
   C. otherwise      D. else

## ANSWERS

| 1 | 2 | 3 | 4 | 5 | 6 | 7 | 8 | 9 | 10 |
|---|---|---|---|---|---|---|---|---|----|
| D | D | C | D | D | A | D | C | D | A |
| **11** | **12** | **13** | **14** | **15** | **16** | **17** | **18** | **19** | **20** |
| C | B | B | B | A | C | B | B | A | C |
| **21** | **22** | **23** | **24** | **25** | **26** | **27** | **28** | **29** | **30** |
| B | B | B | A | B | C | A | C | D | D |

## PREPOSITIONS

A *Preposition* is a word which is placed before a noun or a pronoun to show its relation to some other word in the sentence.

     1. I saw a goat *in* the field.

     2. I am fond *of* hot coffee.

In sentence 1, the word *in* shows the relation between two things—*goat* and *field*.

In sentence 2, the word *of* shows the relation between the attribute expressed by the adjective *found* and *tea*.

The words *in* and *of* are here used as prepositions.

The noun or pronoun which is used with a preposition is called its object. The noun or pronoun is in the objective case. It is governed by the preposition. Now it is absolutely clear that in sentence 1, the noun *field* is in the objective case. The word *field* is governed by the preposition *in*.

A preposition may have two or more objects.

The road runs over *hill* and *plain*.

Here, the words *hill* and *plain* are used as objects.

### Use of Important Prepositions

     **1. Among, Between**

'**Among**' is used for more than two persons or things; '**Between**' is used only for two.

**Examples :**

(i) Distribute these sweets *among* the poor students of the class.

(ii) Distribute these books *between* Ram and Shyam.

   **2. Among, In**

'**Among**' is used before collective plural nouns. '**In**' is used before collective singular nouns.

**Examples :**

(i) I found him standing *among* the crowd.

(ii) I saw him in the crowd.

   **3. Beside, Besides**

'**Beside**' means 'by the side of'. '**Besides**' means 'in addition to'.

**Examples :**

(i) The daughter was sitting *beside* her mother.

(ii) *Besides* his relatives, he invited his friends also.

   **4. In, Within**

'**In**' means at the expiry of a period of time in future, '**Within**' means before the expiry of a period of time in any tense.

**Examples :**
(i)   She will return *in* a week.
(ii)  I shall finish my work *within* a weak.

**5. On, Upon**
'**On**' is used for things at rest; '**Upon**' is used for things in motion.
**Examples :**
(i)   He is sitting *on* the floor.
(ii)  The dog sprang *upon* the table.

**6. By, With**
'**By**' denotes the agent or doer, '**With**' denotes the instrument with which anything is done.
**Examples :**
(i)   The bird was killed *by* the hunter with an arrow.
(ii)  He beat the dog *with* a stick.
(iii) I shall reach here *by* five o'clock.

**7. After, In**
'**After**' means at the end of a period of time in the past. '**In**' means at the end of a period of time in future.
**Examples :**
(i)   I shall return your book *in* a week.
(ii)  He returned the book *after* a week.

**8. For, From, Since**
'**For**' is used before a noun denoting a period of time with all the tenses. '**From**' is used before a noun or phrase denoting a point of time, it is used in all the tenses. '**Since**' is used before a noun or phrase denoting some point of time and is always produced by a verb in the perfect continuous tense or third form of a verb.
**Examples :**
(i)   We have been playing cards *for* two hours.
(ii)  She stayed with her uncle *from* the 15th of March to the 15th of May.
(iii) I have been reading this book *since* morning.

**9. Above, Over**
'**Above**' means 'higher from', **Over** is used in the following four senses :
(i)   In the sense of 'above' :
At noon, the sun is *over* our heads.

(ii)  In the sense of 'beyond' :
I cannot get *over* my disappointment.
(iii) In the sense of 'Superiority' :
God *over* all blesses for ever more.
(iv)  In the sense of 'Conclusion' :
It is all *over* with me.

**10. At, Towards**
'**At**' denotes the idea of aim, '**Towards**' denotes the idea of destination.
**Examples :**
(i)   He threw the stone *at* the cat.
(ii)  He went *towards* the house.

**11. At, In, On**
'At' is used as follows :
(i)   '**At**' is used with small towns and villages.
**Examples :**
(a)   He was born *at* Sonepat.
(b)   He lives *at* village Bangra. (Bangra is a village)
(ii)  '**At**' is used before a noun denoting a definite point of time.
**Example :**
He called on me *at* 9 p.m. yesterday.
'In' is used as follows :
(iii) '**In**' is used with the names of big cities, provinces and countries.
**Examples :**
(a)   His father lives *in* England.
(b)   His younger brother lives *in* Calcutta.
(iv)  '**In**' is used before the names of months and years.
**Example :**
His elder sister was born *in* 1972 *in* the month of May.
'**On**' is used with dates and names of days.
**Examples :**
(a)   I joined college *on* the 26th April.
(b)   He will leave for Kolkata *on* Wednesday next.

## Important Information

1. '**In**' is also used in the following phrases :
In the morning; In the evening, In winter, In summer.

2. 'In' also denotes a place inside anything.
   He travelled *in* a crowded bus.
3. 'At' is used in the following phrases :
   *At* home, *At* the station, *At* work, *At* play.

**12. Below, Beneath**

*Below* means 'of lower level in position, dignity and expectation' etc. *Beneath* means 'under'.

**Examples :**
 (i) It is *below* my dignity to talk to her.
 (ii) They rested *beneath* the shade of a tree.

**13. In, Into, To**

'**In**' expresses Rest or Motion inside anything. '**Into**' expresses Motion towards the inside of anything or change from one medium to another. '**To**' denotes motion from one place to another.

**Examples :**
 (i) The boys are *in* the room.
 (ii) Translate this passage from English *into* Hindi.

(iii) Every morning he goes *to* the temple.

**14. Till, By, Of, Off**
 • 'Till' means upto or not earlier than.
 • 'By' means not later than.
 • 'Of' shows cause, source, separation, quality, contents, possession, apposition, point of reference, space in time etc.
 • 'Off' shows separation at a near distance, and detached condition.

**Consider the following examples:**
 (i) I shall work *till* 5 a.m.
 (ii) Madhu died *of* cancer.
 (iii) The nib *of* the pen is made *of* gold.
 (iv) He presented me a bottle *of* perfume.
 (v) Our principal is a man *of* principle.
 (vi) He lived in the house *of* his friend.
 (vii) *By* this time tomorrow, I'll have finished my job.
 (viii) My house is *off* the road.
 (ix) The book fell *off* the table.

---

## MULTIPLE CHOICE QUESTIONS

**Directions:** *Tick the correct preposition for the blank in each of the following sentences.*

1. He applied ...... the manager.
   A. for
   B. to
   C. with
   D. by
2. Trust ...... God and do the right.
   A. in
   B. for
   C. to
   D. with
3. She is worthy ...... a prize.
   A. with
   B. for
   C. to
   D. of
4. Mr. Gomes has no taste ...... music.
   A. of
   B. for
   C. with
   D. to
5. You are hard ...... hearing.
   A. at
   B. of
   C. with
   D. for
6. He is sure ...... his success
   A. for
   B. with
   C. on
   D. of

7. Preeti was warned ...... the danger ahead.
   A. for
   B. at
   C. of
   D. about
8. I am thankful ...... you for a good advice.
   A. for
   B. with
   C. to
   D. of
9. Deepak would not surrender ...... the police.
   A. with
   B. to
   C. for
   D. on
10. The small plant in your lawn is very sensitive ...... touch.
    A. on
    B. with
    C. to
    D. about
11. Divya was sure to succeed ..... the examination.
    A. for
    B. in
    C. to
    D. with
12. Geeta was jealous ...... Ravina's beauty.
    A. to
    B. with
    C. for
    D. of

**13.** He was ignorant ..... what was happening there.
  A. for          B. of
  C. to           D. with
**14.** Your pen is inferior ...... mine.
  A. than         B. with
  C. from         D. to
**15.** Reenu is no match ...... Meenu.
  A. to           B. for
  C. with         D. upon
**16.** It is necessary ...... you to apply for this job.
  A. on           B. with
  C. for          D. to

**17.** Be loyal ...... your country.
  A. for          B. to
  C. on           D. with
**18.** Mukesh is junior ...... me.
  A. than         B. to
  C. from         D. of
**19.** Deepika was innocent ...... the crime.
  A. of           B. with
  C. from         D. to
**20.** I am desirous.... joining the Indian cricket team.
  A. for          B. of
  C. to           D. on

## ANSWERS

| 1 | 2 | 3 | 4 | 5 | 6 | 7 | 8 | 9 | 10 |
|---|---|---|---|---|---|---|---|---|----|
| B | A | D | B | B | D | D | D | B | D |

| 11 | 12 | 13 | 14 | 15 | 16 | 17 | 18 | 19 | 20 |
|----|----|----|----|----|----|----|----|----|----|
| B | D | B | D | B | D | B | B | A | B |

## SYNONYMS

A synonym is a word which conveys a meaning similar to the given word.

### REMEMBER

| Words | Synonyms |
|---|---|
| Add | Increase |
| Adequate | Enough |
| Adjust | Adapt |
| All | Aggregate |
| Allow | Permit |
| Abode | Dwelling |
| Apt | Proper |
| Assess | Appraise |
| Accuse | Calumniate |
| Abashed | Timid |
| Annoy | Displease |
| Ample | Enough, Sufficient |
| Amplify | Increase |
| Apathetic | Unenthusiastic |
| Accost | Address |
| Authentic | True |

| Words | Synonyms |
|---|---|
| Adjust | Fit |
| Approve | Assent, Allow, Accept |
| Adapt | Conform |
| Adversary | Opponent, Rival, Competitor |
| Beat | Whack |
| Benign | Kind |
| Breeze | Zephyr |
| Baffle | Puzzle |
| Booty | Spoil |
| Beauty | Charm |
| Beast | Animal |
| Bandit | Robber |
| Blaze | Shine |
| Bond | Tie |
| Bend | Twist |
| Bate | Diminish |
| Beg | Plead |
| Barbaric | Wild, Savage |
| Bashful | Shy, Reserved |

| Words | Synonyms |
|---|---|
| Begin | Start |
| Blend | Mix, Mingle |
| Bizarre | Funny |
| Below | Under |
| Bedevil | Confuse |
| Bemoan | Lament |
| Babble | Nonsense |
| Blame | Fault |
| Behaviour | Demeanour |
| Call | Accost |
| Copy | Imitate |
| Close | Shut |
| Caress | Love |
| Camp | Stay |
| Connect | Attach |
| Cut | Injure, Curtail |
| Cling | Stick |
| Conical | Funny |
| Convey | Carry |
| Conspicuous | Prominent |
| Cheerful | Happy, Pleasant |
| Curtail | Decrease |
| Cheerless | Sad, Dejected |
| Curious | Strange |
| Circumstance | Factor, Situation, Condition |
| Competent | Capable |
| Congruent | Overlapping |
| Cope | Deal, Endure |
| Confident | Sure |
| Complex | Intricate |
| Cajole | Coax, Flatter |
| Cunning | Crafty |
| Delectable | Joyful, Delightful |
| Devilish | Diabolical |
| Delicate | Soft |
| Devil | Fiend |
| Delay | Postpone |
| Dislike | Repugnance |
| Destroy | Ruin |

| Words | Synonyms |
|---|---|
| Dwell | Live, Dilate |
| Declare | Pronounce |
| Drunk | Flushed |
| Deficient | Lacking |
| Damn | Condemn, Curse |
| Decrease | Diminish |
| Destruction | Devastation |
| Efficient | Competent |
| Ethnic | Racial |
| Enthral | Enslave |
| Earnest | Serious |
| Envious | Jealous |
| Ending | Final |
| Egg | Incite |
| Extempore | At once |
| Extensive | Far-ranging |
| Extra | Surplus |
| Existence | Life |
| Exceed | Overstep |
| Enormous | Vast |
| Excessive | Superfluous |
| Free | Unhindered |
| Frigid | Cold |
| Feed | Cater |
| Fame | Reputation |
| Frame | Make |
| First | Initial |
| Frighten | Terrorise, Intimidate |
| Fervent | Fervid |
| Fall | Decline |
| Feeble | Frail |
| Fickle | Changeable |
| Finish | Conclude |
| Fraud | Deception |
| Forgiving | Placable |
| Grow | Develop |
| Greed | Avidity |
| Greet | Welcome |
| Grave | Serious |
| Group | Constellation |

| Words | Synonyms |
| --- | --- |
| Given | Bestowed |
| Gratitude | Thankfulness |
| Have | Possess |
| Hire | Rent |
| Hit | Strike |
| Handsome | Beautiful |
| Hinder | Prevent |
| Heap | Pile |
| Hope | Expect |
| Hard | Harsh |
| Help | Aid |
| Hymn | Song |
| Henpecked | Enslaved |
| Hoodwink | Mystify, Cheat |
| Humble | Polite, Urbane, Modest |
| Harass | Vex, Trouble |
| Impart | Instil |
| Intact | Untouched |
| Instal | Establish |
| Indict | Impeach |
| Imitate | Ape |
| Instigate | Incite |
| Initiate | Start, Introduce |
| Inimical | Unfriendly |
| Insufferable | Intolerable |
| Impartiality | Justice |
| Jolly | Merry |
| Joyful | Delectable |
| Join | Conjoin |
| Kind | Benign |
| Kill | Murder |
| Kindred | Similar |
| Kinship | Relationship |
| Keen | Sharp |
| Knowledge | Scholarship |
| Lazy | Slothful |
| Large | Substantial, Gargantuan |
| Listless | Careless, Lackadaisical |
| Lax | Loose |
| Little | Small |
| Lifelike | Realistic |

| Words | Synonyms |
| --- | --- |
| Lofty | High |
| Lenient | Soft, Gentle |
| Lacking | Deficient, Wanting |
| Lessen | Decrease |
| Middleclass | Bourgeois |
| Mitigate | Lessen, Abate |
| Modesty | Humility, Lowliness |
| Mix | Mingle, Blend |
| Mixture | Mingling |
| Mixed | Assorted |
| Modify | Decrease |
| Mean | Imply |
| Multifarious | Varied |
| Miscarry | Abort |
| Note | Notice |
| Noble | Stately |
| Native | Indigenous |
| Needful | Necessary |
| Notify | Declare |
| Nervous | Shaky, Tremulous, Timid |
| Natural | Spontaneous |
| Near | Close |
| Normal | Natural |
| Offend | Displease |
| Oppress | Persecute, Tyrannize |
| Opponent | Adversary |
| Obstruct | Hinder, Check |
| Offence | Fault |
| Offender | Villain |
| Overstep | Exceed |
| Overlapping | Congruent |
| Occult | Mystic |
| Profane | Unholy |
| Patience | Forbearance |
| Pornographic | Obscene |
| Plenitude | Abundance |
| Prominent | Important |
| Prodigal | Spender |
| Procrastinate | Postpone |
| Promote | Develop, Honour |
| Persecute | Tyrannise |

| Words | Synonyms |
| --- | --- |
| Profess | Claim |
| Pliant | Flexible |
| Plebian | Common |
| Polished | Sophisticated |
| Quake | Shake |
| Quit | Leave |
| Queer | Eccentric |
| Quell | Suppress |
| Quantify | Allot |
| Reply | Answer |
| Relinquish | Retire |
| Read | Peruse |
| Relation | Reference |
| Render | Do |
| Remainder | Residuals |
| Repeat | Reiterate |
| Repentant | Contrite |
| Retaliative | Retaliatory |
| Rumour | Hearsay |
| Reveal | Divulge |
| Ritualistic | Ceremonious |
| Soft | Delicate |
| Sort | Kind, Choose, Select |
| Selfish | Egoistic |
| Sensual | Earthly |
| Suppress | Quell, Check |
| Stimulate | Provoke |
| Tasteless | Insipid |
| Travel | Journey |
| True | Authentic, Faithful, Truthful |
| Turbulence | Turmoil |
| Tragedy | Calamity |
| Tasteful | Tasty, Delicious |
| Touching | Painful |
| Thankful | Grateful |
| Tremendous | Great, Huge |
| Tough | Strong |
| Terminate | Conclude, End |
| Theory | Doctrine |
| Tell | Relate |
| Tremble | Shake, Shiver |
| Urge | Spur |

| Words | Synonyms |
| --- | --- |
| Unbeaten | Unsubdued |
| Use | Utilize, Practise |
| Underhand | Unfair, Undue |
| Unfair | Unjust |
| Unravel | Reveal, Divulge |
| Unimportant | Common |
| Unconcerned | Apathetic |
| Unimitated | Inimitable |
| Unfortunate | Unlucky |
| Understand | Perceive, Comprehend |
| Vain | Proud, Haughty, Conceited, Shameless |
| Vale | Valley, Dale, Dell |
| Vice | Fault |
| Virtue | Quality |
| Veracity | Reality |
| Value | Price, Prize |
| Vex | Tease |
| Vibrate | Quiver, Shake |
| Violent | Excessive |
| Vivid | Clear, Lucid |
| Victory | Triumph |
| Vulgar | Indecent |
| Virtuous | Honest |
| Variegated | Varied, Multifarious |
| Well | Good |
| Yell | Cry, Shout |
| Yonder | There |
| Yearn | Wish, Desire |
| Yoke | Slavery |
| Zest | Earnestness, Enthusiasm |
| Zealous | Earnest |

## ANTONYMS

A antonym is a word which conveys a meaning opposite to the given word.

### REMEMBER

| Words | Antonyms |
| --- | --- |
| Abhor | Love |
| Abnormal | Normal |
| Able | Unable |
| Acceptable | Unacceptable |
| Adequate | Inadequate |
| Amusing | Boring |

| Words | Antonyms | Words | Antonyms |
| --- | --- | --- | --- |
| Angry | Calm | Hard | Soft |
| Apex | Bottom | Hate | Love |
| Attract | Repel | Honest | Dishonest |
| Bad | Good | Idle | Busy |
| Barren | Fertile | Immoral | Moral |
| Beautiful | Ugly | Include | Exclude |
| Bitter | Sweet | Incorrect | Correct |
| Brave | Cowardly | Intelligent | Unintelligent |
| Brief | Lengthy | Kind | Cruel |
| Bright | Dull | Like | Dislike |
| Calm | Violent | Long | Short |
| Careful | Careless | Lucid | Vague |
| Clear | Vague, Cloudy | Major | Minor |
| Cold | Hot | Naive | Experienced |
| Cruel | Kind | Nadir | Apex |
| Dear | Cheap | Neat | Clumsy |
| Deep | Shallow | Obedient | Disobedient |
| Difficult | Easy | Obscure | Clear |
| Direct | Indirect | Oppose | Support |
| Dishonest | Honest | Optimistic | Pessimistic |
| Disobey | Obey | Out | In |
| Encourage | Discourage | Patience | Impatience |
| Enormous | Tiny | Peaceful | Belligerent |
| Excellent | Bad | Pious | Impious |
| Expensive | Cheap | Polite | Impolite |
| Eat | Fast | Potent | Impotent |
| Fair | Unfair | Prominent | Unimportant |
| Fake | Authentic | Proper | Improper |
| False | True | Pure | Impure |
| Famous | Notorious | Quick | Slow |
| Fool | Genius | Quiet | Disturbance |
| Generous | Miserly | Real | False, Unreal |
| Genius | Fool | Reject | Select, Choose |
| Genuine | Unauthentic | Reliable | Unreliable |
| Gigantic | Tiny | Respect | Disrespect |
| Glad | Depressed | Right | Wrong |
| Good | Bad | Robust | Feeble, Weak |
| Great | Little | Sad | Happy |
| Happy | Sad | | |

| Words | Antonyms |
|---|---|
| Secret | Open |
| Sensible | Insensible |
| Severe | Mild |
| Sharp | Blunt |
| Simple | Complex |
| Sociable | Unsociable |
| Tall | Short |
| Tidy | Untidy |
| Uncanny | Canny |
| Violent | Calm |
| Vivid | Vague |

| Words | Antonyms |
|---|---|
| Strong | Weak |
| Big | Small |
| Easy | Difficult |
| Fast | Slow |
| High | Low |
| Catchy | Unattractive |
| Ugly | Handsome, Beautiful, Tidy |
| Tasty | Insipid |
| Sonorous | Harsh |

## MULTIPLE CHOICE QUESTIONS

**Directions (Qs. 1 to 20):** *In the following questions choose the word which best expresses the meaning of the given word.*

1. ABSURD
   - A. Foolish
   - B. Simple
   - C. Courageous
   - D. Silly

2. ABANDON
   - A. Lose
   - B. Profit
   - C. Vacate
   - D. Foil

3. CAJOLE
   - A. Pause
   - B. Lenient
   - C. Blast
   - D. Lure

4. COMBAT
   - A. Fight
   - B. Conflict
   - C. Shoot
   - D. Quarrel

5. LAMENT
   - A. Condone
   - B. Console
   - C. Complain
   - D. Contribution

6. DEBACLE
   - A. Disgrace
   - B. Defeat
   - C. Collapse
   - D. Decline

7. SHIVER
   - A. Fear
   - B. Tremble
   - C. Shake
   - D. Ache

8. TORTURE
   - A. Terror
   - B. Harassment
   - C. Torment
   - D. Tranquility

9. LAUDABLE
   - A. Lovable
   - B. Commendable
   - C. Profitable
   - D. Oblivious

10. FIXED
    - A. Sterile
    - B. Static
    - C. Stubborn
    - D. Parennial

11. QUEER
    - A. Unfamiliar
    - B. Cute
    - C. Curious
    - D. Strange

12. SUFFICIENT
    - A. Fit
    - B. Proper
    - C. Adequate
    - D. Vast

13. GLOSS
    - A. Brightness
    - B. Soothing
    - C. Rubbing
    - D. Miracle

14. LONGING
    - A. Prune
    - B. Apathy
    - C. Curtail
    - D. Craving

15. JEER
    - A. Applaud
    - B. Magnanimity
    - C. Avoid
    - D. Scoff

16. ZENITH
    - A. Minimum
    - B. Nadir
    - C. Plant
    - D. Peak

17. GARB
    - A. Distort
    - B. Dress
    - C. Trivial
    - D. Rage

**18.** ABHOR
A. Rude          B. Reconcile
C. Crave         D. Detest

**19.** YIELD
A. Shum          B. Incisive
C. Retain        D. Surrender

**20.** YOKE
A. Twist         B. Release
C. Link          D. Extra

**Directions (Qs. 21 to 38):** *In the following questions choose the word which best expresses the opposite of the given word.*

**21.** TRAGIC
A. Dramatic      B. Strong
C. Gentle        D. Comic

**22.** ORAL
A. Verbal        B. Sane
C. Minor         D. Written

**23.** ADMIRE
A. Hate          B. Unlike
C. Dislike       D. Enough

**24.** VIOLENT
A. Gentle        B. Savage
C. Haughty       D. Decline

**25.** ADVERSITY
A. Windfall      B. Inprosperity
C. Prosperity    D. Slave

**26.** GENUINE
A. Spurious      B. Obscure
C. Countless     D. Apathetic

**27.** GRUDGE
A. Essence       B. Guile
C. Goodwill      D. Ill-will

**28.** STIFF
A. Soft          B. Courteous
C. Lively        D. Flexible

**29.** VANITY
A. Conceit       B. Pride
C. Ostentious    D. Humility

**30.** FRONT
A. Upper         B. Unusual
C. Back          D. Rear

**31.** ATTRACT
A. Lured         B. Longing
C. Repel         D. Disguise

**32.** COMFORT
A. Discomfort    B. Discontent
C. Uncomfort     D. Miscomfort

**33.** WELCOME
A. Repel         B. Accept
C. Resist        D. Fight

**34.** TACTFUL
A. Naive         B. Loose
C. Strict        D. Uncivilized

**35.** DUTIFUL
A. Harmful       B. Watchful
C. Forgetful     D. Remiss

**36.** RIGID
A. Flux          B. Adoptable
C. Yielding      D. Adaptable

**37.** RARE
A. Petty         B. Poor
C. Small         D. Common

**38.** ZEAL
A. Despair       B. Calmness
C. Passiveness   D. Indifference

## ANSWERS

| 1 | 2 | 3 | 4 | 5 | 6 | 7 | 8 | 9 | 10 |
|---|---|---|---|---|---|---|---|---|----|
| D | C | D | A | C | C | B | C | B | B |

| 11 | 12 | 13 | 14 | 15 | 16 | 17 | 18 | 19 | 20 |
|----|----|----|----|----|----|----|----|----|----|
| D | C | A | D | D | D | B | D | D | C |

| 21 | 22 | 23 | 24 | 25 | 26 | 27 | 28 | 29 | 30 |
|----|----|----|----|----|----|----|----|----|----|
| D | D | C | A | C | A | C | D | D | D |

| 31 | 32 | 33 | 34 | 35 | 36 | 37 | 38 |
|----|----|----|----|----|----|----|----|
| C | A | C | A | D | D | D | D |

# 3. Sentence Completion

It is such an exercise which starts with the primary schools and continues in the highest level of competitive examinations. One must practise it regularly to score well.

**Directions (Qs. 1 to 15):** *Pick out the most effective word(s) from the given words to fill in the blanks to make the sentence meaningfully complete.*

1. The student ...... that book from the library to study at home.
   - A. issued
   - B. borrowed
   - C. hired
   - D. lent

2. I wish I ...... a king.
   - A. was
   - B. am
   - C. should be
   - D. were

3. He ...... to listen to my arguments and walked away.
   - A. denied
   - B. disliked
   - C. objected
   - D. refused

4. The flow of blood was so ...... that the patient died.
   - A. intense
   - B. adequate
   - C. profuse
   - D. extensive

5. When I met her yesterday, it was the first time I ...... her since Christmas.
   - A. saw
   - B. have seen
   - C. had seen
   - D. have been seing

6. Can you pay ...... all these articles?
   - A. for
   - B. of
   - C. off
   - D. out

7. I ...... you to be at the party this evening.
   - A. expect
   - B. hope
   - C. look forward to
   - D. desire

8. ...... being a handicapped person, he is very cooperative and self-reliant.
   - A. Because
   - B. Although
   - C. Since
   - D. Despite

9. The child broke ...... from his mother and ran towards the painting.
   - A. away
   - B. after
   - C. down
   - D. with

10. With his ...... income, he finds it difficult to live a comfortable life.
   - A. brief
   - B. sufficient
   - C. meagre
   - D. huge

11. He could ...... a lot of money in such a short time by using his intelligence and working hard.
   - A. spend
   - B. spoil
   - C. exchange
   - D. accumulate

12. Though the brothers are twins, they look ......
   - A. alike
   - B. handsome
   - C. indifferent
   - D. different

13. Unfavourable weather conditions can ...... illness.
   - A. cure
   - B. detect
   - C. treat
   - D. enhance

14. No sooner did the bell ring, ...... the actor started singing.
   - A. when
   - B. than
   - C. after
   - D. before

15. If I ...... realised it, I would not have acted on his advice.
   - A. was
   - B. had
   - C. were
   - D. have

**Directions (Qs. 16 to 25):** *In each question, an incomplete statement (Stem) followed by four fillers* *is given. Pick out the best one which can complete the incomplete stem correctly and meaningfully.*

**16.** Unless you work harder you will fail, means .....
 A. if you fail you will work harder.
 B. you must at least plan well than you will not fail.
 C. hardly you will fail if you do not desire so.
 D. if you do not put more efforts, then you will fail.

**17.** Even if it rains I shall come, means .....
 A. if I come it will not rain.
 B. if it rains I shall not come.
 C. I will certainly come whether it rains or not.
 D. whenever there is rain I shall come.

**18.** Dinesh is as stupid as he is lazy means .....
 A. Dinesh is stupid because he is lazy.
 B. Dinesh is lazy because he is stupid.
 C. Dinesh is either stupid or lazy.
 D. Dinesh is equally stupid and lazy.

**19.** He is so lazy that he .....
 A. cannot depend on others for getting his work done.
 B. cannot delay the schedule of completing the work.
 C. can seldom complete his work on time.
 D. dislike to postpone the work that he undertakes to do.

**20.** He always stammers in public meetings, but his today's speech .....
 A. was fairly audible to everyone present in the hall.
 B. was not received satisfactorily.
 C. could not be understood properly.
 D. was free from that defect.

**21.** In order to raise the company's profit, the employees .....
 A. demanded two additional increments.
 B. decided to go on paid holidays.
 C. requested the management to implement new welfare schemes.
 D. offered to work overtime without any compensation.

**22.** Although, he is reputed for making very candid statements, .....
 A. his today's speech was not fairly audible.
 B. his promises had always been realistic.
 C. his speech was very interesting.
 D. his today's statements were very ambiguous.

**23.** I felt somewhat more relaxed .....
 A. but tense as compared to earlier.
 B. and tense as compared to earlier.
 C. as there was already no tension at all.
 D. and tension-free as compared to earlier.

**24.** With great efforts his son succeeded in convincing him not to donate his entire wealth to an orphanage .....
 A. and lead the life of a wealthy merchant.
 B. but to a home for the forsaken children.
 C. and make an orphan of himself.
 D. as the orphanage needed a lot of donations.

**25.** Even though it is a very large house, .....
 A. there is a lot of space available in it for children.
 B. there is hardly any space available for children.
 C. there is no dearth of space for children.
 D. the servants take a long time to clean it.

## ANSWERS

| 1 | 2 | 3 | 4 | 5 | 6 | 7 | 8 | 9 | 10 |
|---|---|---|---|---|---|---|---|---|----|
| B | D | D | C | C | A | A | D | A | C |

| 11 | 12 | 13 | 14 | 15 | 16 | 17 | 18 | 19 | 20 |
|----|----|----|----|----|----|----|----|----|----|
| D | D | D | B | B | D | C | D | C | D |

| 21 | 22 | 23 | 24 | 25 |
|----|----|----|----|----|
| D | D | D | C | B |

# 4. <u>Spotting Errors</u>

The most common errors in English are of spellings, grammar and usage of words. By regular practice, the errors can be easily spotted and minimised.

## MULTIPLE CHOICE QUESTIONS

**Directions:** *In the following questions some of the sentences have errors and some are correct. Find out which part of a sentence has an error, the number of that part is your answer. If a sentence is free from errors, then your answer is D i.e., No error.*

1. (A) Either Ram or/(B) you is responsible/(C) for this action./(D) No error.

2. (A) The student flatly denied/(B) that he had copied/(C) in the examination hall./(D) No error.

3. (A) By the time you arrive tomorrow/(B) I have finished/(C) my work./(D) No error.

4. (A) The captain with the members of his team/(B) are returning/(C) after a fortnight./(D) No error.

5. (A) After returning from/(B) an all-India tour/(C) I had to describe about it./(D) No error.

6. (A) The teacher asked his students/(B) if they had gone through/(C) either of the three chapters included in the prescribed text./(D) No error.

7. (A) Do you know/(B) how old were you/(C) when you came here?/(D) No error.

8. (A) Beware of/(B) a fair-weather friend/(C) who is neither a friend in need nor a friend indeed./(D) No error.

9. (A) Copernicus proved/(B) that Earth/(C) moves round the Sun./(D) No  error.

10. (A) The property/(B) was divided/(C) among the two brothers./(D) No error.

11. (A) I am quite certain/(B) that the lady is not only greedy/(C) but miserly./(D) No error.

12. (A) The brilliant success in the examination/(B) as well as his record in sports/(C) deserves high praise./(D) No error.

13. (A) I cannot find/(B) where has he gone/(C) though I have tried may best./(D) No error.

14. (A) If I was/(B) the Prime Minister of India/(C) I would work wonders/(D) No error.

15. (A) If it weren't/(B) for you,/(C) I wouldn't be alive today./(D) No error.

16. (A) He looked like a lion/(B) baulked from/(C) its prey./(D) No error.

17. (A) Widespread flooding/(B) is affecting/(C) large areas of the villages./(D) No error.

18. (A) If we really set to/(B) we can get the whole house/(C) cleaned in an afternoon./(D) No error.

19. (A) It's arrogant for you/(B) to assume you'll/(C) win every time./(D) No error.

20. (A) The two books are the same/(B) except for the fact that this/(C) has an answer in the back./(D) No error.

**21.** (A) Your husband doesn't/(B) believe that you are older/(C) than I./(D) No error.

**22.** (A) I could not/(B) answer to/(C) the question./(D) No error.

**23.** (A) Two years passed/(B) since/(C) my cousin died./(D) No error.

**24.** (A) I am learning English/(B) for ten years/(C) without much effect./(D) No error.

**25.** (A) Ramesh has agreed/(B) to marry with the girl/(C) of his parent's choice./ (D) No error.

**26.** (A) When he was arriving./(B) the party was/(C) in full swing./(D) No error.

**27.** (A) The most studious boy/(B) in the class/(C) was made as the captain./(D) No error.

**28.** (A) I am participating/(B) in the two-miles race/(C) tomorrow morning./(D) No error.

**29.** (A) When the boy committed a mistake/(B) the teacher made him to do/(C) the sum again./(D) No error.

**30.** (A) Whenever a person lost anything/(B) the poor folk around/(C) are suspected./(D) No error.

## ANSWERS

| 1 | 2 | 3 | 4 | 5 | 6 | 7 | 8 | 9 | 10 |
|---|---|---|---|---|---|---|---|---|----|
| B | D | B | B | C | C | D | D | B | C |

| 11 | 12 | 13 | 14 | 15 | 16 | 17 | 18 | 19 | 20 |
|----|----|----|----|----|----|----|----|----|----|
| C | D | B | A | C | C | C | A | A | C |

| 21 | 22 | 23 | 24 | 25 | 26 | 27 | 28 | 29 | 30 |
|----|----|----|----|----|----|----|----|----|----|
| C | B | A | A | B | A | C | B | B | A |

## EXPLANATORY ANSWERS

**1.** Replace 'is' by 'are'.

**2.** No error.

**3.** Replace 'have' by 'would have'.

**4.** Replace 'are' by 'is'.

**5.** Replace 'had to describe' by 'described'.

**6.** Replace 'either' by 'any'.

**7.** No error.

**8.** No error.

**9.** Omit 'that'.

**10.** Replace 'among' by 'between'.

**11.** Add 'also'.

**12.** No error.

**13.** Replace 'has he' by 'he has'.

**14.** Replace 'was' by 'were'.

**15.** Replace 'wouldn't be' by 'would not have been'.

**16.** Replace 'its' by 'his'.

**17.** Replace 'areas' by 'area'.

**18.** Replace 'set to' by 'set on'.

**19.** Replace 'for' by 'of'.

**20.** Replace 'in' by 'on'.

**21.** Replace 'I' by 'me'.

**22.** Omit 'to'.

**23.** Replace 'passed' by 'have passed'.

**24.** Replace 'am' by 'have been'.

**25.** Omit 'with'.

**26.** Replace 'was arriving' by 'arrived'.

**27.** Omit 'as'.

**28.** Replace 'in' by 'at'.

**29.** Omit 'to'.

**30.** Replace 'lost' by 'loses'.

# 5. <u>One Word Substitution</u>

There are many single words in English language which can be perfectly used for a number of words. These words help in expressing ideas in a short and correct manner for the right occasion. Such words not only increase the vocabulary but also enable you to economise in the use of words to a great extent.

| *Multiple Word Expression* | *Substitution* |
| --- | --- |
| One who always looks towards the bright side of things | Optimist |
| One who always looks towards the dark side of things | Pessimist |
| The time when one develops from a child into an adult | Adolescence |
| The process of growing more plants in order to form a forest. | Afforestation |
| The science which deals with farming | Agriculture |
| From some other country or place etc. | Alien |
| A term, etc. giving more than one meaning | Ambiguous |
| A vehicle which is used to carry sick persons | Ambulance |
| An animal which can live both in water and on land | Amphibian |
| A lawless situation when there is no government | Anarchy |
| Belonging to the history of thousands of years old | Ancient |
| Once a year | Annual |
| A very old object but still valuable | Antique |
| Words of opposite meanings | Antonyms |
| Words of similar meanings | Synonyms |
| Signatures of a famous person | Autograph |
| A government led by one person with absolute authority | Autocracy |
| A written work of one's own life history | Autobiography |
| A person who has never been married | Bachelor |
| A person usually having no hair on his head | Bald |
| A place where one can deposit money and get interest | Bank |
| A person who cuts our hair | Barber |
| A building/group of buildings where soldiers live | Barracks |
| A person who makes buns and biscuits | Baker |
| A person who lives by asking people for food and money without doing any useful job | Beggar |
| The crime of having married to two persons at the same time | Bigamy |
| The branch of science which deals with the study of plants | Botany |
| Able to speak two languages | Bilingual |

| *Multiple Word Expression* | *Substitution* |
| --- | --- |
| Able to speak more than two languages | Polyglot |
| The branch of science which deals with the living organisms | Biology |
| A powerful snow storm | Blizzard |
| A great successful book or movie | Blockbuster |
| A short news on the radio or TV | Bulletin |
| A system in which the most important works are organised by the government officials | Bureaucracy |
| A person who has no vision in his eyes | Blind |
| A page or a series of pages on which the information of days, weeks, months, etc. is given | Calendar |
| A person who eats human flesh | Cannibal |
| A complete list of items often arranged alphabetically | Catalogue |
| A sudden disaster | Catastrophe |
| A period of 100 years | Century |
| A branch of science which deals with chemicals | Chemistry |
| A printed leaf usually issued by banks that we sign to carry certain financial deal | Cheque |
| A person who makes or mends shoes | Cobbler |
| A group of people who has been chosen by others to make decisions on their own | Committee |
| A building in which nuns live | Convent |
| An animal which feeds on other animals | Carnivorous |
| A person who does criticism | Critic |
| A person who cannot hear | Deaf |
| A condition in which one loses a lot of water from one's body because of vomiting, etc. | Dehydration |
| A system of government in which the people cast their votes to elect their leaders | Democracy |
| The study of skin problems | Dermatology |
| A long piece of land covered with sand | Desert |
| The art of managing relationships between countries | Diplomacy |
| A piece of information about the words in a book form | Dictionary |
| A piece of information about the telephone numbers of the people in a book from | Directory |
| A person in charge of a newspapers, magazine etc. | Editor |
| A person who thinks he is better than the others | Egoist |
| To leave your country and settle in some other country | Emigrate |
| A book or series of books giving almost all knowledge about an area or some persons etc. | Encyclopaedia |
| Study of insects | Entomology |
| Time when day and night are of the same duration | Equinox |
| To sell things out of the country | Export |
| To purchase things from some other country | Import |
| A plant or animal no longer in existence | Extinct |
| A situation when there is a shortage of food for a long period of time | Famine |
| An amount of money that we pay for some action or services | Fee |
| Related to women | Feminine |
| An animal strong and aggressive | Ferocious |

| *Multiple Word Expression* | *Substitution* |
| --- | --- |
| A piece of land where plants grow easily from the soil that is favourable to them | Fertile |
| A work of literature having some imaginary events | Fiction |
| A large amount of water covering certain area | Flood |
| A person who sells flowers | Florist |
| A religious ceremony for burying or cremating a dead person | Funeral |
| A substance which kills fungus | Fungicide |
| A person studying or having studied the diseases and the related things of female reproductory system | Gynaecologist |
| The murder of the person of the same group race or country | Genocide |
| A substance which kills germs | Germicide |
| A situation in which many people die because of fire during war | Holocaust |
| The act of killing a person deliberately | Homicide |
| A word having the pronunciation as the other one does but it differs in meaning | Homophone |
| A word having the same spelling as the other one does but it is pronounced in some other way | Homonym |
| A person who is attracted towards the person of the same sex | Homosexual |
| Go across and parallel to the ground | Horizontal |
| A substance which kills the insects | Insecticide |
| That cannot be corrected | Incorrigible |
| That cannot be defeated | Invincible |
| That cannot be eaten | Inedible |
| That cannot be seen | Invisible |
| A place in a school or college where books are kept for the benefit of students, teachers etc. | Library |
| A place in a school or college where scientific experiments are performed | Laboratory |
| An official who is a judge in the lowest court | Magistrate |
| A piece of music or a book before it is printed | Manuscript |
| Related to men | Masculine |
| One who believes in the existence of God | A theist |
| One who does not believe in the existence of good | An atheist |
| That can be believed | Credible |
| That cannot be believed | Incredible |
| That which dissolves in a solvent | Soluble |
| That which does not dissolves in a solvent | Insoluble |
| Hard writing that can be read | Legible |
| Hard writing that cannot be read | Illegible |
| A person who does jobs beneficial to mankind | Philanthropist |
| A person who goes on foot | Pedestrian |
| A person who fights for his own country | Patriot |
| An act of killing oneself | Suicide |
| A woman whose husband is dead | Widow |
| A man whose wife is dead | Widower |
| A person who eats vegetarian and non-vegetarian diets | Omnivorous |

| *Multiple Word Expression* | *Substitution* |
| --- | --- |
| Something which is everywhere at the same time | Omnipresent |
| One who knows everything | Omniscient |
| A child who does not have parents | Orphan |
| An award etc. given after the death of the person | Posthumous |
| The place where animals are kept for amusement and to increase the knowledge of the public | Zoo |
| The science which deals with the study of animals | Zoology |

## MULTIPLE CHOICE QUESTIONS

**Directions:** *In questions given below, out of the four alternatives, choose the one which can be substituted for the given words/sentences.*

1. Something that relates to everyone in the world
   A. General     B. Common
   C. Usual     D. Universal

2. An expression of mild disapproval
   A. Warning     B. Denigration
   C. Impertinence     D. Reproof

3. One who is not easily pleased by anything
   A. Maiden     B. Medieval
   C. Precarious     D. Fastidious

4. Murder of a king
   A. Infanticide     B. Matricide
   C. Genocide     D. Regicide

5. A remedy for all diseases
   A. Stoic     B. Marvel
   C. Panacea     D. Recompense

6. A dramatic performance
   A. Mask     B. Mosque
   C. Masque     D. Mascot

7. Study of birds
   A. Orology     B. Optology
   C. Ophthalmology     D. Ornithology

8. Ready to believe
   A. Credulous     B. Credible
   C. Creditable     D. Incredible

9. Incapable of being seen through
   A. Ductile     B. Opaque
   C. Obsolete     D. Potable

10. One who eats everything
    A. Omnivorous     B. Omniscient
    C. Irresistible     D. Insolvent

11. A place where bees are kept is called
    A. An apiary     B. A mole
    C. A hive     D. A sanctuary

12. One who cannot be corrected
    A. Incurable     B. Incorrigible
    C. Hardened     D. Invulnerable

13. One who is in charge of a museum
    A. Curator     B. Supervisor
    C. Caretaker     D. Warden

14. Continuing fight between parties, families, clans, etc.
    A. Enmity     B. Feud
    C. Quarrel     D. Skirmish

15. A voice loud enough to be heard
    A. Audible     B. Applaudable
    C. Laudable     D. Oral

16. A paper written by hand
    A. Handicraft     B. Manuscript
    C. Handiwork     D. Thesis

17. Habitually silent or talking little
    A. Serville     B. Unequivocal
    C. Taciturn     D. Synoptic

18. To slap with a flat object
    A. Chop     B. Hew
    C. Gnaw     D. Swat

19. A person who speaks many languages
    A. Linguist     B. Monolingual
    C. Polyglot     D. Bilingual

20. A light sailing-boat built specially for racing
    A. Canoe     B. Yacht
    C. Frigate     D. Dinghy

21. A fixed orbit in space in relation to earth
    A. Geological     B. Geo-synchronous
    C. Geo-centric     D. Geo-stationary

**22.** A style in which a writer makes a display of his knowledge
   A. Pedantic       B. Verbose
   C. Pompous     D. Ornate

**23.** A religious discourse
   A. Preach        B. Stanza
   C. Sanctorum    D. Sermon

**24.** A place that provides refuge
   A. Asylum        B. Sanatorium
   C. Shelter      D. Orphanage

**25.** Detailed plan of a journey
   A. Travelogue    B. Travelkit
   C. Schedule     D. Itinerary

**26.** A person who insists on something
   A. Disciplinarian   B. Stickler
   C. Instantaneous   D. Boaster

**27.** A drawing on transparent paper
   A. Red print      B. Blue print
   C. Negative     D. Transparency

**28.** One who believes that all things and events in life are predetermined is a
   A. Fatalist       B. Puritan
   C. Egoist        D. Tyrant

**29.** A school boy who cuts classes frequently is a
   A. Defeatist     B. Sycophant
   C. Truant       D. Martinet

**30.** The act of violating the sanctity of the church is
   A. Blasphemy    B. Heresy
   C. Sacrilege    D. Desecration

**31.** A place where monks live as a secluded community
   A. Cathedral    B. Diocese
   C. Convent     D. Monastery

**32.** One who is fond of fighting
   A. Bellicose     B. Aggressive
   C. Belligerent    D. Militant

**33.** Tending to move away from the centre or axis
   A. Centrifugal    B. Centripetal
   C. Axiomatic    D. Awry

**34.** Words inscribed on tomb
   A. Epitome      B. Epistle
   C. Epilogue     D. Epitaph

**35.** Leave or remove from a place considered dangerous
   A. Evade        B. Evacuate
   C. Avoid        D. Exterminate

**36.** Original inhabitants of a country
   A. Abroge       B. Aborger
   C. Aborgory    D. Aborigins

**37.** Government by the officials
   A. Theocracy    B. Plutocracy
   C. Bureaucracy   D. Democracy

**38.** Incapable of being exhausted
   A. Inexhaustible   B. Inaexhaustible
   C. Exhaustable   D. Non-tired

**39.** A person of good understanding, knowledge and reasoning power
   A. Expert       B. Intellectual
   C. Snob        D. Literate

**40.** One absorbed in his own thoughts and feelings rather than in things outside
   A. Scholar      B. Recluse
   C. Introvert    D. Intellectual

## ANSWERS

| 1 | 2 | 3 | 4 | 5 | 6 | 7 | 8 | 9 | 10 |
|---|---|---|---|---|---|---|---|---|----|
| D | D | D | D | C | C | D | A | B | A |

| 11 | 12 | 13 | 14 | 15 | 16 | 17 | 18 | 19 | 20 |
|----|----|----|----|----|----|----|----|----|----|
| A | B | A | B | A | B | C | D | A | B |

| 21 | 22 | 23 | 24 | 25 | 26 | 27 | 28 | 29 | 30 |
|----|----|----|----|----|----|----|----|----|----|
| D | A | D | A | D | B | D | A | C | C |

| 31 | 32 | 33 | 34 | 35 | 36 | 37 | 38 | 39 | 40 |
|----|----|----|----|----|----|----|----|----|----|
| D | A | A | D | B | B | C | A | B | C |

# 6. Spelling Errors

There are thousands of words in English language. It is difficult to remember the spellings and meanings of all at once. Try to learn as many as you can. Use a dictionary regularly.

**Directions:** *Find the correctly spelt words.*

1. A. Damage  B. Dammage  C. Damaige  D. Dammege
2. A. Efficiant  B. Effecient  C. Efficient  D. Eficient
3. A. Schedule  B. Schdule  C. Schedale  D. Schedeule
4. A. Occurad  B. Occurred  C. Ocurred  D. Occured
5. A. Grieff  B. Grief  C. Grieef  D. Grrief
6. A. Guarantee  B. Garuntee  C. Guaruntee  D. Gaurantee
7. A. Meddicine  B. Medicine  C. Medicene  D. Medicinne
8. A. Benefeted  B. Benefitted  C. Benifited  D. Benefited
9. A. Acommodation  B. Acomodation  C. Accomodation  D. Accommodation
10. A. Querrelsome  B. Quarrelsame  C. Quarrelsome  D. Querralsome
11. A. Sympathetic  B. Smypathetic  C. Sympothetic  D. Sympethetic
12. A. Prograssive  B. Progressive  C. Progresive  D. Prograsive
13. A. Uncivilized  B. Uncevilized  C. Uncivillized  D. Uncevelized
14. A. Extravagant  B. Extreragent  C. Extreregant  D. Extravegent
15. A. Missunderstood  B. Miesunderstood  C. Misunderstood  D. Misunderstod
16. A. Belligerent  B. Beligirent  C. Belligarant  D. Belligerrent
17. A. Astonished  B. Astronished  C. Astoneshed  D. Asstonished
18. A. Sincerely  B. Sencerely  C. Sincerelly  D. Sincerrely
19. A. Rigourous  B. Rigerous  C. Rigorous  D. Regerous
20. A. Satellite  B. Sattellite  C. Satelite  D. Sattelite
21. A. Pesanger  B. Passenger  C. Pessenger  D. Pasanger
22. A. Humurous  B. Humorous  C. Humoreus  D. Humorrous
23. A. Exeggerate  B. Exaggerate  C. Exadgerate  D. Exagerate
24. A. Fariegn  B. Forein  C. Foriegn  D. Foreign
25. A. Excesive  B. Excessive  C. Exccessive  D. Exccesive
26. A. Forcaust  B. Forcast  C. Forecast  D. Forecaste
27. A. Paralleted  B. Paralelled  C. Parralleled  D. Parallelled

28. A. Ocasion      B. Occassion
    C. Occasion      D. Ocassion

29. A. Boquet      B. Bouquet
    C. Bouquete      D. Bouquette

30. A. Chettering      B. Chaterring
    C. Chattering      D. Chatering

31. A. Discourage      B. Disscourage
    C. Discourege      D. Discaurage

32. A. Curageous      B. Courageous
    C. Courrageous      D. Couregeous

33. A. Abandon      B. Abanddon
    C. Abendon      D. Abbandon

34. A. Embarassment
    B. Emberrassement
    C. Embarrassment
    D. Embbaresment

35. A. Eccintric      B. Eccentrie
    C. Eccentric      D. Eccintrie

36. A. Occasional      B. Occassional
    C. Occesional      D. Occessional

37. A. Querrel      B. Querral
    C. Quarrel      D. Quarel

38. A. Contrebution      B. Contribution
    C. Contributtion      D. Conterbution

39. A. Desgrace      B. Disgrece
    C. Disgrice      D. Disgrace

40. A. Harassment      B. Herassment
    C. Harasment      D. Harassmient

41. A. Imaginative      B. Imeginative
    C. Imagenative      D. Imaginetive

42. A. Suficient      B. Suficiant
    C. Sufficient      D. Sufficiant

43. A. Adequate      B. Edequate
    C. Adaquete      D. Edaquete

44. A. Exparienced      B. Experianced
    C. Experienced      D. Experrienced

45. A. Flatering      B. Fletering
    C. Flattering      D. Fletaring

46. A. Cuttiveted      B. Culltrivated
    C. Cultivated      D. Caltivated

47. A. Praiceworthy      B. Peiseworthy
    C. Praiseworthy      D. Praisaworthy

48. A. Profesional      B. Professionel
    C. Professional      D. Profissional

49. A. Ameteur      B. Amateur
    C. Amataur      D. Amateor

50. A. Unfevourable      B. Unfevaurable
    C. Unfavourable      D. Unfivourable

## ANSWERS

| 1 | 2 | 3 | 4 | 5 | 6 | 7 | 8 | 9 | 10 |
|---|---|---|---|---|---|---|---|---|----|
| A | C | A | B | B | A | B | B | D | C |

| 11 | 12 | 13 | 14 | 15 | 16 | 17 | 18 | 19 | 20 |
|----|----|----|----|----|----|----|----|----|----|
| A | B | A | A | C | A | A | A | C | A |

| 21 | 22 | 23 | 24 | 25 | 26 | 27 | 28 | 29 | 30 |
|----|----|----|----|----|----|----|----|----|----|
| B | B | B | D | B | C | A | C | B | C |

| 31 | 32 | 33 | 34 | 35 | 36 | 37 | 38 | 39 | 40 |
|----|----|----|----|----|----|----|----|----|----|
| A | B | A | C | C | A | C | B | D | A |

| 41 | 42 | 43 | 44 | 45 | 46 | 47 | 48 | 49 | 50 |
|----|----|----|----|----|----|----|----|----|----|
| A | C | A | C | A | C | C | C | B | C |

www.ingramcontent.com/pod-product-compliance
Lightning Source LLC
LaVergne TN
LVHW060352200726
843506LV00003B/190